Seductions of Fate

Seductions of Fate

Tragic Subjectivity, Ethics, Politics

Gabriela Basterra

First published 2004 by
PALGRAVE MACMILLAN
Houndmills, Basingstoke, Hampshire RG21 6XS and
175 Fifth Avenue, New York, N.Y. 10010
Companies and representatives throughout the world

PALGRAVE MACMILLAN is the global academic imprint of the Palagrave Macmillan division of St. Martin's Press, LLC and of Palgrave Macmillan Ltd. Macmillan® is a registered trademark in the United States, United Kingdom and other countries. Palgrave is a registered trademark in the European Union and other countries.

ISBN 1–4039–2171–7

This book is printed on paper suitable for recycling and made from fully managed and sustained forest sources.

A catalogue record for this book is available from the British Library.

Library of Congress Cataloging-in-Publication Data

Basterra, Gabriela.
    Seductions of fate : tragic subjectivity, ethics, politics / Gabriela Basterra.
        p.   cm.
    Includes bibliographical references and index.
    ISBN 1-4039-2171-7
    1. Subjectivity.   2. Tragic, The.   3. Ethics.
    4. Tragic, The, in literature.   I. Title.

BD222.B37   2004
128 – dc22   2003066180

10   9   8   7   6   5   4   3   2   1
13   12   11   10   09   08   07   06   05   04

Printed and bound in Great Britain by
Antony Rowe Ltd, Chippenham and Eastbourne

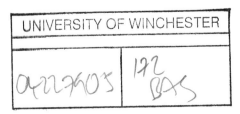

Carmen y Saturnino, para vosotros

Contents

Acknowledgements

New York University has actively contributed to this project, most materially in a Research Challenge Grant in 1999–2000 and a Remarque Institute Fellowship in Autumn 2000. Articles related to this book have appeared in *Anales de la Literatura Española Contemporánea* 24 (1999) and *Journal of Romance Studies* 3.2 (2003). I am grateful to these journals for their permission to use those ideas here. Very special thanks to Jennifer Nelson, of Palgrave Macmillan, for her excellent way of bringing this book into existence.

This book has been written in conversation with many people whom I wish to thank here.

First of all, I want to acknowledge my incommensurate debt to the thinkers and writers whose work has engaged and defined my personal space for so many important hours. To them much more than this book is due.

My deep thanks to Jonathan Strauss, Mitchell Greenberg, Mary Gaylord, Dru Dougherty, Gerard Aching, Erna Von der Walde, Miguel Ángel Balsa, Jo Labanyi, Clive Dilnot, Timothy Reiss, Bruno Bosteels, Irene Mizrahi, Anthony Geist, Nick Nesbitt, and Erin and Joshua Graff Zivin. With your insight, questions and encouragement you bettered this project. I thank you for the strength of your friendship.

I am grateful to my colleagues and students at New York University for creating the intellectually stimulating medium that opened up my work and for sharing its different moments. Special thanks to James Fernández, Kathleen Ross, Ana Dopico, George Yúdice, Gigi Dopico-Black, Helene Anderson, Mary Louise Pratt, Diana Taylor, Alberto Medina, Gabriel Giorgi, Stephanie Kirk and Daniel Grunberg.

I feel very fortunate to be in infinite conversation with Elaine Scarry, James Creech, Sylvia Molloy, Simon Critchley and Leo Steinberg. You, as my interlocutors, ceaselessly exhilarate me with your intellectual inspiration. I am full of gratitude for your generosity and brilliance, and moved by your unconditional presence.

Finally, I would like to express my appreciation for those conversations, already so inspiring, which I anticipate with intense excitement. With you, Judith Butler, Ernesto Laclau, Christoph Menke, Alberto Moreiras, Hagi Kenaan, Tom McCarthy, Bracha L. Ettinger, Julio Ramos, Peter Zeillinger, Adrián Hernández, Lena Burgos-Lafuente and Nathalie Bouzaglo, the future feels full of promise.

Introduction: Self-Denying Creativity

In our present world we often resort to the tragic mode of arranging experience in order to give sublime sense to traumatic events. When we interpret a particular event (genocide, a terrorist attack) as tragic, however, we ultimately justify it by reference to a transcendent agency. By extricating that traumatic irruption in our lives from its historical context, by declaring it ineluctably imposed on us, what we ultimately do is occlude our own involvement in the decision-making process that led to so much suffering, as well as our own responsibility for its outcome.

This book argues that if the tragic interpretation of experience is still so current in spite of the disastrous ethical consequences it entails, it is because beyond constituting a mode of sense-making that we can choose to adopt or ignore, it shapes our subjectivity.

Since the onset of modernity, as a crucial part of the Enlightenment's representation of Western culture, reason and artistic creation share the emancipatory task of liberating individuals from alienating destinies. Only by freeing people from the alienation of any essentialized form of power, whether monarchic, religious or based on custom and tradition, it seemed, could they assume individual and collective responsibility for history. And yet, if we look back to what precisely the modern *invention of tradition* recovers as the first work of fiction, Greek tragedy, we find that the Western self takes as its first self-representation, paradoxically, the denial of the human capacity for action and decision. When the tragic protagonist acts, its action manages to postpone only momentarily the fulfilment of fate. Although tragic heroes such as Agamemnon or Eteocles take action, their decisions and acts recoil against them with fatal results. Their agency is ultimately usurped and reversed by an inexorable force, fate, which provokes their death.

1

Precisely at the moment of its emergence as a concept, autonomous action is reduced to a transitory challenge to the power of destiny, a short-lived resistance that only provokes fate's reinvigoration. Given this ultimate denial of human agency, why has tragedy been considered the birthplace of agency and rationality? Why should we still fashion our identities after a model in which destiny usurps human agency and leads characters to die, apparently denying the possibility of autonomy, modernity's great invention? Here I interrogate modernity's interest in locating the origin of emancipatory political initiative in the very tragic setting in which deciding and acting are most radically denied. But my primary focus is not what modern philosophers have to say about tragedy (that is, tragic theory). Rather, I trace what I perceive as the tragic foundations of their descriptions of modern subjectivity, exploring the connections between two such seemingly irreconcilable notions as the modern autonomous subject and the determinism of the destiny to which tragic subjects submit.

Seductions of Fate initially proposes two interrelated arguments. First, although the emancipatory project of modernity presupposes the self's ability to make rational decisions, and thus expects individual and collective responsibility for history, the modern self constitutes itself in subjection to coercive forces that function like tragic destiny. I refer to this modern and contemporary pattern of self-identity as *tragic subjectivity*. Though it would seem that the abandonment of the belief in God should have eliminated the need for any source of transcendence that confers our identity, in fact, I argue, the secular modern subject embraces a tragic fate in order to become intelligible. The subject achieves a position in the social order by assuming guilt within the framework of destiny. But because in modern times tragic destiny no longer applies, the subject replaces it with essentializing constructs such as law, power, history or the state. Hence the paradoxical fact that the subjective agency that enables democratic politics is premised on deterministic sense

My second starting point is that tragic destiny or *objective necessity* derives its appearance of inevitability from the tension between essentiality and artificiality that structures it. Recognizing this tension is more complex than simply unmasking an essentializing process, because this is the very tension that constitutes who we are. If tragic fate appears to be an inevitable source of control, I suggest, it is because we have erased the traces of our participation in constructing it. Thus it appears that the imagination simultaneously enables and thwarts agency by producing destructive inventions, such as tragic fate, which in spite of being themselves created, radically contradict the human capacity for action and creation. This erasure of our creative activity also takes place in all other ostensibly essential sources of control. It guarantees, in fact, the efficiency of the essentialized sites of authority that produce us as subjects, to whose coercive nature we must blind ourselves. The more invisible and effective the power that subjugates us, the more active our participation in it.

So what would we gain by becoming aware of our participation in the powers that subject us, producing us as subjects? Indeed, assuming that objective necessity is a human fabrication, that it is not necessary but contingent, would seem to neutralize inevitability and restore human agency. If objective necessity is fictional, one could conclude, the origin of decision and initiative shifts from an ineluctable destiny to human hands. Yet, that acknowledgement of contingency places an infinite responsibility on the human self, who becomes accountable to others. The self can no longer attribute its actions to an external source of control and depict itself as a victim. But becoming aware of destiny's contingent nature does not necessarily liberate us from the coercive grip it has on us. Although fate-like sources of power may be a fabrication, that fabrication is constitutive of who we are.

This heteronomous relation with a necessary fiction of power is enabling and fertile, since it generates autonomy and agency. But while this tragic pattern produces the human agents of social and political emancipation, it is based on evading responsibility, and therefore forecloses ethical relations to real people. My goal is thus to explore whether realizing that objective necessity is constructed might help us reassume individual responsibility, and how acknowledging our political agency could revitalize the process of democratization. Awareness of our own contribution to political decision and action should indeed invigorate the always ongoing process of revising, creating and implementing political initiatives based on universality (however problematic their consequences, or precisely because they are problematic).

But while this is crucial, it is not enough. For how can the self's responsibility – its obligation to respond – coexist with the subjective agency presupposed by the order of political rationality, which is enabled precisely by displacing responsibility onto an external source of coercion? Beyond obeying social rules, we are called to act on the infinite responsibility that a demand coming from a living other places on us. I trace this demand primarily in the thought of Levinas, in dialogue with Kant's moral Law. Only in attempting to act on that demand and fulfil an unending duty, can we create a space for political decisions that exceed institutions and rules, a space for political invention. From this perspective, remaining faithful to 'the experience of the unconditional in an entirely conditioned universe'[1] constitutes the first step towards creating a 'beyond the political within the political'.[2] The very possibility of political creation hinges on the tension between acting on one's infinite responsibility and feeling ineluctably controlled.

*

The link between tragedy, subjectivity and subject-based politics can be traced back to the Greek *polis*, where the same surge of creativity invented tragedy, created law and democracy, initiated rational philosophy and inaugurated self-sufficient man. Legal courts, tragic contests and athletic competitions, the three social institutions of the *polis*, coincide in enacting both a struggle and a reconciliation, according to Walter Benjamin.[3] Martha Nussbaum argues, furthermore, that the dialectical, debate-filled and non-conclusive aspects of the public debate that tragedy stages are continuous with the political discourse of Athens. This continuity is substantiated by the fact that Plato's rejection of tragedy and his repudiation of Athenian democracy are linked.[4] If tragic drama is inseparable from public political debates, politics relies in turn on the tragic explorations of different sources of power, of their ambivalent encounters with human self-sufficiency, and of the emergent possibility of human action. If we think, for instance, of the depiction that Sophocles' *Antigone* offers of Creon, the quintessential legal and political ruler, as oscillating between assuming agency, decreeing legal rules and attributing control over his actions to the gods, we can begin to discern the extent to which tragedy must have constituted a laboratory for experimenting with emerging legal and political concepts such as autonomy, rationality and law. On the tragic stage, the values of the city are simultaneously rehearsed and revised without the pressure of having to offer a solution or closure.

By re-enacting the deadlocks of subjective agency, political decision and responsibility, tragic drama has the potential to open up possible spaces for action. This creative potential comes to a large extent from the fact that tragedy is, above all, an invention. It is enabled by the fact that the artistic framework within which tragic drama re-enacts ethical and political tensions announces its fictionality overtly. As a work of art, tragedy reveals the workings of the human imagination even as the imagination denies itself by creating coercive fictions such as tragic fate. While, on the one hand, tragedy anticipates the determinations of modern subjectivity in rehearsing the self's division and cooperation with necessity and in reaffirming a superior causality at the cost of individual death, on the other, as work of art, it reveals the fictional nature of subjectivity's *necessary* constraints. It is important to keep in mind, however, that the given and the fictional often coexist inextricably in tension, as happens in the structure of tragic fate. We should also be aware that notions such as *objective necessity*, tragic destiny or fate, just as *tragic subjectivity* or the *modern subject*, bear the paradoxical status of *necessary fictions*.

Because the tragic artistic framework displays the activity of the human imagination, it suggests crucial philosophical questions concerning the nature of action and creativity. Could the realization that constitutive concepts that are seemingly essential – such as destiny, the law or the subject – are constructed prove in any way liberating? What is the agenda behind the creation and mystification of sources of authority such as tragic fate? What is the contribution of poetic creation to our relation to other essentialized artefacts (certain institutions, gods), particularly to those which, like the modern subject, are at once created and necessary? What insights can art, acting as a self-conscious repository of human making, afford into human agency, as well as into our relations to other people, which we create but are not fictional?

Necessary fate

Tragic subjectivity emerges in tension with an essentialized synthesis of power. Whether denominated *destiny*, *fate* or *objective necessity*, the construct that constitutes tragedy's driving force encompasses competing sources of power responsible for the internal fractures that secure its authority. In Chapter 1, I explore the process of creating the idea of destiny and the tragic view of life in Greek classical drama, drawing primarily on instances from Aeschylus' *Agamemnon* and *Seven against Thebes*, and Sophocles' *Antigone*. Distancing myself from the traditional interpretation that sees tragedy as restoring an initial order, I argue that the complexity of tragic fate and the tensions that structure it contradict any simple idea of an order to be restored.

But if fate is not infallible, how are we to understand the characters' cooperation with objective necessity? If the protagonists of tragedy cooperate in their own death, I propose, they do so in order to occlude the fact that the gods themselves are at fault.[5] Tragic theology constitutes, in other words, an attempt to dissimulate the transcendent origin of guilt, an origin that we may also denominate the Father, the

Past, Objective Necessity or the Law. (I use the word *gods* or *God* in this ample sense of transcendent origin or source of authority.) Based on a displacement of culpability from the gods to the human self, tragic victimization must then disguise this reversal of responsibilities by inducing the innocent protagonist to cooperate in an inverted redemption. He willingly assumes a fault for which he is not responsible in order to avoid recognizing divine fallibility. Since acknowledging God's guilt would unleash chaos, with his own death the protagonist prevents the collapse of the tragic universe on which his own intelligibility depends.[6] If the tragic subject blinds itself to a transference of culpability from the gods, it is in order to preserve the integrity of the tragic order that gives him an identity.

What is the substance of this transcendent originary fault? None. It is precisely by virtue of its insubstantial character, of the emptiness that it disguises as a compelling promise of content (as intimated in the question 'what have the gods done?'), that the figure of divine guilt attains its power. Transcendent defilement is a function that structures the tragic system of intelligibility precisely by virtue of its emptiness, of the fact that it lacks content. Ultimately, the cooperation of tragic subjects with destiny can be explained as an attempt on their part to blind themselves to what I call the *other side* of fate. What they avoid seeing is that the very objective necessity that constitutes them as tragic subjects through a transference of guilt is an empty structure.

If considered from the perspective of preserving the integrity of the tragic world that makes subjects intelligible, tragic death no longer seems such a high price, since it averts something more terrible. Recognizing the emptiness of objective necessity would undo the characters as tragic subjects, suspend sublime sense, and demand from them a more radical commitment to the course of action they take. It would precipitate them into an unintelligible abyss that seems worse than tragic.

The allure of tragic guilt

Should we then conclude that tragic characters desire to die? Inspired by Lacan's analysis of tragedy in *Seminars VII, VIII and XI*, Chapter 2 reads the tragic cooperation with objective necessity as the subject's attempt to fulfil the unknowable desire of the Other, of the social symbolic order. Through a reading of Jean Racine's *Phèdre*, I propose that undergoing tragic death represents the self's ultimate approval of its constitution as a subject (a subjectivation that Oedipus and Antigone, because of their exceptional relation to death, ultimately refuse). Tragedy thus reveals the heteronomous determination of subjectivity that the death-based modern subject reiterates.

Yet, however terrible and compelling, tragic death is not heroic, but an evasion, an escape. An escape from what? What could be so fearful as to make us prefer to become tragic victims? Perhaps it is acting beyond the social rules that legitimate our actions. Perhaps it is daring to decide what our duty is, to give it substantial content, and then to act on it without any external confirmation or support. Perhaps it is taking the risk of acting without being in debt with destiny, without the shelter provided by the framework of guilt in which we have our place, beyond the safe realm of institutions and laws. When confronted with this infinite responsibility that undoes us as intelligible subjects, the tragic death that reaffirms our position in the symbolic order comes as a relief.

But how is tragic sublimation achieved in practice? How does tragic art manage to naturalize the tragic structure of interpretation of reality? In the second part of the chapter I examine the tragic plot described in Aristotle's *Poetics* as an engine of tragic sense-making and of representation in general, trying to account for its success. A question that arises, regarding the relevance to the present of the tragic causality as a mode of interpreting human action, is how tragic self-representation manages to survive the modern pre-eminence of reason. That modern reason and self-consciousness are precisely based on it is one of the arguments of this book. Because modern subjectivity follows tragic patterns, an exploration of the weaknesses of the tragic plot as generator of sense may reveal the vulnerability of reason and its ways of apprehending reality. I thus examine the tragic plot in relation to Kant's antinomies of pure reason, which emerge at the point in which the synthesis of phenomena realized by the imagination seems to fail. To simplify rather violently, theoretical reason fails to provide an insight into the moral Law that constitutes practical reason or ethics, because the moral Law is incomprehensible, according to Kant. The ethical obligation that escapes reason, the infinite responsibility that cannot be apprehended as an object of knowledge, is precisely that from which tragic death provides an escape.

Tragic modern subjectivity

This tragic evasion of responsibility still inflects modern and contemporary subjectivities. Whether it is described in terms of a constitutive division in Hegel's unhappy consciousness, Kant's separation of pure and practical reason, the Nietzschean conscience, Freud's distinction between ego and superego and his description of melancholic self-beratement, or Althusser's ideological interpellation as an originary assumption of guilt, subjectivation presupposes the existence of a transcendent force of otherness (power, Law, the state) that produces a rent and bound identity, the self-conscious modern subject. Though most modern philosophers do offer a theory of tragedy (which constitutes the main focus of studies on tragedy and modernity), it is significantly not there, but rather in their descriptions of the processes through which the subject achieves an identity, that I perceive a re-enactment of the tragic. The self-conscious subject must internalize authority, blind itself to the conditions of its emergence, accept a doubly bound agency, disown responsibility paradoxically by assuming guilt, and make constrained decisions under the appearance of free choice. Following the grammar of fate, the displacement of culpability from the source of authority to the subject depends on dissimulating the origin of defilement, in order that the individual can perceive it only as provider of social identities and civil liberties. In tragic style, one blinds oneself to the originary guilt that comes from the Father or the Law by taking it on one's shoulders, which seems preferable to recognizing it. In this way, the social symbolic order that makes one intelligible as a subject is preserved. There is a direct correlation between becoming a subject, assuming guilt and depicting oneself as victim. Guilt is therefore the last thing tragic subjects (both classical and modern) would be willing to renounce.[7]

This self-depiction as victims allows us, (tragic) modern subjects, to invoke an inexorable fate as an alibi – 'I was acting under fate's control', 'I was following the law (or enforcing it)', 'I did it in fulfilment of my duty, however hard' – and thus to disclaim responsibility for our actions. Being responsible for one's actions implies being responsible before someone else, and if we deny our responsibility we also deny our accountability to other people. Unlike guilt, which reaffirms the self's self-centred sameness, responsibility disposes the self towards the others, to *act for* the others. It is the real people affected by our actions that we blind ourselves to – that we manage to obliterate, when we assume guilt and depict ourselves as victims. The ethical consequence is obliterating the suffering inflicted on the real people with whom the tragic self does not relate.

But perhaps more important than refusing responsibility, the tragic self-depiction responds to an irresistible aspiration to intelligibility. The self strives to protect the social symbolic order that produces it as subject from the potential disruption of real people. While the abstract otherness of fate, Law or the Father configures the self as an intelligible subject, real people, with their presence and needs, question the centrality of the self. Paradoxically, the eagerness to depict oneself as inexorably controlled – as a victim – despite the disempowerment it entails, betrays a fear of leaving oneself, an urge to preserve the pre-eminence of sameness that only a real person can disrupt. That disruption might break through the self's autonomy and sink it into a void that seems more unbearable than the tragic. It would expose the self to the terrible *other side* of destiny and the Law that sublime tragic sense seeks to occlude. This is the paradox of heteronomy at the service of preserving autonomy.

Is it then possible, I ask, to break with the pattern of self-victimization and restitute the possibility of agency? As long as agency is contingent on the fiction of the modern subject, the answer seems to be no. Given its association with the autonomous self, itself a heteronomous construction, we must assume that human agency does not exist except when it is denied, at risk of imminent peril, in the face of constraint. Only this constrained idea of agency supplies the foundation for an acceptable self-representation as agent that leaves one's sense of autonomy intact.

However problematic, this *autonomous* subject premised on assuming guilt and depicting itself as victim constitutes the basis of democratic politics, since it is the locus of the rational principles of universality and equality. Therefore, the very egalitarian principles that found democracy, enabling constitutions, the rule of law, and courts of human rights, may result, paradoxically, in an inability to reach out to others, if not in their suppression. This does not imply, however, that we should renounce subjectivity, for it is a necessary creation that constitutes who we are. Even supposing that we could renounce it, with it we would give up agency (however precarious), the possibility of political struggle and of the rule of law (however imperfect), as well as all work that universals do on our behalf. We would relinquish, in the first place, the constitutional arrangements that aim at securing the bodily inviolability of the other, as well as mine. By renouncing subjectivity we would give up ourselves, that is, the very position from which such a renunciation is made.

The fiction of fate

Since tragic subjectivity precludes the irruption of others by constructing fate as an alibi, what would be the consequences of realizing that fate is a fiction? Some modern tragedies at once re-enact the inevitability of classical destiny and at the same time disturb it, suggesting that fate – and by extension all essentialized sources of control – is *also* constructed. In Chapter 4, I propose the possibility that fate is fictional, and I trace the process of its creation in Federico García Lorca's tragedy *Bodas de sangre* (*Blood Wedding*). While this play does indeed re-enact fate's victory through the death of the characters, it simultaneously questions fate's existence. In the middle of lamenting that they are controlled by destiny, the protagonists project a narrative onto the present and obliterate the other characters on stage, relinquishing, in effect, their ability to act and interact. This new reading suggests that fate is not an inexorable given, but rather a fiction constructed by the characters in order to displace responsibility from themselves.

This displacement of responsibility is as characteristic of the tragic consciousness as the control by an inexorable force with which it coexists. Tragedy thus enacts the interplay between two apparently opposing tensions, one that turns characters who have no agency into victims (when the actions of the characters are usurped by fate), and one in which potentially acting and responsible characters relinquish agency and accountability (by projecting a narrative of the past upon the present time of the play). By simultaneously depicting fate's power and showing that it is a human fabrication, this drama reformulates human relations to otherness, moving away from victimization by a transcendent Other and stressing the self's responsibility for real people. From this perspective, characters no longer appear as fate's victims.

It would seem that realizing that fate is contingent would undermine the illusion of external control, relocating both initiative and responsibility in human hands: the self is now accountable to real people. But though this potential liberation affirms the possibility of human agency against fate's control, it is conditioned by its interaction with fate's victory. Hence tragedy simultaneously prevents and enables agency through the interplay between a necessary and a fictional fate. The coexistence of fate's fictionality with fate's victory intimates that however responsible and well intended human action may be (fictional fate), action is fragile and potentially destructive (fate's victory).

Becoming aware of our role in creating fate, in other words, does not cancel fate's power, as one might expect. Abolishing objective necessity would only be the obverse – and thus the complement – of confirming it. The moments of fate's victory and fate's fictionality, which symmetrically prevent or demand action, are inextricably intertwined. This interplay between an essential and a constructed fate thus speaks of the vulnerability of action, an action we must take in spite of its tendency to fail.

In terms of subjectivity, realizing that the subject is not necessary but contingent means that the subject is invested as an infinitely responsible agent, and called to take high risks, such as deciding how to respond to others in a relation which is asymmetrical and non-reciprocal (Levinas), daring to posit its duty outside of any legitimizing paradigm (Lacan), acting in the absence of any external support, radically exposing itself. What politics may now learn from this new reading of tragedy is how to commit itself to situations that exceed sublimation (tragic and otherwise). In this sense, to act politically would be to assume responsibility for decisions and actions whose failure can no longer be attributed to a transcendent source of control, not even to the obedience of rules. Political emancipation requires resisting the allure of tragic sublime sense.

Tragic autonomy meets ethical heteronomy

At this point, we have seen different modes of intelligibility at play: the tragic subjectivity that premises the rational political order, and the infinite responsibility imposed on the self by an ethical demand prior to any subjectivation. Before and beyond the identity conferred by regulated society, the self is invested as an infinitely responsible subject by an order of obedience coming from an other. Whether that ethical demand is placed by the moral Law (Kant), by the face of the other (Levinas), or by fidelity to one's desire (Lacan), it obliges the self to act in ways that lie outside social legitimation and support. These distinct modes of intelligibility presuppose two different forms of heteronomy (or obligation to another) that I tentatively call *tragic* and *ethical*.

Chapter 5 stages an initial conversation between the *tragic* heteronomy that premises autonomy and the *ethical* heteronomy that is evaded through tragic death. I trace this structure of ethical demand and response in the work of Levinas, in conversation with Kant's moral theory. According to these accounts, the subject is constituted by a command it receives from elsewhere, by a decision made by another that the self finds in itself only in so far as it responds to it. Does this mean that we are fully responsible for deciding, even though decision does not entirely come from us?

This heteronomously constituted subject becomes autonomous and free by believing itself the author of what it has received. But Kant's and Levinas's accounts differ in the position they attribute to the principle of autonomy. Because autonomy is the basis of Kant's moral theory, one becomes a free subject by coming to desire the Law, by making one's will and duty coincide. Whilst Kant's self-conscious, rational subject recasts the obligation that constitutes it as self-given, as a decision freely made by the self, Levinas's sensible subject is traumatized and obsessed by its infinite responsibility for the other to the point of substituting itself for the other. In privileging heteronomy over autonomy, Levinas underscores the constitutive structure of heteronomous obligation that runs through Kant's moral philosophy, but that Kant leaves aside for the sake of the primacy of autonomy.

Tragic heteronomy consists in dying as a victim of a terrible destiny with which one cooperates in exchange for becoming a subject. If, as I argue in this book, tragic death constitutes an evasion from *ethical* heteronomy, what exactly is the rapport between the two heteronomies? Since they both refer to an *externally* imposed obligation, might they not come to coincide at some point? How would the ethical demand ultimately differ from the heteronomy imposed by the very tragic subjectivity that it questions, disrupts and exceeds? How are we to understand my claim that the ultimate goal of tragic heteronomy is to assert autonomy?[8] I contend that both heteronomies refer to the same experience from different perspectives. Tragic heteronomy constitutes a perception, from the limited perspective of autonomy and of knowledge (that is, from the perspective of the self-conscious rational subject), of the ethical experience that occurs outside temporality and escapes comprehension. Consciousness, in Levinas's account, arises with the presence of the third in the midst of my responsibility for you. The entry of the third is 'the birth of the question' of consciousness and politics.[9]

And it is in relation to life in community and politics that problems seem to arise. How can the radical responsibility placed by the demand coexist with the social rules that enable political life, whose reliance on the autonomous subject may result, as I propose in Chapter 3, in avoiding responsibility to the point of suppressing other people? Is it possible to abide by a social contract without betraying the infinite responsibility imposed by the demand? What is the relation, in other words, between (Levinasian) ethics, which is asymmetrical, and the contemporaneousness and universality that premise the institution of justice and political life?

It is in the political space that *tragic* and *ethical* subjectivities, autonomy and heteronomy, meet. And it is precisely in order that politics can devise itself on the basis of autonomy that heteronomy must be emphasized. Unlike *ethical* heteronomy, autonomy is not a primordial experience. Becoming manifest in the dimension of reason, not of ethical responsibility, autonomy consists in the illusion of authoring the decision that the other has made in me. Self-consciousness constructs the demand from the other as self-imposed. Since autonomy constitutes the basis of modern liberal politics, politics is inseparable from the originary *ethical* heteronomy upon which it rests. And because the third is already present in the demand, my political responsibility has always already been imposed (primordially and anarchically) as responsibility for the other. It is in this sense that the relation between ethics and politics has always already taken place within the subject, within me.

Already constituting subjectivity, the tension between heteronomy and autonomy, between ethics and politics, inflects the political space. While as a subject of the state I must follow the rules of the community that dictate and legitimize my action, in responding to the demand of the other (which includes that of the third) I must exceed those rules and act on a duty that I posit without any external acknowledgment or confirmation. It is in this sense that responding to the demand of the other is impossible, that my responsibility only increases the more I act on it. If seen from the perspective of a political space created by the self's attempt to respond to that demand, what has been theorized in various ways as a distance or hiatus between ethics and politics constitutes, in my view, a tension within the political.

Now energy can be deflected from the ethics/politics divide and devoted to constructing the political space as inflected by an ethical demand. Acting politically in this sense would mean risking a decision and an action that are fully aware of their own contingency. It would be giving substantial content to my duty in each particular context without any *external* acknowledgment or support. It would be acting creatively on that duty with no guarantee of success while seeing my responsibility increase the more it is fulfilled.

1
Necessary Fate

The art of tragic composition arranges events in a narrative that secures the victory of a superior necessity or fate. This fable of the futility of human agency is repeated from one drama to another, engendering the self-representation that we call tragic consciousness as we know it today. Each tragedy re-enacts the reaffirmation of fate's power through the hero's death, rehearsing an expected, announced and inexorable story.

It might thus seem surprising that the modern invention of Western tradition recovers tragedy both as its first self-conscious work of fiction and as the birthplace of human agency. And yet, there are good arguments in favour of looking back to tragedy, since tragedy was conceived in the rise of creativity that created law, initiated rational philosophy and inaugurated self-sufficient man in the Greek *polis*. The city provided the necessary conditions for the human self to begin to perceive itself as autonomous from the transcendent forces that had dictated human destinies thus far. Indeed, as a depiction of the hero's impulse towards action, tragedy constitutes an emblematic starting point for the modern invention of the Western autonomous self, if we understand modernity as 'the adoption of the principle that human beings individually and collectively (that is, societies) are responsible for their history',[1] that is, as a conception of social and political life based on responsible agency.

Furthermore, the first expressions of the need for democratization as we conceive it today were promoted by the thinkers of Enlightenment. And since modernity is linked with democracy, the Greek *polis* seems a suitable site to rely on in any process of recovering origins. Looking back to classical Greece offers the added advantage of sweeping away the historical periods in which external coercion becomes tangible, such as the 'obscure' early Middle Ages or seventeenth-century absolutism. This contributes to modernity's dissociation from any historical or religious force that alienated the human self.

But when the tragic protagonists, believing themselves self-sufficient and free, act, their action manages only to postpone momentarily the fulfilment of fate.[2] Precisely as autonomous action emerges as a concept, its scope of effectivity is reduced to a transitory challenge of fate's power, a short-lived resistance that only provokes fate's reinvigoration. Although the characters believe they can steer the course of their lives, their decisions and actions recoil against them with fatal results. Their agency is usurped by a transcendent force. The protagonist, as the plaything of the gods, can only delay their final victory, but not avoid it. This delay constitutes tragedy. The tragic model thus poses an implacable causal system with a resistance – the hero's intentionality – inscribed on it. Although in the end tragedy celebrates the ultimate victory of fate over man, each tragic drama plays out the illusion that human power can be equal to fate, that the hero's self-sufficiency and freedom constitute a real obstacle to the ironclad causality of the gods. However, because transcendent design is inflexible, it is ultimately the hero's threat to this order that is crushed. The time of a tragedy seems to coincide with the time it takes fate to reassert itself.

A fractured source of authority

Where does the tragic concept of usurped agency come from? Jean-Pierre Vernant contextualizes it in the clash, at the time of tragedy's emergence, between two competing sources of authority: on the one hand, the still prevailing mythical, heroic and religious traditions; on the other, incipient rationality enabled by the legal and political configuration of the *polis*. Action in Greek tragedy participates in two opposed levels, between which it oscillates.[3] While the emergent definition of the individual as a legal being stimulates debates on autonomy and self-sufficiency, the origin of human agency is still deeply ambiguous. Although waning, the hold of the demonic world-order continues to be very powerful.[4] Even if the protagonist believes to be acting rationally within the realm of city law, often his or her deeds provoke the wrath of the gods, whose authority invariably prevails.

Tragedy had a very short life. It was born in the Athenian *polis* at the end of the sixth century BC, and flourished and died in the narrow margin of a hundred years (Euripides, the youngest great tragedian, died in 406 BC).[5] The birth of tragedy in the *polis* coincides with the birth of law and politics, whose ways of producing subjects, as I shall argue later, still bear the traces of tragedy today. Tragic contests, which together with legal courts and athletic competitions constituted the three main public events of the *polis*, were spectacles open to all citizens, theatrical stages on which the city dramatizes itself, becoming the subject of tragic performance.[6] In its public exploration of civic values, tragedy is continuous, as Martha Nussbaum points out, with the political debates of Athenian democracy.[7] Its experimentation with power and authority, with human rationality and agency, contributed to consolidate the practices of political and legal institutions, be it by expanding their ideals, by preserving the complexity of the human relation to power, or by underscoring the inscrutable conflicts that the city would need to expel from its walls for the sake of rationality. But where rational philosophy dismisses tragic conflict as irrational, tragedy remains a repository of complex experience and unmediated conflict. On the tragic stage, the city tests the limits of inconsistency, the strength of rationality, the loyalty to belief, the ability (of the city and of its citizens), but also the costs, when not (as is more often the case) the impossibility, of incorporating conflict. Through tragic fiction the values and institutions of the city are simultaneously rehearsed and challenged.

Because of its inextricable link with the *polis*, its values and institutions, tragedy ends with the *polis*'s demise. When Aristotle wrote his *Poetics* he was no longer familiar, at least from experience, with the tragic concept of action (the description of tragic action in the *Poetics* – with the possible exception of its mystifying argument on catharsis – is done not from the viewpoint of the philosopher of action who wrote the *Nicomachean Ethics*, but from that of a practical literary critic accounting for narrative ways of arranging action).[8] The debate between the mythical and heroic past and the civic present was no longer at issue, since law and the institutions of political life had finally established themselves over myth. The discussion of agency and responsibility was taken over by philosophical thought, which got rid of the contradictions of the tragic universe by rationalizing human action. The divine and the human levels ceased to be perceived as simultaneously inseparable and opposed.[9]

It is not the case, though, that tragedy *reflects* the legal, mythical or religious beliefs it sets in conflict (beliefs that exist in Greek society in a raw, non-systematic state). Rather, tragedy constructs them narratively, in the same way as it elaborates the materials taken from legend, inventing the tragic view of life.[10] It is important to clarify, therefore, that what we identify today as the social and psychological conditions of classical Greece, frequently studied as the background to tragic drama, is often derived from the individual tragedies, and then reapplied to the plays as valid interpretive tools, as Raymond Williams remarks – it is no wonder the tragedies illustrate the 'sociological features' of their time so neatly.[11] It is possible, of course, to list particular beliefs ('in fate, in divine government, or in a sense of the irreparable'[12]) as tragic meanings, but those meanings are very limited historically.[13] Any historical conditions deduced from sources other than the tragedies, while useful, are also of limited interest. They document, at best, less than a century of classical Greek culture, and do not account for the success of tragedy in different places, circumstances and moments. Ultimately, what the currency of sociological explanations confirms, when taken as the only source of insight, is the ability of the tragic fiction to pass for real.

Tragedy is not shaped by those orders of belief: it creates them. Tragedy creates its own world, a world in which conflicts are never mediated. The legal, mythical and religious spheres appear rent by internal contradiction, pervaded by ambiguity and lacking clear boundaries. Although the hero's loyalty seems split between the religious and the legal paradigms for organizing experience, he eventually becomes aware that he does not really have to choose between the gods and the laws of the *polis*. Ultimately indistinguishable, the divine and the legal contribute to an undifferentiated reserve of transcendent power that constitutes tragedy's most brilliant and productive invention: tragic fate.

The invention of fate as an essentialized source of authority allows tragedy to create an inexorable causality to which it submits human action. This causality must be inflexible in order to compensate for the inconsistencies and contradictions that rend both the religious and legal realms. Interestingly, the tragic causality is a narrative concept, yet because of its inflexibility (compounded by both religion and law), because it seems necessary and inevitable, it is perceived as transcendent, as divine, and thus is usually referred to as the causality of the gods. The tragic plot, a precise narrative structure, gives shape to the paradoxes that spring from the tension between the transcendent and the human. Re-enacting an invariable pattern of reversal from one drama to another, tragedy configures its signature creations, the tragic consciousness and the tragic view of life.

Although after its first impulse towards action the tragic self generally eludes conflict by cooperating with necessity, tragedy is the art of unmediated conflict. And while the tragic self constructs its subjectivity as internalized fate in order to preserve its intelligibility, the tragic play, by displaying the traces of the human hand, points to fate and to itself as constructions. What the tragic self believes, in short, is what the play as artefact contradicts. Tragedy creates a productive tension, in other words, between the essentialized sources of authority that it constructs, and the fact that it (the tragedy itself), as work of art, openly announces its fictional nature, the trace of the human hand. In the next chapters I will explore the insights that this tension affords into a conception of human agency born under constraint. We could go as far as venturing that the concept of subjective agency, a concept inextricably linked to the fiction of the autonomous self, is premised on positing an objective necessity that provides the constraints under which agency may emerge.

A note on essentialization might prove useful at this point. In spite of the negative historical effects produced by essentialized sources of power such as tragic fate, this inquiry into the seductions of fate will consider essentialization as a creative faculty crucial to human life. Since it is not essentializing processes themselves that must be indicted, but rather the agenda behind some of them, here the art of tragedy will come again to our help. Tragic art displays the enabling power of essentializing, but also the negative impact that certain essentializations have on the essentializer, the human self.

Agent and victim at once: Creon

Because rationality and human self-sufficiency, though gradually enabled by the legal and political institutions of the *polis*, are still emerging at the time the tragedies were written (a time in which the idea of will did not yet exist),[14] tragic plays depict them in full confrontation with mythical and religious influence. Thus tragedy represents the double binds of agency. Even though action seems to spring from human initiative, from *ethos* (the human self as self-sufficient agent), at a certain point of each tragedy it appears manipulated by *daimon* (demonic, transcendent powers).[15] This tension between the human and the demonic is conveyed, for example, in the Ode of Man that the Chorus of *Antigone* intonates, a praise of man's matchless ability to control the natural world. On the one hand, the Chorus affirms that man's skills will procure individual and civic greatness only if 'he weaves in the laws of the land, and the justice of the gods that binds his oaths together'.[16] But the tasks of following civic norms and honouring the gods are often irreconcilable.[17] Instantiated in the 'reckless daring' or man's inability to control itself that the Chorus condemns, the contingency of human self-control is set in sharp contrast to the human skills it celebrates, most notably, that man has taught himself language and thought.[18] This double origin of action, religious and legal, makes the tragic subject appear simultaneously as agent and as controlled from outside.[19] In the midst of the tension between these two contending sources of authority, writes Vernant, 'the tragic sense of responsibility emerges when human action becomes the object of reflection and debate while still not being regarded as sufficiently autonomous to be fully self-sufficient'.[20] Consequently, tragic subjects commit themselves to a conflict whose resolution always escapes them, since at a particular moment of each drama the weight of necessity disrupts the previous state of equilibrium, foreclosing any possibility of responsible initiative, or what is called human freedom.[21]

It is not the case, though, that the divine and legal universes existed as neatly organized domains. The conflict between religious and civic duty is further complicated by the insoluble contradictions that rend each of these sources of authority. Perhaps unexpectedly if one considers their influence, in classical Greece neither religion nor law formed a consistent whole, and it is precisely this indeterminacy that secures their success as sources of power. With its inclination towards depicting tension and conflict, tragedy offers an extended description of the discrepancies at the heart of each. Since tragedy is often studied as the materialization of the sociological or psychological conditions of its time (conditions to which we have little access), I would like to make it clear at the outset that in the next paragraphs I will speak of religion and law *as depicted* in the individual plays. Instead of illustrating pre-existing orders of belief that tragedy reflects, therefore, the dramatic passages quoted below *shape* the conceptions of agency and authority at stake in this discussion.

Religion in Greece did not constitute a coherent system that can be described as a Greek theology. Diverse cults and religious syntheses overlapped, without allowing one to prevail, in a confusion that tragic plays, in their taste for conflict, cultivate.[22] On the tragic stage old and young gods alike fight their past in an attempt to secure their future authority, rending the divine world with their hostility. Hence the polarity of the Olympic and the Titanic in *Prometheus Bound*,[23] the fight of the Erinyes against Apollo in *The Eumenides* (before they become the tutelary spirits of Athens at the end of the play) or the temporary questioning of Apollo's authority by Dionysus' frenzy in the *Bacchae* constitute instances of the clash between different divine genealogies.[24] Individual gods send contradictory orders or – just like the human protagonists – are unable to decide who is right and who is wrong, as is the case in *The Eumenides*.[25] Here Orestes appears simultaneously pursued by the angry Erinyes for the murder of his mother, Clytemnestra, and supported by Apollo (from a younger genealogy), who commanded her death. When the estranged parties apply to Athena for help, the goddess, unable to come down in favour of one, appoints a court of jurors to decide whether Orestes should be absolved or condemned.[26]

These instances and others allow us to discern one of the most powerful strategies that tragedy adopts to alienate the human self, namely, the ability to synthesize diverse powers as a mystifying transcendent force. The idea of *daimon*, writes Ricoeur, 'represents the divine as close to undifferentiated power; and so it provides an apt designation for the sudden, irrational, invincible apparition of the divine in the emotional and volitional life of man. Thus the theology of fault tends to sustain a reserve of divinity that resists the tendency, triumphant everywhere else, to individualize and visualize divine powers.'[27] Beyond the conflict between distinct divine figures, divine influence over the human self is most efficient when it manifests itself as an intangible reserve of power that resists individuation.

Which of the competing divine commands should one follow? The success of divine authority depends on its elusiveness, that is, on the uncertainties provoked by the coexistence of diverse cults and contending genealogies of gods. Divine power thus represents a confused and confusing Other whose desires are ultimately inscrutable. Hence the ability of this indeterminate power to alienate the human self, who is produced as a subject in the process. By being subjected to elusive divine control, the tragic self achieves a position within the divine causal system that makes it intelligible. The impulse to preserve that intelligibility accounts for the tragic subject's otherwise unexpected cooperation with the divine command that alienates it. Its often impassioned complicity with the source of its doom, and its eagerness to assume as voluntarily chosen a course of action that was imposed as inevitable in the first place, can be explained by the urge to persist in the subjective position conferred by a transcendent causality. Though alienating, this inexorable but identity-conferring symbolic order crystallized around a transcendent form of control must be protected at all costs.

This fruitful elusiveness of authority is further intensified by the fact that the legal order against which religious powers clash is also inconsistent. Indeed, one of the most significant practices of tragedy consists in rehearsing the emergence of the human self as a subject of law: 'I shall select judges', says Athena in *The Eumenides*, 'and swear them in, establish a court into all time to come. Litigants, call your witnesses, have ready your proofs. . . . They shall swear to make no judgment that is not just, and make clear where in this action the truth lies.'[28] But the meaning of the concept of law (as well as that of the truth that Athena seeks to discern) is unclear. Even though technical terminology of law abounds in individual plays, its use does not amount to a description of a coherent legal system. As Vernant writes, 'We find [legal] terms used imprecisely, shifts of meaning, incoherences and contradictions, which betray internal clashes and tensions at the very heart of a system of legal thought that lacks the elaborated form of that of the Romans.'[29] The legal sphere is thus perceived in 'degrees and separate layers of law, some of which overlap or are superimposed upon one another'.[30] Far from reaffirming legal principles through its use of legal terminology, then, tragedy exercises its taste for ambiguity and contradiction by setting them in tension and displaying their inconsistency.

The public display of the uncertainties and incompleteness at the foundations of the social and political orders would be unthinkable today, when the inconsistency and violence at the origin of power are occluded from human sight. How do tragic plays manage to stage these inconsistencies, and to do so uncompromisingly? If tragedy succeeds in enacting the instabilities at the heart of power, it is because it submits them to an arbitrary causality of its own invention, the tragic causality. Tragedy's ability to make the tragic causality appear inevitable accounts for some of its most remarkable creative achievements. Para-doxically, by making tragic action undergo an inevitable course, tragedy is able to destabilize and disorder the orders it creates. Tragedy 'is designed', in Walter Benjamin's words, 'not only to bring about the restoration but above all the undermining of law in the linguistic con-stitution of the renewed community'.[31] So much for the idea that order is restored.

Furthermore, beyond the inconsistencies provoked by the internal fractures of religion and law, there is a lack of clear boundaries between the two domains which makes it difficult to decide where the religious ends and the legal begins. It is not the case that the divine and the legal worlds, though internally rent by contradictions, clash neatly, their limits clearly drawn – if it were so, discerning one's allegiance to one or the other would be easier. Rather, since both religious authority and legal justice aspire to occupy the same position of control, they perme-ate each other. However emphatically Greek law introduced the categories of human intention and responsibility, it was still deeply penetrated by religion. Apollo, the guarantor of civic justice and peace, and the counsellor of legal activity, is also 'the great master of ritual purifications'.[32] Although his counsel guides and heals, it does not exonerate or absolve the tragic self, remarks Ricoeur, since purification is still necessary. In this sense, from the perspective of our legal society, we tend to assume that in the *polis* civic law was fairer to the human self than divine design. Though that is the perception that would soon prevail in philosophy (albeit only for the sake of citizens, and thus only from the perspective of a few), the equanimity of law is not what the tragedies show. The inseparability of law and religion may be better understood by looking to the power strategies of the modern state. In spite of its association with the rule of law (or perhaps precisely because of that), the modern state still relies heavily on essentialized constructs (Law, tradition) that function like transcendent sources of authority. Just think, for example, of the way in which, according to Althusser, ideology interpellates individuals and produces them as subjects in the form of divine naming.[33]

In its enactment of this overlap of law and religion, each individual play locates the source of maximum authority alternately in the gods and in the city. This oscillation makes it hard to decide whether it is religion or human rationality that rules. In *Oedipus at Colonus*, for example, the only organizing principle would appear to be law (as in the words of reproach with which Theseus addresses Creon, who has dared to abduct Oedipus' daughters in Theseus' land: 'You come to a city-state that practises justice, / A state that rules by law, and by law only').[34] Yet, at the next moment, absolute authority is attached to the oracles of the gods ('You also think it clever,' Oedipus reminds Creon, 'to flatter Theseus, / And Athens – her exemplary government; / But in your flattery you have forgotten this: / If any country comprehends the honours / Due to the gods, this country knows them best').[35] In fact, Theseus proclaims law as the only paradigm for ruling the state ('by law, and by law only') immediately after offering a sacrifice to 'the great god of the sea, Colonus's patron',[36] further blurring the jurisdictions of each form of authority. The curse that Oedipus imposes on his son Polynices demonstrates the inseparability of law and religion even more clearly: 'And so your supplication and your throne / Are overmastered surely – if accepted / Justice still has place in the laws of God.'[37]

Since the divine and the legal orders compete for the same position of control, they must enter into inevitable conflict when, for example, a god's oracle or curse results in a violation of state law. It would be more accurate to say, though, that the one that enters into conflict, caught between the two sources of power, is the human self. If Polynices chooses to follow the prophecy that Apollo expresses through his father Oedipus, he has no alternative other than to turn against the ruler of his native Thebes and attack it with an army from Argos. That is the very act of treason that leads Creon to forbid the burial of his corpse and that triggers tragic conflict in *Antigone*.[38] From a different perspective, however, it would seem that Polynices' act of invading Thebes in fulfilment of Apollo's curse constitutes an attempt to recover the Theban throne which his younger brother Eteocles had usurped from him, the rightful heir. Not surprisingly, in the absence of stable values or firm reference points in relation to which to judge human action, the Chorus of *Antigone* places the weight of certainty in language, as when it entreats Creon: 'Lord, if your son has spoken to the point / you should take his lesson. He should do the same. / Both sides have spoken well.'[39] By equating speaking well with being right, the Chorus remains unable to pronounce itself in favour of one side as long as both contending parties prove persuasive.[40]

The final play in the *Oresteia*, *The Eumenides*, seems to attempt a reconciliation between law and religion by granting both the gods and the city their share of autonomy. When the Erinyes and Apollo apply to Athena for help in judging Orestes' murder, she appoints a court of Athenian jurors, inaugurating civic justice. Even then, confronted with the need to undo the draw in which the tribunal's votes result, it is Athena herself who must cast the deciding vote. 'So it stands. A crisis either way,'[41] she says, recognizing the claims of each party. Not even in this rehearsal of the birth of civic justice, then, does law prevail clearly. Consequently, legal terms as basic as the notion of 'guilt' yield incompatible interpretations. Sometimes guilt refers to a defilement sent by the gods and expatiated through blood from parent to child; at others, it attaches itself to the person who has voluntarily chosen to violate the laws of the city.[42] When at the trial of Orestes the Chorus tells Athena that he 'murdered his mother by deliberate choice', the perceptive Athena asks: 'By random force, or was it fear of someone's wrath?'[43] Her words intensify both the ambivalence of authority and the already ambiguous status of Orestes' deed.

Caught between a rent divine universe and the incipient legal order, human agency exists in a very precarious state. Human action is placed at the crossroads of city law and a tyrant's personal desire, in the tension between family duties and the will of the gods, in the clash of divine and legal justice. This accounts for the contradictory ways in which tragic subjects refer to their own actions, alternately presenting themselves as passive (they acted under the influence of a madness sent by the gods) and active (they are self-sufficient beings who follow the laws of the city), at one moment assuming responsibility for acts to which they feel committed, and at the next attributing their destructive outcome to divine design. Even those characters whose action has been traditionally interpreted as enforcing city law, such as Creon in *Antigone*, oscillate between assuming and disclaiming responsibility for their acts.[44] When Creon decrees that whoever buries his nephew Polynices, a traitor of the city, must die, he appears as a strict and consistent ruler who is loyal to his city, even if that implies denying funeral rites to one of his own kin.[45] Yet, when his command to immure Antigone alive is about to be enforced, he tries to erase all traces of his contribution to her death. He asks her guards to provide her with food, so that when she refuses to eat (as he assumes she must, in order to hasten her death) she can be considered to bring about her death by her own hand, thus absolving the city of guilt.[46]

Why must Creon the ruler disown his part in Antigone's death, rather than stand by it? Of course, one could argue that this is a classic political strategy, instantiated in everyday politics. But since Creon has been considered the quintessential legal ruler, this apparently incoherent change of character calls for further analysis. Why does the Chorus, in turn, vacillate, at one moment energetically affirming that Antigone has chosen to die and goes to death willingly, rather than by any external coercion or violence,[47] and at the next urging Creon to mend his 'misguided' ways?[48] Could these incoherent transformations in the character of the protagonist represent, in fact, back-and-forth shifts from a political register to a religious and mythical one?[49] The key to reading these oscillations is to focus not on character (as Hegel, Freud and so many nineteenth-century philosophers and critics have accustomed us to do), but on action, which is what tragedy is about.[50]

Because its source is indeterminate, human action appears radically ambivalent. On the one hand, action entails reflecting on motivations and aims; on the other, it involves precipitating oneself into inscrutable territory at the risk of one's life.[51] In the latter case, when the actor perceives itself controlled by fate, a rift opens between intention and result.[52] Tragic characters sometimes express awareness of this rift, and thus they refer to the origin of their actions with extreme ambivalence, oscillating between assuming or disowning their acts.

If tragic characters are confronted with a decision without choice that makes them act in spite of themselves, to what extent is the tragic subject responsible for the course of action taken?[53] Since the characters are compelled to accept their fate in order to take action, at a certain point in each play protagonists disown their own agency. Creon says: 'It was a god who struck, / who has weighted my head with disaster; he drove me to wild strange ways, / his heavy heel on my joy'; 'Take me away at once, the frantic man who killed / my son, against my meaning. I cannot rest. / My life is warped past cure. My fate has struck me down.'[54] If considered carefully, their words denote an oscillation between assuming guilt and declaring some kind of innocence, in accordance to the double nature of action, human and divine. Oedipus and Antigone constitute an exception, since they refuse to assume any guilt. Oedipus' awareness of his innocence plays a prominent role in *Oedipus at Colonus*. Perhaps this play manages to exceed the tragic, since it reflects on the possibility of situating oneself, as Oedipus does here, outside of the tragic symbolic order.

In the face of religious or legal constraints, where do human agency and responsibility lie? It would seem that nowhere in tragedy can tragic subjects be called agents if their actions are usurped and reversed. What seems clear, in any case, is that tragic action, which leads well-intentioned characters to their doom, runs counter to a constructive notion of action that promises happiness when chosen well, as Aristotle describes it in his *Ethics*.

The fact that tragic action is governed by an inexorable causality confers a singular status on it. The tragic action is one that recoils against the agent, with results contrary to those intended. In turning agents into victims through a reversal of fortune, tragedy would seem to put the concept of agency radically into question. By destroying instead of creating, doesn't action here run against any notion of action that presupposes the agents' capacity to choose freely, to decide how to influence their circumstances and be in charge of their own *destiny*? Or so goes the common-sense understanding. For the question we will need to ask later is whether a *non-destructive* kind of agency exists. Does the consideration that an action has been chosen *well* guarantee its success? What is, in any case, the standard against which to consider whether an action was *well chosen*? It would seem that the concept of *acting well* is a circular one, since it is applied to an action retrospectively deemed *well chosen* when it yields positive results, that is, when it fulfils the agent's intentions. As compared with the Enlightenment's understanding of a good action, which, according to Kant's categorical imperative, refers to an action that embodies universal principles, it would seem that tragedy offers a concept of agency that is more complex and describes human experience more accurately. I would like to suggest, at least provisionally, that responsibility for one's action is not related to choosing an action well (what does that mean, after all?), but rather to attending to its results, whatever they might be, that is, assuming the action up to the receiving pole, the other person affected by it. Isn't this the gist of Walter Benjamin's affirmation that tragic subjects become 'guilty by their actions, not their will'?

Cooperating with death: Agamemnon, Eteocles

Tragic protagonists must appear 'guilty by their actions, not their will', writes Benjamin.[55] A central strategy of the tragic narrative is to create the illusion of choice, in order that characters can be held responsible for their acts. Fate's presence is relentless from the very moment in which the protagonist must decide between different courses of action. What appears initially as deliberation between two alternatives quickly becomes a 'spoken consciousness of division', according to Roland Barthes.[56] However sincerely the characters seem to debate, their dilemma is formal, a twofold structure without content which makes them recognize that there is only one course of action available, namely, to obey necessity. They do not deliberate between good and evil; their being split does not reflect their individual act (it is not related to their psychology). Their self-division is related to the structure of the action, it is a matter of form.[57] For example, Agamemnon in Aeschylus' tragedy debates between letting his fleet remain becalmed and his men die, and sacrificing his daughter Iphigenia, which is the condition imposed by the goddess Artemis to let him set sail for Troy. Yet not laying siege to Troy does not constitute a viable alternative, since this is, in turn, Zeus' command.[58] In *Seven against Thebes* Eteocles finds himself in a similar dilemma when he tries to defend Thebes from a traitor army. Although he realizes that the opponent he has to defeat at the seventh gate is his brother Polynices, his only alternative is to fight, lest he provoke the wrath of the gods.[59] The tragic subject, in short, has no choice. Martha Nussbaum observes that both men are under the pressure of a controlling force in that a wrong will be done whatever they choose, since breaking with blood relations or breaking with the bonds of civic friendship offers a choice of undesirable alternatives.[60] Thus, when they realize what the outcome of their actions will be, they immediately recognize that the only course of action available to them is to obey necessity, even in those dramas in which such recognition can be expressed only through a brief cry of protest.

In Jean-Pierre Vernant's words, 'tragic man does not have to "choose" between two possibilities; rather, he "recognizes" that there is only one way open before him'.[61] Deliberation in classical tragedy is, in this sense, sterile. If deliberation reveals anything, it is only the 'non-choice of choice', the impossibility to choose one option over another.[62] Taking Troy (in obedience to Zeus Xenio's demand) or fighting a traitor of Thebes does not constitute a viable option, but rather an ineluctable task. Alhough the characters are not given the chance to choose between right and wrong, their deliberation conveys the illusion of freedom and thus an impulse against the tragic, however short-lived. As Nussbaum observes, the existence of deliberation in tragedy, however formal its structure, none the less inaugurates the search for a way out of tragic conflict. Hence, in its display of deliberation, tragedy presents, 'alongside with the "tragic view", the origin of the denial of that view'.[63] 'There is no doubt that, for Aeschylus at least,' says Ricoeur in similar vein, 'tragedy is both a representation of the tragic and an impulse toward the end of the tragic.'[64] What should be added to this is that the representation of the tragic and the impulse towards the end of the tragic exist in a permanent impasse: the latter, a portrayal of incipient agency, would not exist without the former. Though ultimately it will be crushed, human effort to resist fate brings about the emergence of agency.

Given this lack of choice, the eagerness with which the characters come to desire their fate after a brief moment of *formal* deliberation and *voluntarily* become victim to it is surprising.[65] 'Blaming no prophet,' states the Chorus in *Agamemnon*, 'he blew together with the winds of luck that struck against him.'[66] Instead of lamenting the course he has to follow, Agamemnon changes direction, overcomes his self-division and suddenly forgets the force of the opposing claim (his daughter's right to live), to the point of passionately desiring to sacrifice her.[67] He now claims: 'For it is right and holy that I should desire with exceedingly impassioned passion the sacrifice staying the winds, the maiden's blood. May all turn out well.'[68] Eteocles accepts his fate with the same zeal as Agamemnon. As soon as he realizes that the opponent he has to fight is his brother (and after recognizing his father's curse on his sons), he fervently decides to take a stand against him: 'Who else would it be more just to send? Leader against leader, brother against brother, foe against foe, I shall stand against him. Bring me my greaves as quickly as possible, to shield me from the spears and stones.'[69]

What drives these characters to assume the gods' design so keenly, 'with exceedingly impassioned passion'? For Vernant it is a matter of narrative plausibility. Their willingness to cooperate with an imposed necessity allows tragedy to reintroduce the illusion of free choice at the heart of the necessary decision. If the hero apparently complies with his fate, he can be held responsible for his actions, and therefore he can be punished.[70] The ultimate purpose of having the characters' actions appear freely chosen is to bridge the rift between lack of intention and responsibility. Consequently, forced into a situation in which he must inevitably decide, the hero will become guilty of an action to which he would not have chosen to commit himself. Let us anticipate, however, that the narrative requirement of plausibility addresses the enigma of human complicity with objective necessity only partially. As we shall see below, human cooperation with fate may be further explained by the need to ignore divine guilt in order to avoid the collapse of the tragic world.

But tragedy conceals almost all traces of the character's appropriation of necessity, of his collaboration in his own doom, by directing our attention to fate's immemorial origin. Fate's power to make men and women atone for a crime they did not choose to commit lies in its anteriority. Its anteriority allows fate to demand accountability for an unredeemable past that has always already taken place, for an original defilement that the tragic subject re-enacts by acting. Thus human fall adopts a retroactive character which plays a twofold function: theological and narrative. From a theological perspective, the characters' guilt can be traced through their ancestors back to the gods, who are, in turn, the *purveyors* of Fate.[71] The implication of this retroactive character of evil is astonishing. Tragic guilt, in short, does not originate with the hero, but rather with God. According to this theological aspect of tragedy (to which we shall return), the hero assumes God's guilt and purchases God's innocence at the price of his life.

Tragic guilt, in other words, is not individually deserved, but rather transmitted from generation to generation through blood ties. This transmission is dramatically expressed as the irreversible character of the past, and thus the defilement of crime is always transmitted to the whole lineage.[72] The fate of the tragic character is inherited, a fact that underscores the impossibility of individual agency, the human inability to change the course of events. It is inaccurate, therefore, to ascribe the faults for which characters are held accountable to their individual deeds. When Artemis calms the winds, preventing Agamemnon's expedition from sailing, this is not a punishment individually deserved by Agamemnon, but rather divine retribution for the crimes committed by his lineage. By inheritance, the guilt of Oedipus attaches itself to the whole Labdacid lineage, beginning with his children Polynices, Eteocles and Antigone, and Agamemnon inherits the guilt of the House of

Atreus. As the vehicle of expatiation of guilt, blood carries the force of a curse: it literally incarnates in the hero's body a defilement originating in a remote past which transcends individual intentionality and is transmitted to future generations through blood ties.

It is then to be expected that at a certain moment in each tragedy the characters will be compelled to inherit the fate they had initially attempted to avoid. As Roland Barthes remarks, 'by the curse they attach to the Blood, the gods merely guarantee the inexpiable character of the Past'.[73] Guilt's inescapability and power to divide the protagonist and drive him to act against himself comes from its capacity for embodying itself literally in the character's blood. Perhaps more important than blood's transmission of guilt is its role in securing that the tragic subject internalizes it. (This internalization of guilt also premises modern and contemporary subjectivation.) Once internalized, guilt's transcendent origin remains foreclosed to human consciousness, appearing to have emerged from the human self.[74] Hence the passion with which the characters assume guilt. Fate admirably succeeds in passing for an internal defilement that truly divides the hero. In appearing simultaneously external and internal, and in directing the protagonist's action against his suddenly acquired awareness of guilt, fate compels the human self to become a tragic subject by turning against itself. In his discussion of Clytemnestra and the Chorus in *Agamemnon*, for instance, Richmond Lattimore observes that 'they do not collide with purely external forces but act always against a part of their own will or sympathy which is committed to the other side, and what they kill is what they love. The action of the play in itself, of the trilogy [*Oresteia*] as a whole, is thus bound inward upon itself.'[75]

Driven to turn against itself by internalizing guilt, the tragic subject is *reversed*. The hero's acceptance of a predetermined course of action enables a narrative reversal, which according to Aristotle constitutes the formula of tragedy: 'a reversal is a change of actions to the opposite.'[76] The consequence of acting against oneself is that actions, turned into their symmetrical contrary, recoil against their agents, who are now acted upon.[77] In the most famous instance of reversal, Oedipus seeks to discover Laius' murderer and to solve the riddle of the Sphinx, only to discover that he himself is at once the answer to the riddle and his father's murderer.[78] As Barthes persuasively argues, 'what constitutes the special nature of the tragic reversal is that it is exact and, so to speak, measured. Its fundamental design is symmetry. Destiny turns each thing into its contrary as though in a mirror: inverted, the world continues, only the *direction* of its elements is switched.'[79]

Self-division is thus the consequence of internalizing or transposing into the self a confrontation with authority, with a transcendent command that, as I noted above, comes not only from the gods and the demonic domain, but also from civic law. It is this process of assuming guilt that produces the tragic hero as subject. Assuming guilt allows the hero to occupy a position within a system of meaning that makes him intelligible, that makes sense of his life, even if that sense comes at the cost of death.

But beyond producing a divided and self-defeating tragic subject, the self's internalization of *external* guilt also suspends ethical responsibility, since the hero will henceforth disown his agency and attribute his actions to fate.

The figure of a world in recoil, whose conception one must interrogate from both the perspectives of narrative and the production of subjectivity, constitutes the cosmic counterpart to the tragic experience of self-division. But how does the process of internalizing external command and assuming guilt work? (For the sake of narrative simplicity, I will refer to the transcendent command that produces a guilty subject as *God*.)

The constitutive act of self-blinding

The primary tension underlying all tragedies is related to the burden of divine presence.[80] In tragedy the demonic and human are inseparable, intertwined in a venture that leads to the ultimate victory of the gods. Although the victory of the divine over the human does not come as a surprise, it is none the less based on an astonishing fact. Differing from the Aristotelian critical tradition, which still with great predicament situates the origin of conflict in the tragic mistake (*hamartia*), in a flaw in the character of the protagonist related to *hubris* (arrogance), Barthes and Ricoeur (writing, significantly, after the crisis of modernity and rational thought) shift guilt's origin away from human defilement. If the 'predestination to evil' that figures at the core of tragedy affects man, they argue in different ways, it is because of a propensity towards evil in the gods themselves.[81] The tragic theology is so scandalous that it resists being thought.[82] Tragic guilt, in short, does not originate in the hero, but in God.[83]

How can a divine order that is inseparable from the demonic re-create its people? How are we to understand the coincidence of diabolical evil with divine good? The tragic theology must remain evasive in order to occlude that primordial incoherence.[84] When the hero has an inkling of it, he or she becomes speechless. '[I]n tragedy,' writes Benjamin, 'pagan man realizes that he is better than his gods, but this realization strikes him dumb, and it remains unarticulated.'[85] Demonic guilt becomes manifest in the silence of the hero, a silence which by not trying to justify itself (suggests Benjamin in an unusually optimistic reading) inverts its apparent meaning and 'throws suspicion back on to his persecutors . . . : what happens before the public is not the guilt of the accused but the evidence of speechless suffering.'[86] Rather than being concerned, like comedy, with 'ethical denunciation and reform' (Ricoeur), tragedy offers 'an exegesis of moral evil' that allows the character to escape moral condemnation and appear before the Chorus and the audience as the one to be pitied.[87]

Consonant with the divine origin of guilt, God's blinding of man is not a punishment of human defilement; rather, it represents 'the fault itself, the origin of the fault'.[88] Instead of deploying instances of a human defilement that can be expiated only through death, tragedy stages a transference of guilt from the gods to the human self.[89]

What is the substance of this transcendent original fault, what is it that makes it so terrible? Precisely that it has no content, or more exactly, it lies outside the constellation of content. Divine guilt is an empty structure, and it is from its formality that it derives its power. A guilt detached from any action or violation suspends causality and seems to threaten intelligibility – but intelligibility is actually enabled by this threat. According to the logic of the tragic transference of guilt, the gods are not the object, but rather the subject of jealousy: it is the gods themselves who are jealous of man's greatness. Contrary to the usual assumption, therefore, divine jealousy is not incited by human hubris.[90] Rather, hubris, sent by the gods, becomes their excuse for provoking the fall of man: 'human hubris is not . . . the initiative that provokes the jealousy of the gods, but the initiative that is caused by that jealousy through the intermediary of blindness.'[91] Jealous God, in short, inflicts immoderation and arrogance on human beings in order to create a visible justification for His punishment of man. (From this perspective, predications of moderation may be read as an attempt, subsequent to the at least partial human recognition of divine jealousy, to keep it in check while acknowledging the need to remain blind to it.)

This chimes with Barthes' assertion that 'tragedy is essentially an action against God, but an action infinitely suspended and reversed'.[92] Divine aggression provokes a symmetrical reversal of responsibility. God acts against man, and then, reversing the roles of agent and victim, He himself becomes the victim and holds man responsible for the fault, a fault that is as terrible as it is empty. Tragic guilt is therefore not essential, but rather 'an artificial construction intended to naturalize . . . suffering . . . , to change form into content successfully'.[93] The task of guilt, 'to change form into content successfully', that is, to make an empty signifier signify, is impossible by definition, and it is this impossibility that accounts for guilt's success as a structure, as the principle that enables symbolization.

If guilt is an empty structure constitutive of intelligibility, if suffering must be naturalized – that is, if neither guilt nor suffering is a given – why should men and women accept this attribution of an alien fault? Why should they consent to die in atonement for a defilement whose accountability they could have refused, and to emerge as the split subjects of a world in recoil? Recourse to psychoanalytic language might do justice to the human fear on which this process relies. Perhaps the human self assumes the guilt invested by God for fear of having to acknowledge that God himself is guilty.[94] The idea that the gods are at fault is unbearable. Thus tragedy places human beings in a situation in which recognizing a guilty God and having to abandon Him would be more unbearable than assuming God's guilt.

The tragic subject theorizes divine jealousy as a punishment for human hubris in order not to see the divine origin of this constitutive fault.[95] Since the revelation of a transgressive God would bring the world to chaos, the hero's guilt is 'a functional necessity', says Barthes: 'if man is pure, then God is impure, and the world falls apart.'[96] This reversal of culpability, where man must appropriate an alien fault as a lesser evil in exchange for *not knowing*, can result only in an inverted redemption. Having been born 'innocent', the tragic hero assumes another's fault in order to exempt God.[97]

How tragic art manages to naturalize this reversal of culpability, and then to erase the traces of the essentializing process, attests to the creative power of the tragic imagination. The transmission of guilt from God to the human self finds its dramatic expression in the irrevocable character of the past.[98] Whether called 'blood' or 'destiny', the channel for this retroaction of guilt precipitates men and women into the struggle of forces that holds the tragic world together. Blood, a retroactive and diffuse version of the Otherness that victimizes the human self, occludes the divine origin of defilement. Thus in tragedy the bonds of blood become at once the vehicle of guilt and the materialization of the protagonist's fate in his or her body – guilt inherited and incarnated.

Guilt's embodiment as blood brings the tragic internalization of an *alien* fault to the height of paroxysm. Interestingly, the hero's appropriation of external guilt by internalizing it (thus creating through self-division the occasion for punishment), as well as the resulting occlusion of guilt's divine origin, have a paradoxically enabling side-effect. Internalizing guilt allows men and women to escape demonic jurisdiction and regain a sense of agency and of autonomy from the gods. Assuming guilt seems preferable to being enslaved by guilty gods: if I am guilty, it must be because I did it, and therefore I was, and am, an agent – so the reasoning goes.

If we pretend for a moment that it is God's actions that matter instead of human self-representation that narrativizes – invents – them, if we look at God as the subject and man as His object, we can articulate an even more disturbing notion of fate. Fate or destiny would be the name God assumes *as* 'organizer of the tragic spectacle' in order to be able to keep man on his side.[99] Hiding behind the name of destiny allows God to preserve man's fidelity, a fidelity He would otherwise lose if the hero could identify Him as the instigator of his doom. Ricoeur also emphasizes the need for the source of evil to be diffuse, as if springing from a 'surplus of power not distributed among the most distinct anthropomorphized gods', in order that it can blind, alienate and disorder the human self.[100]

Hence Barthes' subtle formulation: 'Destiny is . . . not quite God, it is a *this side* of God. . . . Destiny permits the hero partially to blind himself as to the source of his misfortune, to situate its original intelligence, its plastic content, without designating responsibility for it: Destiny is an act modestly cut off from its cause.'[101] By foreseeing the influence of destiny while ignoring its origin, the hero is then allowed to perceive destiny as a sort of wickedness without having to name it God.[102] Blinding oneself to the source of coercion is thus the prerequisite for internalizing guilt and for becoming an intelligible subject – it is the condition for achieving an identity.

This misrecognition of divine agency allows the human self to take agency. Or, at any rate, it allows the self to believe himself an agent, and therefore provides him with the impulse necessary to resist divine causality by positing his own causality, thereby delaying the final victory of the forces of evil. Since on account of their act of self-blinding tragic subjects are unable to identify the transcendent power that reverses their acts (that makes those very acts recoil against themselves), they deliberate about what course of action they should take. In so doing, they insert with their illusion of choice – if only momentarily – a resistance to the tragic within the very same framework in which the tragic devises itself.

Although apparently this confrontation with the Other throws the human self into his own otherness and out of praxis, alienates him and reduces him to the position of an 'unwelcome guest to the world',[103] the hero's misrecognition of divine agency is in fact productive: it enables tragic intelligibility and (though in unexpected ways) agency, since it is only in confrontation with the tragic causality that agency emerges.

Here we encounter the paradox of the birth of agency, both tragic and modern. Agency depends on its lack, and is created day by day in tension with failure. Already in tragedy, the notion of agency emerges vis-à-vis constraint, it is created in a daily struggle with the possibility of its non-existence. Perhaps it is in recognition of this, and not in spite of this, modernity institutes tragedy as its model. The agency invested on the one who becomes guilty, who assumes what was unchosen and inevitable, takes the form of a recovery of what never existed and will never exist.

However radical and extreme, the tragic internalization of *external* constraint that the plays reenact so seamlessly will become one of the central strategies in the creation of the modern consciousness. In this respect, modernity collapses two elements that in the Greek *polis* were continuous – legal and political discourse with its ability to produce subjects *and* the tragic stage, eventually effecting the disappearance of the latter as a crucial element of civic life. With the disappearance of the tragic stage, what is lost is both the record and the self-conscious practice of fictionality, agency and responsibility in the creation of the state, that is, the opportunity of rehearsing social principles and of testing laws. Reenacting the tragic strategy for conferring both guilt and intelligibility, the modern state produces its subjects on the condition that their internalization of guilt remains foreclosed to consciousness, as we shall see.

Destiny's *other side*

If we turn away from the representation of the human subject as victim and focus on the creative act of human self-representation that tragedy affords (though in doing so, we are admittedly adopting a different strategy, rather than simply undoing the initial one and describing the 'natural state of things'), we can see that the tragic divine kingdom has two sides. On one side are the evil gods, whose wickedness is foreclosed to the hero's consciousness; on the other is divine sublimity and majesty, a source of enabling gestures. This benevolent side where the gods appear as the origin of authority and of law (hence the indistinction with which the divine and the legal occupy the position of authority in tragedy) is the only one the hero's position allows him to perceive. That the tragic gods appear benevolent or evil is thus a matter of perspective, but the tragic subject is allowed (or allows himself?) only one perspective, the finite human one from which destiny appears as the hither-side of God.

What we should note here is that the sublimity of the tragic gods, their ability to enunciate law, depends on their monstrosity. The tragic theology of evil changes when the perspective which looks on it shifts, at one moment appearing as the only *side of God* that tragic subjects are allowed to see, at another as God's cruel nature. But God's wickedness is an unbearable revelation to which tragic subjects must have no access. If the hero could identify God's guilt as the origin of his doom, he would have to reject Him, and with Him he would have to relinquish the faith in a sublime truth from which intelligibility emanates. In the absence of this act of self-blinding, what would be lost is the counterpart of sublime law, a monstrous reserve of undifferentiated power and violence that law negatively affirms, and thus the very possibility of ethical goals. It is therefore in order to prevent the possibility of that revelation that the tragic subject quickly cooperates with necessity and accepts the transference of guilt from the gods, blinding himself to the origin of guilt. As Slavoj Žižek puts it, referring to the identity of the sublime Law and the monstrous implicit in Kant's distinction between the two (an identity whose recognition Kant avoids), what 'our finite mind perceives as the sublime majesty of the moral Law is in itself the monstrosity of a crazy sadistic God'.[104]

In tragedy law reveals itself to be the combination of the monstrous, whimsical, cruel gods (what the hero constructs as objective necessity, as I shall soon propose) and the beneficial enabler of social and political life. The nexus between monstrous and moral Law is the hero, whose act of self-blinding to transcendent evil in order to see objective necessity as 'this side of God' premises the possibility of subjectivation and identity. From this perspective, the tragic subject is not a sacrificial victim on whom all the destructive tensions of the community are displaced, and through whose death the community is redeemed. Rather, the tragic subject embodies the blind spot that allows the community to get rid of the perspective which, by revealing the terrifying emptiness of the gods as principle of authority, would undo the foundation of law.

This brings us back to the emptiness of divine guilt. What is the fault of the gods? Precisely that as source of authority and regulation, the gods are an empty structure. This would explain why that fault has been attributed to jealousy and envy. A divine order which is jealous of man has nothing to offer him, least of all redemption: it exhausts itself in the act of jealousy. It is therefore not the gods' wickedness, but rather their emptiness, that the tragic hero refuses to see.

Divine monstrosity, the obverse and condition of possibility of Law, consists in its emptiness. Such emptiness is so terrible that it constitutes and guarantees, paradoxically, the foundation of Law: Law exists in a void, it is just formal, as we will see in Chapter 2 concerning Kant's ethics. It is that emptiness that makes Law revolutionary. Under the appearance of regulating human actions, Law is nothing but the obligation to fulfil one's duty, a duty that is not specified or described. Since Law does not offer a set of positive, concrete rules with content, following its injunction – i.e. fulfilling one's duty – precipitates the self into uncertain territory. It demands that one act in the void, with no support from any positive system that will legitimize those acts. This emptiness imposes on the self the unbearable responsibility of deciding what a good action is, without ever receiving, either before or after acting, the confirmation that its choice was right. This would explain why the self always feels guilty beforehand. This guilt is productive of the tragic subject, but also of the modern autonomous self and of the notion of subjective agency, as we shall see in the next chapters. In fact, the temporality presupposed in the word 'beforehand', in the guilt felt for having infringed a law whose content one ignores even before acting, is suspended. From the viewpoint of the formality of the Law, in the absence of positive confirmation, the 'before' and the 'after' of acting are collapsed into the same movement: after acting I'm going to confront the same lack of confirmation as before. My action does not take me any further into a route, defined by a positive symbolic system, which has as its finality the fair or the good. The act coincides with the non-act.

This is what tragedy, if read from a different perspective, so brilliantly expresses: well-intended action only makes a difference for the worse. Thus, one might as well cooperate with an imposed necessity, *create* a tragic fate with which to cooperate. Such a creative act allows, at least, for a conception of agency as the voluntary assumption of what was inevitable in the first place.[105] It allows the self to perceive action as its willed effect, to fancy itself the origin of action, an agent. Agency and decision, in other words, necessarily depend on constraint. They cannot exist except in confrontation with failure, with external control, by being denied.

Without internalizing objective necessity, the operation that secures the tragic subject's (and our) perception of the Law as sublime, the emptiness of the Law would cause vertigo. Assuming the ethical need for that emptiness would entail the abyssal act of determining our duty and fulfilling it without being supported by a positive symbolic order. It would entail, in effect, that I as subject give substantial content to the empty Law while assuming responsibility for the concreteness of moral norms. Speaking of Kant's ethics and paraphrasing Hegel, Žižek expresses the extreme responsibility inherent in the subject's act of translating the abstract demand of the Law into concrete positive norms, as conceiving ' "the moral Absolute not only as Substance but also as Subject": the ethical subject bears full responsibility for the concrete universal norms he follows – that is to say, the only guarantor of the universality of positive moral norms is the subject's own contingent act of performatively assuming these norms'.[106] Later, I will ask whether the ability to respond to the empty injunction of the Law would require a different framework, a mode of intelligibility other than the tragic one.[107] But tragic intelligibility founds a social order whose organizing principle the self must preserve at the price of its death, and the modern tradition of the self-conscious subject is based on this model. What is at stake here is the way in which these death-based identities liberate the self from ethical responsibility. The alienating relation of the tragic subject with what it posits as the objective necessity which deprives it of its autonomy paradoxically allows it to avoid relating to real people – precisely those who ultimately suffer the consequences of the self's acts and misdeeds. It is before other people that the self becomes truly accountable. Thus, in the very same alienating act that deprives the self of its autonomy, autonomy is preserved, because cooperating with objective necessity protects our autonomy from a more *real* threat: the experience of the actual people who suffer from our actions. Real persons are the only others who can indeed disrupt this intelligible universe which the subject enables by assuming guilt, and whose central position it occupies, albeit at the cost of its life.

2
The Allure of Tragic Guilt

It is time to look at the tragic subject's cooperation with objective necessity from the perspective of desire. In Euripides' *Hippolytus*, the play that inspired Jean Racine's *Phèdre*, the nurse speaks of 'something other dearer still than life':

> But something other dearer still than life
> the darkness hides and mist encompasses;
> we are proved luckless lovers of this thing
> that glitters in the underworld: no man
> can tell us of the stuff of it, expounding
> what is, and what is not: we know nothing of it.
> Idle we drift, on idle stories carried.[1]

Something 'other', a 'thing' 'dearer still than life', of which 'we know nothing', of which nobody can tell us. '[W]e are proved luckless lovers of this thing.' Is 'this thing' death, the ultimate object of desire? Is death, in this case, an otherness that desires, whose unknowable desire we attempt to interpret and fulfil? Is it, in this sense, an ethical imperative so foreign, excessive and incomprehensible that it is impossible to meet?

Objective necessity as the desire of the Other: *Phaedra* with Lacan

Desire, ethical duty, death and tragedy meet in the last session of Lacan's Seminar VII, on *The Ethics of Psychoanalysis* (1959–60). Here Lacan characterizes ethics as acting in conformity with one's unconscious desire. Since, according to him, one should not give way on one's desire – 'ne pas céder sur son désir' – an ethical action is one taken in conformity with one's desire to the end. Lacan then turns turns to tragedy to illuminate the interplay of action, desire and death in the constitution of the self as subject:

> [T]he relationship between action and the desire which inhabits it in the space of tragedy functions in the direction of a triumph of death [*dans le sens d'un triomphe de la mort*]. I taught you to rectify the notion as a triumph of being for death [*triomphe de l'être-pour-la-mort*] that is formulated in Oedipus' *me phunai*, a phrase in which one finds that *me*, the negation that is identical to the entrance of the subject, supported by the signifier. There lies the fundamental character of all tragic action.[2]

Me phunai, 'Not to be born is best when all is reckoned in, but once a man has seen the light the next best thing, by far, is to go back where he came from, quickly as he can.'[3] According to Lacan's teaching in *The Ethics of Psychoanalysis*, in other words, the desire of the tragic protagonist is not associated with life, but rather is bound to death. 'The negation that is identical to the entrance of the subject, supported by the signifier' indicates, furthermore, that the death that triumphs here is a death that identifies. In Seminar VIII, *Le transfert*, Lacan refers again to Oedipus' *me phunai* ('this *could I not be*, which means *not be born*') in order to emphasize the self's entrance in 'the implacable game of debt'.

> *Me phunai*, this *would that I were not* or *would that I had not been* to be more precise (ce *ne sois-je*, ou ce *ne fus-je* pour être plus près), this not being there which in French in so curiously confused with the verb of birth, this is what happens in the case of Oedipus. And what is indicated here? – if not the fact that through the imposition of a destiny upon man, through the exchange prescribed by parental structures, there is something there, something concealed, which brings on, with its entrance into the world, man's entrance into the implacable game of debt. In the final analysis, Oedipus is guilty because of the charge that he receives from the debt of the *Ate* that precedes him.[4]

This being-towards-death, which radically differs from the death drive (a drive that is indifferent both to death and to life),[5] gives the self a subjective position in the symbolic order ('the negation that is identical to the entrance of the subject, under the support of the signifier') as soon as it takes upon itself a symbolic debt by assuming guilt. There is a correlation between desire, death, subjectivation, debt and guilt.

What is it exactly that tragic subjects desire? I would like to read this link between desire, death and subjectivation in the light of Lacan's dictum that 'desire is the desire of the Other'. The force that drives tragedy is objective necessity, which receives several denominations: tragic destiny, divine command, fate. One of the most perplexing aspects of tragedy is the passion with which tragic subjects cooperate with the fate that brings on their doom ('with exceedingly impassioned passion', says Agamemnon, who deems 'right and holy' his act of desiring his own destiny).[6] Given the characters' willingness to die in order to become reconciled with their destiny, could we venture that their object of desire is objective necessity *as* the desire of the Other, as the inscrutable desire of the Other?[7] What I am proposing is that one becomes a tragic victim by constructing what one imagines that the Other desires (from oneself) as the dictates of fate. In using the word 'constructing' I wish to underscore that inevitable as objective necessity may appear, it is none the less an illusion, a fiction fashioned by the self that plays a crucial role in its constitution as subject. Objective necessity thus acquires the strange status of 'necessary fiction'.[8] The problem – as well as the guarantee – of subjectivation is that the Other's desire remains a secret to which we have no access. We desire 'something dearer still than life', a thing 'that glitters in the underworld', of which 'we know nothing'.

Objective necessity responds nevertheless to the aspiration to give some positive content to the secret of the Other's desire, but since that desire is unknowable, since, furthermore, 'we are proved luckless lovers of this thing', then the only way the subject can commit to fulfilling that desire is by renouncing life.

Having to die in order to become a subject seems an extraordinary thing. The question that arises is who is the Other whose desire tragic subjects want to fulfil by abandoning life. What could one gain by desiring to die? The words that Lacan attributes to Oedipus, *me phunai* (it is first best not to have been born, and second to die as fast as one can) are 'identical to the entrance of the subject, supported by the signifier'. The Other is the social order, call it the Symbolic or the Law, which gives us an identity, which constitutes us as subjects. We achieve a position in the social system of meaning by assuming guilt.

Oedipus constitutes an intriguing exception to subjectivation through death, because of his unusual relation to desire and necessity. Since at the moment of acting in order to avoid the fulfilment of the prophecy

Oedipus is unaware that he is actually fulfilling it, he is deprived of the chance to desire objective necessity, and therefore of the occasion to become guilty, which only desiring could have afforded him. Alenka Zupančič describes the case of Oedipus with Lacan's words in his reading of Paul Claudel's *The Hostage* in *Le transfert*: 'someone has his desire taken away from him and, in exchange, he is given to someone else – in this case, to the social order'.[9] Oedipus' destiny could then be summed up, she suggests, as 'the theft of desire and the mother in exchange'.[10] Is there more shocking a fate, being Oedipus without the complex? Having one's mother seems a pale substitute for desiring one's mother, and so, stubbornly claiming he is innocent, Oedipus refuses to die and be reconciled with his destiny by assuming a symbolic debt.[11] His lack of guilt and renunciation of death provokes an unusual dénouement, a tragedy whose protagonist does not die.[12] Now, if we agree that Oedipus refuses the pattern of subjectivation through death, why would he pronounce the words that Lacan attributes to him, *me phunai*, thus undermining his obstinate refusal to die? It so happens that *me phunai* is not enunciated by Oedipus, but rather by the Chorus.[13] Yet Lacan's attribution of these words to Oedipus is significant, for Oedipus constitutes the perfect example of the relation between desire and death *in negative terms*.

If tragic characters desire necessity, indeed if they construct necessity, it is in an attempt to give a content to the desire of the Other. Because of the intense impulse to fulfil that desire, their desire for the desire of the Other is one in relation to which the possibility of their own death and the death of others no longer seems terrible. It is from this perspective that to be driven by the desire of the Other means to assume responsibility for a course of action that was initially imposed, and to do so passionately. Within the context of tragedy, assuming as individually chosen what appeared inevitable in the first place does appear to be the appropriate action. But this heroic gesture is not selfless. In fact, it is not even heroic, as we shall see.

There is no worse way of insulting tragic characters than by absolving them from their guilt. 'It is a point of honour with such great characters that they are guilty,' writes Hegel in the second of his *Lectures on Fine Art*.[14] 'They have no desire to avoid the blame that results therefrom [deeds that are both injurious and wrongful]. On the contrary, it is their fame to have done what they have done. One can in fact urge nothing more intolerable against a hero of this type than by saying that he has acted innocently.'[15] By assuming guilt, tragic subjects achieve identity and sense, which is why they do want to be guilty, why the idea of being innocent is intolerable, why they need to preserve their blame at any cost.

Guilt is crucial. In fact, guilt is so alluring that it provokes erotic ecstasy. The nurse who in Euripides' *Hippolytus* speaks about our desire for 'something dearer than life' addresses her words to Phaedra, wife of King Theseus and mother-in-law of Hippolytus. In this tragedy Phaedra is agonically divided between desire and honour – between her illicit desire for Hippolytus and the respect due to Theseus, as well as her own position as a queen. Twenty centuries later, Jean Racine re-enacts this story in his tragedy *Phèdre (Phaedra)*.[16] The context in which Racine writes is the beginning of the absolutist state, whose form the Enlightenment would critique but also retain by replacing the monarchic power legitimized by God with the moral Law dictated by Reason that constitutes the modern subject.[17] A significant difference between the two plays, if conceived as artistic artifacts that rehearse human experience, is the weight Racine's *Phaedra* places on its restrained use of language, apparent in the precedence of speaking over physical satisfaction in the pursuit of sexual desire. Moreover, if in Euripides' *Hippolytus* sexual desire exemplifies human impotence to escape divine design, the eroticism of a guilty conscience becomes the center of Racine's play. It is therefore to Racine's *Phaedra* that I now turn to explore what it is that makes guilt so alluring.[18]

Phaedra's subjectivity is rent between desire and conscience, between the virus of Venus that she inherits from her mother, Pasiphaë, and the prohibition that she inherits from her father, Minos, the guardian of Hades, and her maternal grandfather, Helios, the Sungod. Phaedra is thus torn between two imperatives, the overwhelming desire she inherits from her mother and the restriction of conscience embodied by her grandfather. Hers is a dilemma between two impossible alternatives that characterizes tragic choice. But, as in classical tragedy, her division between desire and conscience is just formal, it is a dual structure without content, as Barthes observes.[19] Its terms, desire and conscience, constitute the two sides of the same thing: of her desire *for* conscience, *for* guilt.

What does Phaedra desire, what is the object of her desire? Hippolytus, her husband Theseus' son? (The other, another's body?) Hippolytus *as* a substitute for the absent Theseus, as a blank screen on which to project her desire? Not really. In an acknowledgement that would make many husbands shudder, and that Hippolytus does his best to misinterpret, Phaedra loses her sight and speech in Theseus' presence because she sees his son Hippolytus in him.[20] In a moment of rapture, transfigured by the intense erotic desire that invades her, she confesses her passion to Hippolytus, asking him to end her life by striking her with his sword (*frappe*), or to give her his sword to kill herself (*donne*).[21] Terrified and shocked, Hippolytus the hunter, the chaste, runs away.

But is Hippolytus indeed the object of Phaedra's desire? Lacan says that there is no such thing as a desired object. Hippolytus seems the ideal object of desire (the object of desire that Lacan says does not exist, that is, the excuse to displace one's desire), because he himself is incapable of desiring. Phaedra is in love with prohibition, and from this perspective choosing the frigid Hippolytus as object of desire proves appropriate, since he will neither respond to her desire nor satisfy it. True, when Phaedra learns that Hippolytus desires another woman, Aricia, she is full of jealousy and rage. But her rage should be read in light of her investment in Hippolytus' frigidity, that is, less as a consequence of jealousy than as an anticipation of the terrible threat that a desiring Hippolytus would pose to her own desire. What disrupts Phaedra's integrity is the fact that he desires at all. And terrified she might well be, since what a desiring Hippolytus would ultimately threaten is Phaedra's desire *for* necessity, the continuity of her desire that his frigidity guaranteed. Only by virtue of remaining insensitive to desire can Hippolytus keep Phaedra's desire, and hence her self-division, alive.

Hippolytus becomes the alibi that Phaedra needs to devote herself entirely to the inscrutable desire of the Other, the symbolic order that dictates necessity. Though Phaedra laments not having reaped the fruits of her love, she also rejoices over her guilt-ridden existence:

> Hélas! Du crime affreux dont la honte me suit
> Jamais mon triste coeur n'a recueilli le fruit.
> Jusqu'au dernier soupir, de malheurs poursuivie,
> Je rends dans les tourments une pénible vie.[22]

> *Alas, my sad heart never plucked the fruit*
> *Of pleasure from the frightful crime of which*
> *I stand accused by shame.*
> *To my last gasping breath by griefs pursued,*
> *I here surrender my tormented life.*[23]

Which makes us wonder: What is it exactly that Phaedra wants? Does she want to enjoy physical satisfaction, or to preserve her own burning conscience, her consciousness of guilt, thus accomplishing her self-division? In 'I Want to Die, I Hate my Life – Phaedra's Malaise', Simon Critchley writes:

> Phaedra is a paradox: she detests her desire, yet she cannot give way on it; she fears the burning conscience of the sun, yet she constantly calls to him. The gravity of her desire is constituted by her will to pull free of it in the experience of conscience. The promised ecstasy of libidinous transgression is directly proportionate to the power of moral prohibition.[24]

She is more libidinally attached to the Sungod than to Venus, to her tormented conscience more than to her desire. *'Soleil, je te viens voir pour la dernière fois'*, she says as a final farewell to the one she really desires before taking her own life. Phaedra's choice of Hippolytus seems made out of fidelity to prohibition (embodied by her grandfather, the Sungod), out of attraction to punishment (to be administered by her father). Running through her veins, the prohibition that she inherits from the men of her lineage Oedipally rouses her attachment to guilt. More exactly, what Phaedra desires is the Sungod's inscrutable desire, which manifests itself as objective necessity, that is, as the social order that forbids her desire. In other words, the unknowable desire of the Other (of objective necessity) becomes the desire of the subject (of Phaedra), who in desiring necessity becomes guilty.[25]

Although Phaedra's illicit love for Hippolytus would seem to profane the rules of the social order, in effect her investment in adultery and incest comes to reassert the symbolic world. Though she murders and lies, her acts of murdering and lying are still carried over as transgressions to that order, *within* it. Perhaps the revelation of intelligibility, of the sense that the social order promises, constitutes Phaedra's ultimate – and impossible – object of desire. Of course, the fascination of these transactions of desire lies in the fact that what the Other desires is a secret (Lacan's *'Che vuoi?'*) to which the self has no access, try as it may. Latent in desiring what the Other desires is an unlimited ethical potential. The compulsion to fulfil the Other's unknowable desire dares the self to fill an empty structure (such as Kant's incomprehensible moral Law) with substantial content, that is, to posit its own duty. Nevertheless, the line between positing a duty for which one takes responsibility *and* using blind necessity as an excuse for not fulfilling one's duty is very thin. If the subject initially hesitates to take an imposed course of action, it is because it harms the other (Agamemnon must sacrifice his daughter, Eteocles must stand against his brother). Thus the enjoyment derived from killing the other in fulfilment of one's 'terrible duty' (Agamemnon's 'desire with exceedingly impassioned passion') places tragic protagonists even further away from the ethical.[26]

Death as evasion

The tragic subject dies in response to the desire of objective necessity. But why would the symbolic order *want* us to die? In requiring our death, the social symbolic order prevents us from dying an absolute death that falls out of its jurisdiction. Or, speaking from the position of the subject as agent rather than as victim, we choose to die so as to preserve our subjective position. Hence the paradox of these stories on death called tragedies: in them the ultimate death is avoided. Seen from this perspective, tragic death is not a true death – it does not provide an exit from one's existence, which is why Phaedra, appalled by her own crimes of incest and murder, is horrified at realizing that she cannot die.[27]

> Mes crimes désormais ont comblé la mesure.
> Je respire à la fois l'inceste et l'imposture.
> Mes homicides mains, promptes à me venger,
> Dans le sang innocent brûlent de se plonger.
> Misérable! Et je vis? Et je soutiens la vue
> De ce sacré Soleil dont je suis descendue?
> J'ai pour aïeul le père et le maître des Dieux;
> Le ciel, tout l'univers est plein de mes aïeux.
> Où me cacher? Fuyons dans la nuit infernale!
> Mais que dis-je? Mon père y tient l'urne fatale.
> Le sort, dit-on, l'a mise en ses sévères mains:
> Minos juge aux enfers tous les pâles humains.
> Ah! Combien frémira son ombre épouvantée,
> Lorsqu'il verra sa fille à ses yeux présentée,
> Contrainte d'avouer tant de forfaits divers,
> Et les crimes peut-être inconnus aux enfers!
> Que diras-tu, mon père, à ce spectacle horrible?
> Je crois voir de ta main tomber l'urne terrible,
> Je crois te voir, cherchant un supplice nouveau,
> Toi-même de ton sang devenir le bourreau.
> Pardonne.[28]

> Guilt has passed
> all bounds. Hypocrisy and incest breathe
> At once through all. My murderous hands are prompt
> To vengeance; eager to spill innocent blood.
> Do I yet live, wretch that I am, and dare
> To face this holy sun from which I spring?
> My father was the master of the Gods;
> My ancestors fill all the Universe.
> Where can I hide? In the dark realms below?
> But there my father holds the fatal urn;
> His hand awards the irrevocable doom;
> Minos is judge of all the ghosts in hell.
> Ah! How his shade will shudder with surprise
> When he shall see his daughter brought before him,
> Forced to confess sins of such varied dye;
> Crimes, it may be, unknown to hell itself!
> What wilt thou say, my father, at a sight
> So horrible? In my mind's eye I see
> The fateful urn crash from thy hand. I see
> Thee seeking some unheard-of punishment
> Thyself become my executioner.
> Forgive me![29]

It is quite an irony that Phaedra cannot die after courting guilt so insistently, after cursing her black flame. For that is how Phaedra refers to her passion, as 'such a black flame'. *Une flamme si noir. . .* In *Phaedra* world and underworld are strictly complementary, hence the contrasts of light and darkness, what Barthes denominates *chiaroscuro*.[30] In strident complementarity, light and darkness – flame and shadow ('shadow about to be penetrated by a burst of light'),[31] hell and world, white and black – announce their strict identity. *'Une flamme si noir'*: as long as the symbolic universe is shaped by contrasts (light, dark), by polarities (world and hell), it reaffirms itself, preserves its integrity and remains a *safe* place both for us (*its* dutiful subjects), and particularly for itself (the world). Where to escape? No wonder that Phaedra cannot die, since dying and inhabiting hell, in the terms she conceives of it, would be no different from remaining in the world. Rather than 'something [...] that glitters in the underworld', of which 'we know nothing', hell here is a familiar (and familial) place that Phaedra can describe in detail. The night of Hades is no more than the world's other side, and thus still part of the symbolic order. It is not Hades that Phaedra fears most, since in going there she would be returning to the place she never left, to her father's scale of justice – she would go back home. Unable to die, Phaedra languishes, lulled by an awesomely sensual guilt, which descending to the underworld would only intensify.[32]

From Phaedra's inability to die does not follow that the (symbolic) world dies. Her vigil attests to the world's vitality, to its success. It cannot die, the symbolic world that Phaedra embodies with all its impossible eroticism, nor should it, perhaps. What seems tragic is having to die in order to save the world, having to disappear so as to preserve the world's intelligibility intact, securing one's intelligibility in the same movement as one ends. Only those who ignore the monstrous lack of intelligibility that horrifies the tragic subject will survive.

It has been argued that dying is not possible in the tragic universe, that in it death is, in Barthes' words, *une mort durée*, 'a lasting death'.[33] But I would like to add: dying is not possible in the tragic universe *as long as one refuses to leave that universe*. As long as death is still part of the tragic universe, as long as one cannot envisage a way of dying *to* the tragic universe, one cannot die.

What then is tragic death? In my view, the death that Phaedra so much wishes but momentarily postpones actually constitutes the space for evasion. Though Phaedra's desire for the desire of the Other (negatively embodied in the prohibition of adultery and incest) leads her to desire her death, the death she anticipates is still an escape from something more terrible. She refuses to die to the social symbolic order and to be undone as a subject. She never acts outside of intelligibility; she avoids facing sheer monstrosity and indeterminate nothingness because that act would amount to dismantling the symbolic frame that guarantees her guilt, her being. What drives her existence is the impulse to preserve her symbolic debt – when prohibited by social norms, the virus of Venus is so sensuous that Phaedra must languish in erotic ecstasy. When she does die, she achieves her subjectivity retrospectively, and also secures the subjectivity of others. By dying the kind of death she foresees, the one her father imposes, Phaedra evades the monstrosity of emptiness, the murmur of nothingness.

Tragedy bears the traces of the emptiness of authority in the invisible form of the *other side* of Destiny. That monstrous emptiness, the void around which the tragic universe is structured, can only be perceived in the rejection it provokes. Tragedy suggests the existence of the 'worse than tragic' in its depiction of the subject's act of avoiding it by blinding itself and passionately cooperating with necessity. The emptiness that supports the symbolic order is, of course, not specific to tragedy –

it powers up any symbolic framework. What is specifically tragic is the structure of desire and horror whereby the self assumes the traumatic injunction placed by objective necessity in order not to confront the monstrous nothingness that constitutes its other side. 'Tragic' does not refer to any external constellation of competing forces, but rather to the position that the human self adopts in relation to desire/horror. I would further suggest that the very act of avoiding emptiness is what makes subjects specifically tragic.

Tragedy is larger than objective necessity. It also depicts in negative terms a heteronomous constellation (destiny's *other side*) that the tragic subject evades by accepting another situation of heteronomy (objective necessity as *this side* of destiny). The heteronomous situation provoked by the other side of destiny might be considered ethical in so far as it places all the weight of the decision on the human self. This would be a decision taken in the absence of objective necessity, beyond any organizing source of transcendence or control, without any external determination that dictates the coordinates of ethical activity in advance. Because this ethical responsibility exceeds tragic sense, because it lies beyond sublimation, it may appear more terrifying than tragedy. By contrast, the obligation imposed by objective necessity – an alien injunction that characters such as Agamemnon or Eteocles passionately assume as a path to the desire of the Other – requires a legitimizing source of control. This form of subjection is not ethical, it is tragic, because it is embraced for the sake of preserving the intelligibility of the tragic universe as well as and one's position in it: though I die (literally if I am a tragic subject; as material and sensible being if I am a modern subject), the order that gives me an identity is preserved. Precisely because I am aware of the impossibility of becoming intelligible, I must remain faithful to my desire for intelligibility by blinding myself. Tragic death as evasion, as escape.

This is, to my mind, the driving force of tragedy: enacting the traumatic possibility of the collapse of the world, and then reaffirming the symbolic order that sustains that world when it fragments. If the moment of breakage were not necessitated for that reassertion, tragic reversal would be pointless and the tragic causality would have no bearing on human existence (if we pretend for a moment that the former could exist independently of human invention). And the giving way of the symbolic, or what I call the temporary delay of the fulfilment of fate, necessitates the energetic, if short-lived, performance of autonomy that tragic personae insert as a temporary resistance to necessity. A short-lived threat this is, an aborted seed of denial that tragedy engenders, where the two predispositions of the tragic subject, desire and death (*as* escape from death to the symbolic), meet in the form of self-sacrifice. Phaedra assumes a transference of culpability for the guilt and the desire that tear her apart, and cultivates that self-division for the sake of the survival of the symbolic world: although the individual dies, subjectivation, the possibility of producing the subject, survives. In dying as a consequence of assuming as voluntarily chosen what was initially inherited, the self approves retrospectively of its constitution as subject.

This is perhaps the most important sense in which tragedy is political. When considered a Christian tragedy framed by the hidden Jansenist God, as Critchley proposes following Lucien Goldmann, Phaedra might appear anti-political if compared with classical or modern tragedy.³⁴ However, what makes *Phaedra* a tragedy is less the elusiveness of the *Deus absconditus* than the fact that its protagonist undergoes subjectivation through death. From this perspective, Racinian tragedy, just as Attic and modern tragedy – the former with an internally-fractured source of transcendence (which is both divine and legal), the latter without a God – embodies the conditions of possibility of the political. Indeed, *Phaedra* enables the political, since it bears witness both to attachment to prohibition and to internalization of ideological repression working at their best: it rehearses the conflictual constitution of the political subject. Tragedy creates the political space by displaying the claims of each kind of justice to the empty position of authority, and by placing the human self in a situation of intense desire for it, a desire that none of the existing sources of power is able to fulfil. Moreover, the conditions of the tragic subject's decision are political: it must decide which realm of authority to follow, even though the boundaries between one and the other are unclear, only to realize that there is no actual choice, only a structure of choice, yet it will nevertheless be held responsible for its performance of decision. Confronting the *other side* of power, the empty side that in *Phaedra* supports the symbolic order of both hell and world, would be even worse – and thus the political subject constitutes itself, we might say, by reacting against that emptiness. As a condition of subjective constitution, this vertigo of nothingness must remain foreclosed to consciousness, which is why modernity has pushed it aside.

What characterizes tragedy, whether in its artistic forms (classical or otherwise), or as a mode of organizing experience (as a model of subjectivity), is that it is shaped around objective necessity, itself an empty source of control that the self fills with the illusion of another's desire. It is as if the content of one's obligation were dictated by oneself in the attempt to fulfil the unknowable injunction of another. A similar constellation structures Kant's principle of autonomy, whereby the rational subject gives itself a Law that it receives from elsewhere.[35] This pattern, which is premised on the notions of destiny and debt, structures both modern tragedy and modern subjectivity, as I argue in the next chapters.

Now it becomes clear that the pairs of opposites that divide the subject – world/hell, life/death, desire/conscience – become identical after all. Ultimately, it is not between these terms that one must choose, but rather between the tragic and the non-tragic. As we will see, the ultimate decision, *the* decision for which one takes responsibility instead of attributing it to fate, exceeds the tragic. It might even end it, for one must choose between dying to save the tragic, as Phaedra does, *or* abandoning the tragic and undoing oneself as tragic subject.

If Phaedra does not die an absolute death, if, according to Barthes, in the tragic universe one does not die, who in this tragedy is the subject of death? – asks Critchley. In my view, the corpse at the end of the play is not that of an unlivable world, nor that of the illusion of the political order. Neither is it, emphatically, the corpse of the subject itself, for subjectivity reemerges energized. But there is a death that has disastrous consequences for our present world, a world that we deprive of human responsibility when we choose to interpret it as tragic. It is the death of the ethical impulse, both individual and collective, which the tragic subject must avoid lest it should undo itself. What dies here is no less than the possibility of ethics.

Exceeding sublime tragic sense

Only by not giving way on one's desire *and* by realizing it does one act ethically, says Lacan.[36] It may appear that Phaedra does not to give up on her desire, invested, as she is, in her transgression. But does Phaedra indeed remain faithful to her desire and act in conformity with it? It is important to differentiate between desiring objective necessity as the desire of the other (such as Phaedra or Agamemnon or Eteocles do, securing their constitution as subjects) *and* acting on one's desire and pursuing the death-drive (as Antigone and Sygne de Coûfontaine in Paul Claudel's *The Hostage* do in different ways, according to Lacan). Unlike other tragic subjects, Antigone personifies a desire that ignores objective necessity and breaks through subjectivation.[37] Like her father Oedipus she refuses to assume guilt and be reconciled with her fate, she breaks up with the symbolic (this, perhaps, unlike him), introducing a crack in the ontological edifice of reality. In fact, she does not even recognize the objective necessity imposed by the city laws as her own fate. Antigone looks the emptiness of ethical goals in the face, and suspended there, in the absence of any social support (in fact, resisting social opposition), in the abyss, she gives concrete shape to a formal imperative and assumes responsibility for it. Beyond fulfilling her duty, she dares posit her duty (burying the corpse of her brother), make it determinate, and in doing so she disrupts herself, she excludes herself from social commands and therefore undoes herself as a member of society. Refusing intelligibility, without any external legitimation, she acts 'from the place of that limit where her life is already lost, where she is already on the *other side*'.[38]

From this perspective, Phaedra gives way on her desire after all, and in compromising her desire she might be said to evade a terrifying suspension of intelligibility. She avoids looking at the social order from the *other side*, blinding herself to the emptiness of both social and religious authority, to a realization that would perhaps undo her as tragic subject. Against the traditional postulation of tragic heroism espoused by modern philosophy, the tragic paradigm is not heroic if we consider that most tragic subjects die in order to escape symbolic death (unless enabling legal and political society constitutes a worldly kind of heroism). Tragic subjectivation is instantiated by characters such as Agamemnon, Clytemnestra or Eteocles as depicted by Aeschylus, but persistently refused by Antigone and Oedipus. Lacan notices the strangeness of Sophocles' plays, in whose beginning the race is already run, and whose characters are dead before dying, that is, they *exist* between two deaths ('Dead in life,' says Electra. 'I'm already dead to everything').[39] In the Sophoclean universe as we know it from the few extant plays, the role of the tragic subject is usually played by *secondary* characters: Polynices – who passionately assumes the necessity dictated by the curse of Oedipus in spite of Antigone's entreaties in *Oedipus at Colonus*, or Creon in *Antigone*.[40] Antigone might be heroic, but then she is not tragic (she refuses to enter the game of debt). However, her desire becomes its own cause, the cause to which everything else is sacrificed: seeing life 'from the other side' implies achieving the 'outside' standpoint that allows her to embrace her existence as a whole, or what Lacan calls 'the point of view of the Last Judgment'.[41]

In terms of Kant's ethics, Antigone's desire may be taken to represent the 'highest good' or 'infinite measure' that guides all action. But since for Kant the 'highest good' is not a particular object, but rather the perfect coincidence of will and duty – one must come to desire one's duty, Antigone ultimately instantiates classical ethics.[42] Because in classical ethics one sacrifices everything for an ideal (such as the honour for whose sake one is willing to lose one's life), in Lacan's reading Antigone still exemplifies 'the service of goods' (*le service des biens*) which, in providing an infinite measure of every value and action (that is, some kind of transcendental guarantee), is inadequate to describe modern tragedy and ethics. Therefore, in *Le Transfert*, Lacan proposes instead that modern ethics is represented by Sygne de Coûfontaine, the protagonist of Paul Claudel's drama *L'Otage* (*The Hostage*). Like Antigone, Sygne sacrifices everything for her desire, but unlike Sophocles' heroine, Sygne is asked to give up even the exception that justifies renouncing everything else: she must give up her desire, and she is left with nothing.[43] In the end, Sygne dies an unheroic and incomprehensible death, 'agitated by a nervous twitch of her face'.[44] Since with her desire she has had to sacrifice the infinite measure against which to determine the value of what she has lost – indeed, she has done without the higher cause, exception or external perspective that secures the intelligibility of phenomena, the nervous tic that deforms her face may be read as the act whereby the noumenal infinite comes to invade the field of the finite (formed by no longer intelligible phenomena), parasitizing it.[45] If, in Lacan's terms, desire introduces an infinite measure in subjectivity (enabling the classical ethics of a higher cause exemplified by Antigone), the desire that Sygne must sacrifice as exception (as an infinite source of guidance, legitimation and intelligibility) stands for the missing transcendental guarantee in modern ethics.

We are dealing with three different modes of understanding desire. The first one is the self's desire for the desire of the Other – of objective necessity and the symbolic order – that drives tragic characters such as Agamemnon and Phaedra to death (Oedipus, who is denied this desire and therefore subjectivation, confirms it in negative terms). Action is in this case determined by the illusion of externally-imposed control. Second, a desire that is not evaded, that becomes its own cause, the exception to which everything else is sacrificed. Personified by Antigone, this is the desire that most tragic subjects evade through death. Here the course of action is posited by the self in an act that defies social normativity and leaves one's subjective intelligibility in suspension. Guided nevertheless by faithfulness to a cause, this action, though inserted outside of society, is taken with full individual certainty: what Antigone wants is clear from the outset; rather than being divided by two non-viable options, her decision is irrevocable. Finally, there is a desire (that Sygne must *realize*) that sacrifices everything, even itself as the exception or higher cause to which everything else is sacrificed.[46]

The first kind of desire, which constitutes subjects as tragic, is associated with the possibility of modern subjectivity and politics, as I will claim in Chapters 3 and 5. The second kind, an unbearable desire that tragic subjects evade, exceeds tragedy but still functions as the infinity or limit that defines tragedy. The third kind of desire structures a non-heroic ethics, an infinite ethics that does not service any predetermined higher good and may even destroy. This absolute desire, manifested as the commitment to fulfil an obligation which is ultimately impossible to meet, is related to Kant's perplexing notion that the free subject is constituted as such by desiring its duty, by making its will coincide with the moral Law. Accordingly, one becomes a free subject by desiring the empty injunction placed on oneself by a categorical imperative not as substantial content, but as form.[47] 'The moral law ... looked at more closely, is simply desire in its pure state,' says Lacan.[48] Like intransitive pure desire, this ethical demand has no concrete object, it is empty (it exists outside of content) and impossible to fulfil. We can never have any knowledge of what is being demanded from us.

At this point I hope to have identified two distinct modes of obligation to another that give shape to different types of subjectivity. The first (tragic) mode produces the self-conscious autonomous subject that premises the rational political order. The second (ethical) mode of obligation, in turn, constitutes a vulnerable, endlessly obligated and infinitely responsible subject by placing on it an unconditional ethical demand that is prior to (tragic) subjectivation. Before and beyond the identity conferred by regulated society, in other words, the self is invested as an infinitely responsible subject by an order of obedience coming from an other. Whether the other that imposes the ethical demand is reason (as in Kant's moral Law), the face of the other (as in Levinas's infinite responsibility), or the desire to which one must remain faithful (as in Lacan's ethics of psychoanalysis), it obligates the self to act without receiving any external legitimation. When I trace the rapport between these two modes of subjective constitution in the last chapter, I will tentatively call them *tragic* heteronomy and *ethical* heteronomy.

Failures of the imagination: Aristotle's plot and Kant's antinomies

The desire for tragic death and the 'pure' desire that tragic subjects evade structure two different modes of apprehending reality, of making it intelligible. Here I will begin to explore the first one, the tragic mode of making sense of experience, by analysing the work of synthesis effected by the tragic plot. Can the plot offer any clues to the synthesizing activity of the imagination, to its representation of human action?

In his treatise on literary representation, the *Poetics*, Aristotle underscores the fact that action and fiction – what happens or might happen, and the way of accounting for it – are inseparable. Mimesis, says Aristotle, is the imitation of an action through the mediation of a plot. The implications of this well-known but extremely complex definition are crucial to understand reason's apprehension of the phenomenal world. Although its first half, imitating an action, alludes to the possibility of 'copying' reality, the second half, about the plot's mediating activity, suggests that reality can be imitated only by being recreated or rearranged according to conventional narrative rules (i.e. rules that have been constructed and established as the norm). In one of the most revolutionary insights into the concept of agency, here Aristotle introduces a productive tension between copying an action and constructing it, between repeating reality and fictionalizing it, rendering the practice of reproducing or reflecting 'reality' and the act of inventing it inextricable. Every attempt to account for human action, in short, must have recourse to fiction.

From the irreducible tension between reproducing and fictionalizing an action it follows that an unmediated copy, an exact representation of experience (not to mention of 'reality', which does not constitute Aristotle's object here), is impossible in the strict sense. The poet, says Aristotle, 'cannot undo the traditional stories, e.g. that Clytemnestra is killed by Orestes . . . ; but he should invent for himself, i.e., use the inherited [stories] well'.[49] Interestingly, in addition to suggesting that imitation and invention are intertwined, this explanation presupposes that the initial action to be imitated, 'the traditional stories', is not itself an unmediated manifestation of reality, since it already exists only as a narrative, as a representation. Creativity lies, as Aristotle intimates, in this irredeemable tension between imitating and constructing, between copying and inventing.

The structural principle through which a plot organizes experience, imprinting significance on otherwise meaningless events, is causal intelligibility. Events, according to Aristotle, must be linked according to causality, that is, they must arise 'either by necessity or by probability as a result of the preceding events'.[50] Connections between events must be internal, not external to the plot, in order for the plot successfully to realize the work of synthesis from which intelligibility springs.[51] Universalization is central to poetic creation, and consists in making the intelligible spring from the singular and the necessary from the fragmentary. As Ricoeur says, the plot's 'making is immediately a universalizing "making". The whole problem of narrative *Verstehen* is contained here in principle. To make up a plot is already to make the intelligible spring from the accidental, the universal from the singular, the necessary or the probable from the episodic.'[52] The poet, writes Aristotle, 'should set them [his stories, both those already made up and those he composes himself] out as universals'.[53] Regarding the strategies through which narrative produces universality, we could describe the plot as a work of synthesis that confers universality on selected events by arranging them according to the rules of causality, that is, as if they had taken place not 'one after another', but 'one because of the other'.[54]

But how is causality accomplished and measured? Who is to decide, and by what standards, whether the plot succeeds in presenting events as a result of previous actions, that is, as probable? '[P]ossibility means credibility,' writes Aristotle.[55] A chain of events is probable, that is, not when it reflects reality, but when it convinces the audience that it is believable: 'What is impossible yet probable should be preferred to that which is possible but incredible. . . . Thus in reference to poetic effect, a convincing impossibility is preferable to that which, though possible, is unconvincing.'[56] The probable is therefore partly constructed in the plot and partly defined by the audience.

The audience's verdict about the probability of a particular turn of events takes place retrospectively. Although probable, the convincing events are not foreseeable, they should be impossible to anticipate and therefore come as a surprise. The effect that tragic causality has on the audience must be unexpected. Though Aristotle illustrates this point with examples from the most famous tragic plays, the formulation of this fact is one of the most perplexing in the *Poetics*. In order to become 'terrifying and pitiable' (that is, to achieve what he calls the 'tragic effect'), events should thus take place 'contrary to expectation but because of one another'.[57] Even what appears accidental, seemingly brought about by a stroke of luck, ultimately meets the causal requirement, a fact that will make the recovery of order more convincing. More importantly, 'contrary to expectation but because of one another' introduces a disjunction between expectation and necessity. This disjunction is particularly interesting if we consider it from the perspective outlined above of objective necessity as the unknowable desire of the symbolic order, as a secret impossible to discern. Although events will appear as the result of previous actions, the characters are unable to foresee, let alone plan and assume responsibility for, the effects of their acts. As

Ricoeur writes, 'reversal, recognition, and suffering – particularly when they are joined together in one work, as in Sophocles' *Oedipus* – bring to their highest degree of tension the fusion of the "paradoxical" and the "causal" sequence, of surprise and necessity.'[58] In short, Aristotle's unexpected identification of the causal and the paradoxical would seem to exclude the possibility of human intentionality. Contradictory as this may seem, causality can take place only through happenings that the human self, unaware of transcendent design, must interpret as chance.

But does the plot's requirement of unforeseeable causality indeed deny the human self the ability to declare itself the origin of its acts, to become responsible for them? Or is it the human self who, by constructing objective necessity and cooperating with it, by devising the tragic plot as a predominant narrative model for organizing experience, disavows its own agency and responsibility? We begin to see how, rather than simply describing a destructive kind of action, and rather than characterizing a particular type of story-line, the plot unreservedly reveals the limitations and double-binds of agency and decision that premise the possibility of modern and contemporary subject-based politics.

Moreover, the experience that the plot must organize in an intelligible fashion does not need to have taken place in actuality, as long as it is believable. 'What is impossible yet probable should be preferred to that which is possible but incredible. . . . [A] convincing impossibility is preferable to that which, though possible, is unconvincing.'[59] Does the fact that the events to be represented should be 'impossible yet probable' mean that when imitating human action the plot can do without that action? Though the priority of 'impossible' seems to privilege the representation of something that cannot take place in actuality, isn't that concept of 'actuality' defined not by lived experience, which is impossible to grasp without representation, but rather by previous representations? Doesn't Aristotle mean, indeed, that 'impossible' events are those that have not been convincingly represented before – in mythical, legendary or historical accounts, in oral experience or folkloric memory, in non-dramatic lyric or epic poetry, from which tragedy draws for narrative material? At first glance, the fact that the causal and the intelligible are divorced from lived action would seem to widen the cleavage between representation and action, between theory and praxis. Although the distance between lived experience and representation may seem to deny human activity, perhaps becoming aware of the fictional strategies of representation actually reopens a space for subjective initiative, as I will argue in Chapter 4.

To summarize the work of synthesis of the plot, events must happen by a necessity that is unforeseeable, 'contrary to expectation but because of one another'; the events described in this imitation of human action do not need to have taken place in actuality. In short, the tragic representation of reality can do away with that reality as long as the plot meets the requirements of unforeseeability and causality through which it accomplishes its universal character. Thus achieved, the tragic arrangement of human experience can then be reapplied as the paradigm for organizing life, for imprinting intelligibility on it. Should we conclude, then, that the synthetic activity of the imagination destroys or denies that which it represents?

Does this imply that any attempt to account for the phenomenal world is already to posit that world? This is not to suggest that *reality* does not exist *out there*, that it is only a product of the categories with which the imagination approaches it, but rather that the only possible approach we might have to that reality, the only guarantee that it exists, is negative, since it emerges in contrast to our awareness that reality must be different from the ways in which we synthesize it. As such, in the act of representing, reason posits a reality external to its operations and impassible to them, a reality that can exist only as the imagination's obverse. Given that our knowledge of reality is always mediated by perception, it would follow that reality can exist only as an unknown and unknowable place, as a void, perhaps, sustained by the illusion that there is something to be known.

*

Let us pause to reflect on how we posit the reality 'existing out there' that we deem 'objective', since reality is always already mediated by human experience and the different ways in which the imagination organizes that experience. Aristotle's idea that reality is always already represented seems to antecede the transcendental idealist premiss that '"objective" reality itself is constituted through the subjective act of transcendental synthesis'.[60] That is to say, the reality we call objective, existing out there, is posited by us in opposition to subjective representations, the very representations of which Aristotle speaks. As Slavoj Žižek understands it:

> Idealism claims . . . that the In-itself of 'objective reality' is definitely to be distinguished from merely subjective representations – its point is only that it is the synthetic act of the transcendental subject itself

which transforms the multitude of representations into 'objective reality'. In short, idealism's point is not that there is no In-itself, but that the 'objective' In-itself, *in its very opposition* to subjective representations, is posited by the subject.[61]

In *The Plague of Fantasies* and *The Ticklish Subject*, in a discussion of Jacob Rogozinski's *Kanten: Esquisses Kantiennes*, Žižek sets out to analyse the paradoxical relationship between the sublime Law and the Monstrous in Kant. Here I will turn to both accounts for insight into the empty *other side* of Kant's moral Law, in order to reflect on it in relation to the *other side* of fate.

As Rogozinski points out, the terms of the Kantian triad of the Beautiful, the Sublime and the Monstrous are linked, as in a Borromean knot.[62] Rather than being contraposed and contradicting the previous term, each new term shifts into the next when it realizes its potential to the extreme, and mediates between the other two.[63] This interconnection situates both the Sublime and the Monstrous beyond the sensible world, in the realm of the noumenal, where they exist beyond the grasp of intellectual or sensory perception. Pushing Kant's distinction a step beyond what Kant might have been willing to accept, Žižek proposes that the Sublime and the Monstrous are, in the last analysis, identical. Just as the divine universe that rends the tragic subject, making it turn against itself, the Sublime and the Monstrous constitute two sides of the same coin, of the noumenal domain which, precisely by being beyond intellectual or sensory perception, provides the guarantee of the phenomenal world, enabling its intelligibility.

If the Sublime and the Monstrous appear different, it is because the subject's perspective on them changes: the sublime Law will become monstrous if we come too close to it.[64] This is also the case of the sublime *this side* of fate to which the tragic subject restricts its field of perception, in order to avoid seeing the monstrous *other side*. What the tragic subject avoids seeing is the fact that objective necessity as an organizing and intelligibility-conferring principle, indeed as a moral imperative, transfers to the self a debt that the self willingly assumes. Ultimately, what makes fate's *other side* monstrous is its emptiness, as I argued in Chapter 1. This is the unbearable realization that the tragic subject avoids at the cost of its life: that as a source of authority, as the desire of the symbolic order, objective necessity or the Law is an empty structure. To borrow the words with which Žižek describes the revolutionary insight of Kant's philosophy, 'the divine monstrosity appears as the kingdom of rational Goals only when it is viewed from a certain (finite human) angle'; 'what our finite mind perceives as the sublime majesty of the moral law is in itself the monstrosity of crazy sadistic God'.[65]

The tragic act of self-blinding to fate's *other side* or, in Žižek's and Rogozinski's terms, to the Monstrous side that constitutes the reverse of the Sublime Law and thus enables it, is what secures the integrity of the tragic universe (of the symbolic order, as I have called it above). Keeping this in mind, I propose envisaging two different tensions, the tension between *this side* and the *other side* of objective necessity *and* the tension between the Law and its Monstrous enabling side, as parallel constellations. I will suggest that the synthesis constitutive of reality that Kant attributes to the imagination in the *Critique of Pure Reason*, as well as the failure of that synthesis, are instantiated in the syntheses and compensations for failure effected by the tragic plot. If this parallel proves convincing, one of its implications will be that the Reason whose supremacy premises the principle of universalization that enables Kant's categorical imperative, and thus the Enlightenment's conception of modern subjectivity and liberal politics, *is* fundamentally tragic.

In *Kanten*, Rogozinski argues that Kant fails to see that the synthetic activity of the imagination ('memory, retention, temporality') in constituting 'normal' reality is already violent, because it arranges and orders an otherwise chaotic inconsistent range of impressions of the world.[66] Precisely because that violence on phenomena is a prerequisite for the order that the imagination achieves, the synthesis of the imagination fails in two ways. First, the apprehended phenomena far exceed the comprehended phenomena, and the insufficiency of comprehension is intensified by the fact that the initial apprehension is unable to encompass the totality of phenomena. Second, the task of organizing the inconsistent world requires the intervention of an external principle that belongs to the noumenal and is imposed on the chaotic array of phenomena from the outside. This is the intervention of the Law, which the subject experiences as 'a violent intrusion which disturbs the smooth self-sufficient running of the auto-affection of his imagination'.[67]

These failures are met by the two types of transcendental ideas in conflict, dynamic and mathematical, which structure each of the four Kantian antinomies of pure reason.[68] The dynamic antinomy to which idealism gives priority suspends the phenomenal causal chain from the outside through the intervention of the supra-sensible Law. From this viewpoint, the contingency of the phenomenal world would be the consequence of the inscription of the noumenal Beyond in the phenomenal realm. The mathematical antinomy, by contrast, preserves the inherent inconsistency of phenomena, producing an array of elements that does not amount to a whole that possesses the ontological consistency of reality. In other words, the dynamic antinomy avoids the dissolution that would result in the collapse of the imagination, and thus in chaos and inconsistency. Chaos and inconsistency are the consequence of 'the inherent failure, collapse, of imagination' in the mathematical antinomy.[69] While, as Žižek puts it, the mathematical antinomy dissolves 'phenomenal reality in the direction of the monstrous Real', the dynamic antinomy 'transcends phenomenal reality in the direction of the symbolic Law – that is, it "saves phenomena" by providing a kind of external guarantee of the phenomenal domain'.[70] Ultimately, in giving priority to the dynamic antinomy, and thus to the intervention of the Law as constitutive exception, idealism 'saves' the phenomenal world from the total lack of intelligibility inherent in the mathematical antinomy.

What insights into tragic sense-making does the distinction between dynamic and mathematical ideas afford? Following the mode of operation of the dynamic antinomy, and in an attempt to avert the *dissolution* of reality that would threaten the tragic universe if the hero did not cooperate with necessity, tragedy provides *objective necessity* as the organizing principle of human action. From this perspective, objective necessity intervenes as an external guarantee of the intelligibility of human acts. That intelligibility is accomplished by transposing a contingent inconsistent world to two different domains, the divine (or transcendent) and the human. The interaction between the two domains (and therefore the success of this strategy) depends on the subject's willingness to accept a transference of culpability. Therefore, the act of constituting objective necessity as the unknowable desire of the Other ('something other dearer still than life / the darkness hides and mist encompasses'), which then becomes the self's desire ('we are proved luckless lovers of this thing / that glitters in the underworld'), is crucial in securing human cooperation. The very possibility of cooperating, however, can emerge only if the tragic subject restricts itself to the finite human perspective that misses or misrecognizes the *other side* of objective necessity. From this limited perspective, the Monstrous adopts the form of the Sublime Law.

We are now ready to turn to the tragic plot. At stake in the process of emplotment is the radical violence on *human action* exerted by the reversal that constitutes the main operation of the tragic causality represented by objective necessity. The question that arises is whether the *human* causality that objective necessity violently disrupts, according to which actions should have expected results, is not already violent. The term *causality* presupposes a particular arrangement of experience that is the result of a violent synthesis done by the imagination. Since causality always carries the violence that engenders it, we should ask if what seems initially a violence that reversal exerts on the tragic subject is not itself a side-effect of the initial violence exerted by the subject on the phenomenal world. In this sense, by superimposing the tragic causality on *human causality*, the plot might be considered to inflict a violence (reversal) on a violence. This *previous* violence which is violated is the *human causality* that becomes apparent in the subject's expectations regarding the result of its actions, that is, in its assumption that a particular act must produce a particular result. We cannot posit, in other words, a moment in which the imagination has not always already exerted a violence on events experienced as contingent by submitting them to its work of synthesis. For were we to posit that *prior to representation*, would that act of positing not be inherently violent, always already denying, by virtue of conceptualization, that which it represents?

Tragic reversal is one of the clearest instances of the violence done by the imagination's synthesizing activity. But what seems initially a violence exerted by the plot's reversal on the tragic subject is in itself a side-effect of the violence exerted by the subject on the phenomenal world in the process of comprehending and organizing it, of making it intelligible. Although not as dramatic as reversal (perhaps because in this case we are not aware of the *chaos* from which it emerges) the causality interrupted by reversal creates the expectation that the results of an action will be foreseeable. The fact that the tragic causality disrupts this existing causality suggests a failure in this initial synthesis of the imagination, a failure for which the tragic plot attempts to compensate. How? By replicating, in an exaggerated manner,[71] the way in which the initial causality works, *and then* submitting it to it the figure of a world in recoil.

Changing perspectives slightly, does the intervention of objective necessity in the form of reversal not constitute a violent interruption of the smooth running of the world, an interruption that creates the condition for instituting Law, in the style of the dynamic antinomy? Is not the intervention of destiny, in other words, the consequence of invoking a noumenal order that organizes (that confers intelligibility on) the phenomenal world, of positing a transcendent source of authority and control – objective necessity or fate – to which the tragic subject then attributes the usurpation of its agency? As classical tragedy repeatedly shows, however, this attribution of control to an *external* force is not simply disingenuous. It represents, rather, the narrowing of perspective enabled by the act of self-blinding to the violent irruption of objective necessity, the law around which the tragic universe gravitates. Since this transcendent domain enables and guarantees the subject's intelligibility precisely by virtue of its *external* position, the subject *absorbs* the violence inflicted on itself by cooperating with it. The point of the tragic subject's cooperation with necessity is thus to avoid the dissolution of reality, the dismantling of intelligibility. That dissolution is avoided by averting the revelation of the Monstrous *other side* of the Law (of objective necessity, destiny or fate), a revelation that would make the tragic world collapse, giving way to inconsistency and chaos. From the viewpoint of Kant's dynamic antinomy, then, the recourse to objective necessity provides the 'external guarantee' of the intelligibility of the (tragic) symbolic order.

This process might be said to work as follows: the initial 'phenomenal causal chain' that creates the expectation of foreseeable consequences does not exist out there, but rather is imposed by the synthetic activity of the imagination. Such synthetic activity already presupposes a transcendent source of meaning that produces the causal chain. Then the self-inscription of the noumenal beyond into the phenomenal domain transcends or suspends from the outside the causal chain, resulting in a temporary phenomenal inconsistency. This break that the noumenal beyond causes in the expected concatenation of events, in the anticipated correspondence between the subject's expectations at the moment of acting and the results of its acts, is instantiated in the tragic reversal. Reversal turns everything into its contrary, suspending human causality by imposing on it another causality, tragic causality, which from the hero's viewpoint (and from that of the spectator) seems, at least initially (at the initial moment of deliberation), whimsical. Then, significantly, that whimsical causality imposes itself as the only possible causality. In order to avert the threat of inconsistency, it is accepted not only internally (by the protagonists and the Chorus) but also externally (by Aristotle and the critical tradition that focuses on catharsis and tragic effect).

It is surprising that this tradition of reading tragedy, which is the predominant one, has not ultimately questioned tragic causality, however much it may have gestured towards criticizing its arbitrariness. This lack of criticism is instantiated by the success of the modern understanding of the Aristotelian concepts of *hamartia* and *hubris* – the catalysts of the tragic fall – as referring to the hero's individual mistake. As Naomi Liebler remarks, *hamartia*, which in the domain of action where it belongs means, literally, 'missing the mark', has been displaced to the domain of character,[72] as befits the modern eagerness to assume guilt. What current interpretations of *hamartia* as 'an optional and unavoidable "error" resulting from some inadequacy or "flaw"' of the protagonist obliterate is the fact that in classical tragedy *hamartia* refers primarily to 'positionality'.[73] The tragic fall is not motivated by an individual mistake, but '*happens* in consequence of the complex situation represented in the drama'.[74] Instead of denominating individual mistakes, *hamartia* and *hubris* are strategies through which the plot, operating at the level of action, naturalizes the tragic causality.

To recapitulate, the tragic plot, with its inscription of the dictates of destiny, replicates the violent synthesis of phenomena which was already realized by the imagination. Perhaps this explains why tragic causality, though initially rejected by Plato precisely for its irrationality and monstrosity, has been taken for granted by the Western rational tradition, even inaugurated as its origin, even if (or precisely because) in it the human self is systematically held to be guilty and punished. In terms of subjectivity, the self blinds itself to that monstrosity, desires objective necessity and assumes guilt in order to become a subject. The fact that the empty *other side* of the Law is overlooked, and so much value is placed on the heroic human impulse to act against all odds (as well as on the nobility of human suffering), demonstrates how natural it feels to be constituted in subjection.

The tragic figure of a world in recoil structures our social text, the very symbolic system which produces us as subjects. That the outrageous aspects of tragic causality are overlooked points to a constitutive blind spot on which the very possibility of becoming intelligible is conditioned. This blind spot is produced in the tragic act of self-blinding, which is less a refusal to see or recognize than a dramatic limitation of perspective. If the outrageous functioning of tragic causality is taken so casually, it may be because it is just one more instance (albeit a radical one) of the violence of the imagination's work of synthesis.

Tragedy's refusal of mediation

It should come as no surprise that the violent synthesis realized by tragic causality, just like the initial *human* causality it disrupts, also fails – why shouldn't it? The plot may be considered to function like Hegel's dialectical triad as described by Žižek, where the third term only intensifies the contradiction between the initial two.[75] Above being contraposed, the first two terms (thesis, antithesis) are inextricably linked to each other and to the third term. Rather than contradicting the previous term, each new term shifts into the next when it realizes its potential to the extreme.[76] This is also how the Kantian triad of Beautiful, Sublime and Monstrous functions, according to Rogozinski and Žižek:

> an object which is thoroughly beautiful is no longer merely beautiful, it is already sublime; in the same way, an object which is thoroughly sublime turns into something monstrous. Or, to put it the opposite way: a beautiful object without the element of the Sublime is not truly beautiful, a sublime object which lacks the embryonic dimension of the Monstrous is not truly Sublime, merely beautiful . . .[77]

And this is precisely how tragic emplotment works: the hero's first impulse towards action (Agamemnon's attempt to set sail for Troy, Clytemnestra's scheme to murder her husband, Agamemnon, Oedipus' escape from his native land in order to avoid fulfilling the prophecy, Eteocles' duty to defend Thebes from a traitor army, Creon's decree that the corpse of traitors be left unburied outside the city walls) shifts into its own reversal when it is fully realized, as instantiated in the story of Oedipus. Oedipus' act of abandoning what he takes to be his native land in order to avoid fulfilling the prophecy becomes the very condition for the prophecy to be fulfilled.

As a consequence, the tragic dénouement never mediates or solves anything, it simply intensifies the initial condition, underscoring the failure of any attempt to mediate. In the same way as the first synthesis of reality that the plot interrupts was bound to fail, the dénouement of the play does not bring about harmony, since the phenomena it apprehends are vastly exceeded by those it does not. Contrary to the usual interpretation, the tragic dénouement does not mediate two opposing premises, one human, the other transcendent. Curiously, what is usually taken as a restoration of order in tragedy is in effect the violent victory of one term over the other. One would be tempted to regret the way in which human intention is crushed by objective necessity (supposing one could look at subjectivity from *the outside*), were it not because the prevalence of objective necessity enables subjectivation.

But a tragic play is larger than objective necessity. We could say that tragedy situates itself in the shift from one antinomy to the other, for isn't there a point in the tragedy when these two options meet? Does this reference to the monstrous side of the Law not already point to inconsistency, to a non-contingent law? Doesn't the emptiness of the ethical principle of which I was speaking in the previous section create a self that perceives its actions as contingent, since they are not legitimated by any concrete rule? Isn't this self already precipitated into uncertainty, into a suspension of intelligibility? Isn't this self the one that becomes aware of its own invention in positing tragic fate? Isn't this part of tragedy – the other side of fate, the suspension of intelligibility, the vertigo of nothingness – what modernity has pushed aside, that is, the conditions of subjective constitution that must remain foreclosed to consciousness?

Tragedy does not mediate, it does not offer a stable judgement on the conflicts it depicts, or a particular perspective to interpret them. Indeed, it does not offer a harmonious synthesis of the different modes of approaching reality it proposes, which coexist in tension. Conflicts stay open, and though the hero may have died, nothing has been resolved. The end of many tragedies is arbitrary, it precipitates the protagonist's death as an escape from a situation that would be worse than tragic, that is outside and beyond any intelligible whole. This escape from (symbolic) death through (tragic) death, premised on the subject's desire for objective necessity and reconciliation with *its destiny*, is the condition for subjectivation. The protagonist has been crushed, but from the viewpoint of the play as a whole conflicts remain open, and so does interpretation. Rather than committing to a single perspective, that of the protagonist, tragedy proposes many perspectives. It becomes the locus where perspective shifts.

Tragedy offers many different perspectives: that of a necessary fate or of a fictional fate;[78] that of the sublimity of Law (destiny, tragic causality) or of noumenal monstrosity (what the hero has to blind himself to, the blind spot on which objective necessity and tragic sublime sense are built); that of dynamic or of mathematical antinomies; that of the *objective* power of transcendent forces, or of the open display of the power that essentializations have over the human self; that of fate's power to alienate the human self or of the fictionality of the tragic framework, also revealed by tragedy's awareness of itself as work of art, as a created artefact.

Let us pause for a moment with this last shift of perspective from fate's power to alienate to the fictionality of the tragic framework. While the tragic plot is structured by the irruption of objective necessity, tragedy presents a universe in contradiction, a world divided by conflicts that it refuses to mediate. This affirmation of contingency, manifest in the inconsistency of the sources of authority that tragedy depicts, is what a perspective on tragedy as work of art emphasizes. In the famous Tenth Letter of his *Philosophical Letters on Dogmatism and Criticism* (1795), Schelling describes the contradictions of Greek tragedy as follows: 'A mortal, destined by fate to become a criminal, fights *against* this fate, and yet he is horribly punished for the crime, which was the work of fate!' And then, emphasizing the artistic nature of tragedy, he continues: 'In order not to exceed the limits of art, Greek tragedy was obliged to have the hero *succumb*; but in order to compensate for this humiliation of human freedom imposed by art, it also had to allow him to atone and make amends – even for a crime committed through fate.'[79] Though Schelling's writing on tragedy merits extensive attention, here I will only underscore that tragedy's artistic nature makes the disruption and subsequent reaffirmation of intelligibility that it enacts deeply intriguing. It is indeed extraordinary that such enactment is done within a work of art – precisely the kind of artefact which, in announcing its fictionality overtly, places artificiality in tension with the essentiality of the entities (objective necessity, destiny, divine evil, the law) it creates.

3
Tragic Modern Subjectivity

> [T]he more a man controls his aggressiveness, the more intense becomes his ideal's inclination to aggressiveness against his ego. . . . It is from this, indeed, that the conception arises of a higher being who deals out punishment inexorably.
>
> Freud, *The Ego and the Id*

> [T]he moment the subject is bereft of external obstacles which can be blamed for his failure, his subjective position will collapse on account of its inherent inauthenticity.
>
> Žižek, *Tarrying with the Negative*

Being alienated by a mystifying 'Other' has premised the possibility of conscious subjectivity since Schiller and Kant.[1] According to most readings of Hegel's *Phenomenology of Spirit* – particularly the sections on 'Self-Certainty' and 'Self-Consciousness', which are arguably the most influential model of modern subjectivities – the self is depicted as engulfing the other in order to satisfy desire, but also, paradoxically, as needing that very other it supersedes to achieve external recognition of itself as self-conscious being. When seen in opposition to the self, in turn, the other is perceived as an all-powerful, constraining force that robs the self of its autonomy. In so far as self-realization is based on the conflicting movement of cancelling the externality of the other through which the other recognizes the self, the other becomes the 'most awesome of stumbling blocks in the self's march to fulfilment',[2] a threat that simultaneously constitutes and thwarts the self.

This extreme but actual representation of a threatening other, manifest in the heteronomous obligations of every incipient subject, follows the same pattern as the conception of tragic fate. As if destiny, and with it the *irrational* tragic self-representation for which, according to Nietzsche's *Birth of Tragedy*, there is no longer room in our rational times, were still alive and well.[3] Significantly Raymond Williams writes that arranging the events of a life as if dictated by fate is a choice,[4] and Emmanuel Levinas insists that fate does not precede history, but rather follows it.[5] If men and women no longer choose to represent themselves as blinded by transcendent intervention, why should this insistence on the fictionality of fate, on the fabricated nature of any inexorable otherness, be necessary in the first place?

This chapter argues that the 'autonomous' modern subject is not less constrained than the tragic self, since it is in fact premised on it. Although modernity dissipated the irrational shadow of fate with the putative transparency of reason, I propose that modern theories of subjectivity follow a tragic pattern. They postulate the existence of an alienating force of otherness (power, the father, the law, the state) which produces through internalization a rent and radically bound individual identity, the modern subject. Born in Kant's sublime subject, elaborated in Hegel's dialectical negativity (and especially in the readings of Hegel inspired by Kojève) and reappearing in Freud, Althusser and Foucault (among others), the social being that we call the modern subject is a universal category, the linguistic condition for the individual to occupy a position within an intelligible, identity-conferring framework of meaning.[6]

Achieving an identity therefore entails sacrificing individual experience and materiality, so that, liberated from conflicting desires, the now autonomous subject can freely identify with law. The idea of subjective identity is thus based on death, since it kills the very lived experience it seeks to organize,[7] having recourse to typically tragic devices: reversal of responsibilities, occultation of the source of evil, internalization of guilt, justification of suffering. Characterized as sublimated (by Schiller, Kant, Hegel), death-based and death-bound,[8] estranged from the human other beyond repair, the modern self in its different guises appears extremely vulnerable, even passionately attached, to higher rule (as Freud, Althusser and Foucault point out).[9]

Very importantly, the modern subject is as divided as the tragic self, since it internalizes external coercion as a critical agency that turns against the material and sensitive part of the self. Moreover, that the modern self can experience itself as an agent depends, as Althusser and Foucault have shown, on occluding the state's agency in producing subjects through subjection.[10] Emerging at the price of the death of the sensible individual, cooperating with an authoritarian agency that rules over the self, the subject suffers from the ambivalence of being simultaneously subordinated to social power and constituted by it as an agent.[11] For these reasons, I propose to call these modern and contemporary self-representations 'tragic subjectivities'.

Since this constitutive turn against oneself is so brilliantly instantiated in the tragic cooperation with necessity, the question raised in Chapter 2 remains open and relevant to the present. What could be the gain in representing ourselves as victims of objective necessity? Could it be the case that modern and contemporary (tragic) subjects paradoxically assume guilt and represent themselves as victims in order to preserve the illusion of autonomy? I will argue that the self's cooperation with *external* coercion, aside from affording it a subjective position, fulfils a two-fold task: it allows the self to gather itself as same under pressure, and it creates the conditions to preserve sameness by precluding the irruption of real persons.

*

The tragic character of post-Kantian philosophy has been acknowledged by many thinkers.[12] To explain it briefly, by discrediting dogmatic metaphysics in the *Critique of Pure Reason*, but then affirming, in *Practical Reason*, that the human self is freely subjected to the moral law, Kant opens a deep fissure between nature and freedom, between epistemology and ethics. He then tries to bridge this gap between pure and practical reason in the *Critique of Judgment*. Aesthetics thus replaces religion in the attempt to reconcile the causality of the natural world, which is objective, determined and determining, with the causality of human freedom (practical reason), which is defined by moral necessity. Kant's attribution of such an important role to the aesthetic materializes in the privileging of dramatic art, particularly of classical tragedy, in post-Kantian philosophy, notably in Hegel, Schelling and Hölderlin. Thus, Hegel's famous reading of *Antigone* in the *Phenomenology of Spirit* (1807) is preceded by Schelling's brief discussion of *Oedipus Rex* in the last of his *Letters on Dogmatism and Criticism* (1795), by Hölderlin's comments on *Oedipus Rex* and *Antigone* (1803), and by Hegel's own remarks on tragedy also in 1803, in his essay 'Scientific Ways of Treating Natural Law'. The unprecedented attention devoted to *Oedipus Rex* and *Antigone* in the nineteenth century then takes a different turn in the twentieth century with Freud's resort to the Oedipus myth, Heidegger's commentary of the second *stasimon* of *Antigone* in *An Introduction to Metaphysics* (1935)[13] and Lacan's reading of *Antigone* in his Seminar VII on the *Ethics of Psychoanalysis* (1959–60).

But my goal here is not to focus on the theory of tragedy as developed by Schelling, Hegel or Hölderlin. Rather, I will begin by tracing a tragic pattern (not a Sophoclean, but an Aeschylean one) in accounts of the conception of the subject which do not refer explicitly to tragedy: Hegel's Unhappy Consciousness, Freud's narrative of melancholia and the formation of the ego ideal, and Althusser's understanding of the functioning of ideology. At the moment of studying the tragic structure of these modern accounts of subjectivation, however, it is surprising to note that Sophoclean tragedy, and more precisely *Oedipus Rex* and *Antigone* (that is, the plays that inspire tragic theory), constitute an exception to tragic subjectivity. As I argued earlier, *Oedipus Rex* and *Antigone* break with the pattern of subjectivation through desire, guilt and death that characterizes, for example, Aeschylus' *Agamemnon* or *Seven against Thebes*.[14] If modern tragic theory is inspired in *Oedipus Rex* and *Antigone*, the less explicit tragic character of modern philosophical theories of subjective constitution is better represented by an Aeschylean pattern of formal deliberation, self-blinding, cooperation with necessity, assumption of guilt and subjectivation through death.[15]

Unlike the post-Kantian subject, Oedipus and Antigone are not agonically divided between two impossible options, they do not *have to* decide. Either totally unaware of what he is doing (Oedipus) or clearly determined to do it (Antigone), they do not suffer the divide between necessity and freedom. Since knowledge of the prophecy reaches Oedipus at the wrong place and time (in Corinth, where he takes his adoptive parents to be his birth parents), he is unaware that in trying to avoid it he is in fact fulfilling it. Oedipus is thus not given the opportunity to desire the necessity imposed on him. Without having desired something one cannot become guilty of it, and so Oedipus, lamenting that he is not guilty (that he has been deprived of desire, and therefore of the possibility of subjectivation), refuses to die.[16] Antigone, in turn, has already excluded herself from the identity-conferring social order at the beginning of the play by transgressing Creon's decree that a traitor's corpse should be left unburied.

Unlike other tragic characters, then, Oedipus and Antigone do not experience the cleavage between necessity and freedom. Not needing to bridge that cleavage, they neither desire necessity nor cooperate with it, and so they refuse to assume responsibility for what is objectively determined. That is the task of Aeschylean characters, whose course of action illustrates well Kant's claim that one should come to desire one's duty, that one's duty and one's inclination must coincide (it is in making that coincidence happen that tragic characters lose their lives). There is, in sum, a gap between what Peter Szondi has called the *philosophy of the tragic*,[17] and the depiction of the modern rational subject. Although tragic theory and tragic subjectivity would seem to meet at last in Freud's and Lacan's psychoanalytic accounts, the relation between both terms is inverse, rather than direct. A careful look at Freud's use of the Oedipus myth alongside Sophocles' play, for example, will reveal that Oedipus' terrible destiny consists precisely in being denied the complex named after him. Deprived of the chance to desire his mother by literally *having* his mother, suffering 'the theft of desire and the mother in exchange',[18] Oedipus is denied the opportunity to be guilty, and therefore to become a subject. In this sense, Oedipus' destiny might be said to undo the tragic, were it not because guilt constitutes his impossible object of desire. Oedipus is indeed not guilty, nor can he assume guilt were he to die for it, which is why he does not die, after all.[19] Without a symbolic debt incurred through desire, subjectivation cannot take place.

This disencounter between tragic theory and tragic subjectivity incites a subtle questioning of what it is that modern philosophy ultimately finds in tragedy, beyond and perhaps against explicit recognition. Modern subjectivity is indeed tragic, but it might be more tragic than we think.

Hegel and the double binds of consciousness

In the *Phenomenology of Spirit* Hegel focuses on the negative relation between individual experience and its universal. It is the very annihilation of the individual required by the identification with abstraction that results in freedom. As Hegel argues in 'Sense-Certainty', the 'self only knows itself as a transcended self'. A paradox emerges, for in order to find oneself, to become self-conscious, one has to leave individual sensuousness and experience and identify with the universal, what one is not. Hegel finds the loss of the 'I' in this process instantiated, for example, in language. When the self speaks and takes the position of the 'I' of enunciation, the 'I' becomes an abstract sign that can refer to anybody, in the same way that the universal 'now' can refer to any time.[20] Not unlike Kant's sublime subject, Hegel's consciousness finds its truth, conceived as participation in a universal horizon, in language,[21] even though speaking or writing results in the erasure of the individual self.[22] '[T]he subject has no place for the individual, since it is the sheer reflection of language on itself,' writes Jonathan Strauss.[23] Becoming a subject is an act of abstract negation, a reflection of language on itself that entails the death of individual sensuality and imagination.

The notion of subjectivity as a negative abstraction is further elaborated by Hegel in the section on 'Self-Consciousness', this time in what concerns its profound and complex dependency on otherness. I would like to focus briefly on two ideas that stand out in Hegel's account of self-consciousness. First, the self confronts any other as its object of desire, as that which must be negated and consumed.[24] The other is thus necessary to the self only in so far as the self must supersede alterity in the process of achieving self-certainty: '[i]n order for this suppression [*Aufheben*] to be, this other, too, must be. . . . Thus self-consciousness, by its negative relation to the object, is unable to supersede it; it is really because of that relation that it produces the object again, and the desire as well.'[25] The ultimate goal of self-consciousness, therefore, is not the other it must engulf, but rather the other *as* object of desire, and therefore its own perpetuation as a desiring self.[26] Second, the self needs to be recognized by another self-consciousness, for self-consciousness finds itself only when it is confronted with what it is not. Reflection on itself through reflection in another is precisely the target of desire.[27] Significantly, the act of self-negation effected by each self-consciousness, not unlike the Schillean and Kantian sublimation of the self, presupposes a different understanding of death's origin. Death in self-negation no longer appears to come from the outside. Rather, it originates within the self in the very process of life that the self has to deny in order to identify with abstraction.[28] Hegel explains this identification as a return to unity, as a communion of the self with the universal that cannot take place without the death of the concrete self.[29]

Hence, when confronted with the other 'through a life and death struggle', the task of each self-conscious being is to renounce any material or sensible part that may become a vanishing moment, identify with death, so that it can become self-consciousness 'in its pure state'. '[I]t is only through staking one's life that freedom is won.'[30] 'The presentation of itself, however, as the pure abstraction of self-consciousness consists in showing itself as the pure negation of its objective mode, or in showing that it is not attached to any specific existence, not to individuality common to existence as such, that it is not attached to life.'[31]

Because the self must find itself in another, in superseding the other it also supersedes itself, and thus it 'has lost itself and finds itself again in its alterity'.[32] As Jean Hyppolite remarks, the self 'always poses itself in a determination and, because this determination is, as such, already its first negation, it always negates itself so as to be itself'.[33]

The confrontation with otherness is always a confrontation with oneself in Hegel's *Phenomenology*. Thus, for example, the self's confrontation with another, narrated as the struggle for recognition, does not take place between two individuals, but rather between the two moments of self-consciousness, the self and the other, which are here externalized. This dialectic – which represents, in Hyppolite's reading, 'the splitting and reproduction of self-consciousness within itself'[34] – is materialized when, after the struggle, one (part of) self-consciousness becomes the master by identifying with death and escaping 'the slavement of life', whereas the other consciousness becomes a slave due to its attachment to life. The master–slave division does not represent an external reality, but rather only a momentary separation of the two moments of self-consciousness, the self and the other. This other's otherness hence refers to the other within the self, never to an exterior other that disrupts the self's world.

In the master–slave dialectic, the slave reaches self-consciousness when he perceives himself as a creative being who, by transforming the world through labour, liberates himself from his feeling of transience: he 'rids himself of his attachment to natural existence . . . by working on it'.[35] The master, by contrast, is dependent on the products of the slave's labour which he consumes and negates. Unlike the temporary satisfaction of desire that the master achieves, a desire which depends on the object for its own preservation, the slave's work 'is desire held in check, fleetingness staved off'.[36] The fact that the slave achieves self-consciousness through the creative activity imposed by the master emphasizes the fact that agency emerges in heteronomy. In spite of usurping the slave's capacity for free and voluntary action, the master institutes the slave as an acting and creating being, as a bearer of agency. Formulated in more general terms, agency or productivity is enabled by the imposed demands of a power that subordinates.[37] This ability to transform the world, to create, born in subordination, constitutes the subordinated individual as a self-conscious being or subject. But the slave ultimately fails to secure his permanence because the objects he produces are taken away by the master. Since the products of the slave's labour, aimed at enabling permanence of self, are taken away from him, in the transience of those objects the slave experiences fear of his own transience, of mortality. It is in experiencing fear of death, absolute fear, that the slave becomes self-conscious, because this fear elicits a certain degree of identification with the universal. The master, in turn, without an equal that will recognize him as self-conscious, and no longer needed in the dialectic process, becomes a dead end.

When the master disappears at the end of this section the master–slave division is internalized, following a usual pattern in the *Phenomenology*. This internalization undoes the externalization of the two parts of consciousness that participated in the struggle for recognition (becoming slave and master), and brings about the reunion of the self. What was temporarily presented as an external dialectic, the master–slave division, transposes itself again to the interior of self-consciousness, henceforth split into an internal slave (a life-seeking self) and an internal master (a critical agency that rules over it). Thus, by internalizing the master and the slave, 'consciousness . . . is forced back into itself . . . '.[38]

The master–slave division, as well as the image of the two consciousnesses that struggle for recognition, constitutes a dialectic within the self. The authoritarian master represents a projection of a part of self-consciousness that identifies with the universal in the outside world. External authority, represented here by the master, is, like any other alterity that confronts the self in Hegel's account of self-consciousness, a projection of the self in the process of self-reflection, that is, an other within the self. This 'external' authority is exerted on the material and creative part (the slave), only to internalize itself again as an ego-ideal or critical agency within the unhappy consciousness. Although this is ambiguous at some points of the *Phenomenology*, Hegel does affirm that the process of achieving self-consciousness is strictly self-reflexive: 'I distinguish myself from myself, and in doing so I am directly aware that what is distinguished from myself is not different [from me]. I, the selfsame being, repel myself from myself; but what is posited as distinct from me, or as unlike me, is immediately, in being so distinguished, not a distinction for me.'[39] In short, the external authority that will internalize itself as a constraining imperative consists of a form of otherness created by the self in the process of becoming self-conscious.

This is not to state that external constraints are always created by the self, but rather that the self is particularly vulnerable to power, since in the process of its formation the self produces a critical agency within itself. This critical agency or ethical imperative within the self allows social power to disappear as external coercion. Social power is redou-

bled within the self, becoming, in Judith Butler's words, a psychic operation, whether in the form of an internal master, the ideality of conscience or the ego ideal. It is precisely the ruling of this critical agency
over the life-seeking part of the self that makes the slave, once liberated
from the master, an *unhappy* consciousness. Although the former slave
is no longer subjected to the master's external authority, such authority re-emerges in self-consciousness as the unchangeable part of the self
that rules over its changeable part.[40]

In spite of the fact that this division characterizes self-consciousness
(self-consciousness contains both parts), the '*unhappy, inwardly disrupted*
consciousness' is not yet aware of being constituted by the unity of
both.[41]

> The two are, for the Unhappy Consciousness, alien to one another;
> and because it is itself the consciousness of this contradiction, it iden-
> tifies itself with the changeable consciousness, and takes itself to be
> the unessential Being. But as consciousness of unchangeableness, or
> of simple essential Being, it must at the same time set about freeing
> itself from the unessential, i.e., from itself.[42]

Since the unhappy consciousness finds itself imperfect and in conflict,
it identifies with the changeable that seeks unity with the unchangeable, repressing itself in order to identify with pure thought. Consequently, remarks Butler, the only viable alternative from the viewpoint
of the unhappy consciousness is to marshal its critical agency against
its changeable part, thought against body, enacting, in effect, a turn
against itself.[43]

As Butler observes, the self-reflexive moment in which the changeable part of consciousness identifies with the universal part marks the
birth of an imperative, which summons the self to turn back upon its
possibilities of action and identify with norms. The birth of this critical
agency enables a new transposition of fear. If the bondsman feared
death after becoming aware of his own transience through the transience of the objects that he creates, and such fear had been displaced
on the master, the absence of external domination reintroduces the fear
of transience, the terror of bodily death. But this time fear is reinscribed
'as the inevitable fate of any being whose consciousness is determined
and embodied, no longer a threat posed by another. . . . Absolute fear is
thus displaced by the absolute law which, paradoxically, reconstituted
the fear as fear *of* the law.'[44] Freed from the master but now imprisoned
by the ethical laws of the mind and condemned to the self-reflexive

application of imperatives, the former slave is as constrained – if not more – as before.[45]

Driven by its aspiration to overcome its changeability and identify with pure thought, the unhappy consciousness inaugurates a series of efforts, productive of several dialectical reversals: the more the unhappy consciousness endeavours to repress and deny its changeable part, the more that changeable part is affirmed. Identification with pure thought is attempted through the permanent mortification, negation or 'suppression' of the changeable or inessential part, the body, which limits the self with its transience, desire and need. Whether it is through stoicism, scepticism, renunciation, self-sacrifice, abjection or, finally, religious mediation, the act of bodily denial by the unhappy consciousness consists in relinquishing agency. More exactly, what it does is to perform a renunciation of agency and responsibility by transferring its initiative to external figures such as divine design, a community of religious wills or a priest: 'The action, since it follows upon the decision of someone else, ceases, as regards the doing or the willing of it, to be its own.'[46] It seems appropriate that the self forsake its formative capacity, precisely that which through labour made the slave aware of himself as creative being.

The self's capacity for action, the body dedicated to labour, now becomes the alterity to be suppressed. But as one might expect, such an attempt at denial invariably results in a narcissistic reaffirmation of the self, if only because punishing one's body, performing renunciation, are themselves reflexive and voluntary acts. Whatever effect of self-denial these acts *were intended* to achieve, there is no way around the discretion of the will, because renouncing volition is always an act of will: 'For though consciousness renounces the show of satisfying its feeling of self, it obtains the *actual* satisfaction of it . . . . Consciousness feels itself therein as this particular individual, and does not let itself be deceived by its own seeming renunciation, for the truth of the matter is that it has not renounced itself.'[47] Several dialectical reversals interfere in the process in which the self seeks to identify with its unchangeable or universal part. This reunion proves ultimately impossible, for the more the self attempts to deny itself and identify with the universal, the more it reaffirms itself as a sensible, creative and desiring self.

(From the viewpoint of the self's relation to the other, it is significant that the fear of transience should be averted through the attempted death of the material and sensible part of the self, of the self as the site of will, agency and responsibility. After all, to be accountable for one's acts is to be accountable before the human other who suffers from those acts. The internalization of an ethical injunction, of law, is ultimately done to the detriment of the human other, who, absent from the scene from the start, is twice negated in the self's act of forsaking responsibility. This denial of the other becomes the more evident if we consider that in disavowing itself as acting being self-consciousness sustains itself. If in disavowing its sensitive and creative part the self did not sustain those very qualities, the act of renunciation would be impossible for lack of something to disavow.)

Only a final and seemingly problematic dialectic mediation will allow self-consciousness to be one with itself. So far any effort of the unhappy consciousness to negate its sensuous part and identify with the unchangeable resulted in self-aggrandizement and self-affirmation, that is, precisely in the reassertion of the sensuous and experiential dimensions that were being denied.[48] The pattern of explanation developed up to this point, a pattern that questioned the viability of identifying with abstraction by emphasizing the self's ultimate inability to forsake its materiality, ceases to apply. Given the impossibility to reach spirit through dialectical reversal, Hegel invokes a religious mediation: the unhappy consciousness relinquishes its freedom to decide, as well as its responsibility, and casts them upon a religious mediator or priest. This time, against all expectation, self-renunciation succeeds in identifying with the unchangeable without reaffirming the materiality of the self, as had been the case so far. Hegel's turn away from dialectics and recourse to religion, not infrequent in the *Phenomenology*, has puzzled readers of different orientations with the significant exception of Kojève, who finds no fault with it in so far as it promotes the very identification with abstraction about which Hegel's text is so ambivalent.[49] Kojève's interpretation of Hegel as offering a death-based theory of the subject is highly significant, if we consider its important area of influence – among Kojève's students at the École des Hautes Études in Paris were Jacques Lacan, Alexandre Koyré, Eric Weil, Maurice Merleau-Ponty, André Breton and Emmanuel Levinas.[50]

What are the consequences of this resolution for Hegel's account of the self-conscious subject? If followed consistently, where would Hegel's pattern of explanation have led him? From the viewpoint of a Hegelian reading *against Hegel* such as the one Judith Butler proposes, one which takes the road that Hegel painstakingly opens but eventually abandons, the subject's repeated failure to negate itself as a sensuous being generates a resistance to subjectivation in Hegel's text.[51] If Hegel's dialectic pattern were to be followed to its last consequences, wouldn't the subject it describes represent the site in which the sensuous, pleasure and agency are reaffirmed?[52]

This potential shift from a self-conscious subject to a sensible one seems promising, since it opens the possibility of envisaging the self's relation to the other in terms no longer restricted to annihilation or deadly struggle. At the beginning of *Otherwise than Being*, Levinas portrays the notion that the self-conscious subject has of the other 'as an obstacle to freedom, intelligibility or perfection, or as a term that confirms a finite being, mortal and uncertain of itself, by recognizing it, or as a slave, collaborator or God able to succor'.[53] As a sensible subject, however, the self is vulnerable and passive towards the other.[54] 'This sensibility has meaning only as a "taking care of the other's need".'[55] This is a subjectivity of naked skin,[56] of 'beings of flesh and blood', which is sensitive to pain and suffering and hunger. 'Only a subject that eats can be for-the-other.'[57] Because this sensible subject does not deny its materiality, but rather enjoys the gifts of the material world, it knows what 'snatching the bread from one's mouth' to give it to the other means.[58] Indeed, this conception of the subject is rather distant from Hegel's description of the self-conscious subject as related to the other by interest, clashing with the other as obstacle, encompassing the other or annihilating it.

But the tendency in Hegel's unhappy consciousness to reaffirm its sensuousness in self-punishment, itself a seed of potential resistance to subjectivation inscribed in Hegel's text, will become in other accounts of subjectivity – such as Freud's or Foucault's – precisely what allows subjectivation to work. It is not the case, therefore, that the focus shifts from a self-conscious to a sensible subject. Rather, in a like manner as consciousness incessantly produces the object of desire it negates in order to secure the continuity of desire, in the same way as the repeated disavowal of the body preserves the disavowing act, subjectivation succeeds at the point in which it fails. By failing to identify with abstraction, with universal (state) law, the subject becomes libidinally attached to the very forms of self-punishment through which internalized state authority operates.

Self-created victims: Freud, Althusser, Foucault

What inaugurates Hegel's unhappy consciousness as a reflexive self is a turn against itself provoked by the internalization of norms. This turn against oneself is later elaborated in Nietzsche's bad conscience, the turn towards authority in Althusser's interpellation, Foucault's regulation of bodies, but also in other extremely influential accounts, such as Freud's melancholic turn or internalization of the lost other, and formation of the ego ideal.[59] While in Hegel the imperative emerges as the self's internal reproduction of the disappeared authority of the master, and in Freud the ego ideal springs from a melancholic turn, in Foucault and Althusser such otherness is embodied in state power, which in turn operates psychically by internalizing itself in the subjects it produces. Whatever the alleged origin of an external subordinating force, whether it is created and projected on the world by the self, or whether, existing in the world, it internalizes itself as guilt, or both – for the line that separates internal and external is unclear – all these accounts characterize the modern conscious self as internally divided. These models rely, in sum, on the self's act of marshalling hostility against itself, and then denominating an external agency as the source of conflict.

Despite the important differences between them, then, these phenomenologies of subjectivity account for the production of the ontological effect of self – of subjectivity, identity or conscience – by means of a turn of the will upon itself that prompts the self's identification with norms. They all narrate the subject's emergence as the fictive redoubling of the self in two opposed parts, the material self and the critical agency ruling over it.[60] Whether instantiated by Freud's ego and super-ego or by Foucault's body and soul, this redoubling or turn against oneself, which is typical of the heightening of conscience, produces the subject as a self-reflexive, and therefore as a potentially self-punishing, self. Let us begin by examining how this happens in Freud's account of melancholia and of its role in the formation of the ego ideal.

In Freud's 1917 essay 'Mourning and Melancholia', the ego turns back upon itself after the loss of an object of love (which may be a person, but also 'a loss of a more ideal kind').[61] Since such a loss is foreclosed to consciousness and therefore unavowable, the ego does not acknowledge the death of the object, or the injury inflicted by the object that from the ego's viewpoint has abandoned (or neglected or disappointed) the ego.[62] Because of this disavowal of loss, the libido that would eventually be reattached to another object once mourning is completed is withdrawn into the ego. This self-directed libido produces the identification of the ego with the object, by effecting a redoubling of the self.[63] In it one part of the ego substitutes for the lost object, becoming, like the latter, at once the object of the self's love and the object of the self's aggression for the loss. The part of the ego that embodies the lost object re-enacts the traits of the object, while the other part redirects the reproaches intended for the other to the self. In the process of incorporating the lost other, therefore, a critical agency (corresponding to the super-ego) is split off from the ego, which now becomes the object of condemnation. 'In this way the loss of the object became transformed into a loss in the ego, and the conflict between the ego and the loved person transformed into a cleavage between the criticizing faculty of the ego and the ego as altered by the identification.'[64] In the process, the ego is redoubled as critical agency (ego) and object of criticism (the part of the ego that now substitutes for the object), while the other, initially an external and independent being (at least theoretically), disappears as such and is foreclosed to consciousness as if it had never existed.[65] The ego redirects towards itself the aggression initially directed to the lost other, refusing to acknowledge the loss, and preserving the past in which the object was loved.

This turn from the 'external' other to the self is central to the constitution of the ego:

> [L]et us dwell for a moment on the view melancholia affords of the constitution of the ego. We see how in this condition one part of the ego sets itself over against the other, judges it critically, and, as it were, looks upon it as an object. Our suspicion that the critical institution in the mind which is here split off from the ego might also demonstrate its independence in other circumstances will be confirmed by all further observations. We shall really find justification for distinguishing this institution from the rest of the ego. It is the mental faculty commonly called conscience that we are thus recognizing; we shall count it, along with the censorship of consciousness and the testing of reality, among the great institutions of the ego, and shall also find evidence elsewhere showing that it can become diseased independently.[66]

The internalization of the other as a part of the self marks the division between ego and object, articulating the ego as a psychic or 'internal' space.[67] By creating a 'topographical' distinction between internal and external worlds, the melancholic turn inaugurates the psyche as the locus of confrontation of the self and its critical agency, that is, as 'conscience'.

In *The Ego and the Id* (1923) Freud confirms the key role that melancholia plays in forming the ego, affirming that he has 'come to understand that this kind of [melancholic] substitution has a great share in determining the form taken by the ego', to the point of defining the character of the ego as 'a precipitate of abandoned object-cathexes'.[68]

The ego-ideal, set up to perform the task of repressing the Oedipus complex, is the product of the first melancholic loss, the loss of the mother as object of erotic love. In the Oedipal situation as Freud describes it here the infant channels his erotic impulse towards his mother by identifying with his father, who is taken as a model. The father, however, poses an obstacle to the realization of his Oedipal wishes. In order to overcome this obstacle, 'his infantile ego fortified itself for the carrying out of the repression by erecting this same obstacle within itself. It borrowed strength to do this, so to speak, from the father, and this loan was an extraordinarily momentous act.'[69] The critical agency, constituted in the form of paternal prohibition and deriving its authority from its manifestation as a categorical imperative, takes up the form of the super-ego. The stronger and faster the repression of the Oedipal complex by this father-authority, the stricter the influence of the super-ego will be over the ego, creating unconscious guilt. The superego is therefore, according to Freud, the residue of the first and most important identification with a love object, done, moreover, when the ego is still feeble – hence its special position in the ego. This authoritative critical agency in the form of the 'voice of the father' is soon strengthened by the influence of authority, religion, schooling: the structure for internalizing authority is in place.[70] (In *Ethics of the Real*, Alenka Zupančič argues that the impact of the father's authority does not derive from the father as an authoritarian figure, but rather from weakness of the real father, which accounts for his inability to enact the role of symbolic father.)

It is important to note that in both the Hegelian account of self-consciousness and Freud's melancholic turn, it is desire understood as negation of the other that ultimately provokes the birth of a critical agency that splits and dominates the self. In Freud's account of melancholia, the self internalizes its own image of the lost other, provoking a split of itself between the part that has suffered a loss and the internalized other, towards which the self's reproaches are addressed. In the process of internalizing otherness the ego loses the social world. Although the loss of the loved object is not necessarily produced by death, although the other may still be present and alive in the outside world, the self cannot leave the psychic for the social, establish communication with the other by whom it feels wronged and solve the conflict. Instead of confronting the real other or its real loss, the ego will revile the internalized other, that is to say, itself, avoiding to confront a loss imposed by the world (for the self perceives it as such).[71]

In consonance with the lack of interest in the outside world that Freud observes in the melancholic, the present is lost to the self as a time for relation, agency and change, becoming the scenario for rehearsing past conflicts.[72] Melancholia reinstates the imaginary past as present: one loses the social world and substitutes oneself for the world in which one dwells. In this line, Butler reads melancholia as a failure of address, 'a failure to sustain the other with the voice that addresses', a way, that is, of precluding the loss of an addressee by occupying every position in discourse.[73] Since melancholia is formative of the ego, its way of anni-hilating otherness and turning the other into a part of the self seems to imply, at the very least, that subjectivation precludes all forms of inter-action with another who is truly exterior to the self.

Freud goes so far as to intimate, in fact, that the melancholic may never have acknowledged another different from the self, that he or she may never have encountered otherness in the first place. Although one naturally assumes that the lost other was initially external to the self, Freud insists that those individuals who are particularly predisposed to melancholia choose their object of attachment 'on a narcissistic basis', that is, for their similarity to the self.[74] It is the object's ability to facil-itate identification, in other words, that provokes attachment to it – a fact that would explain that the internalization of the other as part of the self is done with such ease. Does this mean that, by choosing an object of desire for its resemblance to the self, there has not been a real confrontation with alterity at any point?

*

In the social and political fields, melancholia plays an important role in the implementation of prohibition. In her reading of Freud in *The Psychic Life of Power*, Butler argues that we are all victims of melancho-lia, whose influence is not restricted to fostering the internalization of external prohibition. She proposes, rather, that social power regulates which objects will be foreclosed, and therefore become impossible to mourn, that is, which objects may be susceptible of being internalized through identification and thus constitute an unavowable loss.[75] According to this argument, the state spawns objects for melancholic attachment among its citizens by, for example, making power disappear as an external coercion and be incorporated by subjects as a unavow-able loss, on whose model the subject will now constitute itself.[76] In this respect, affirms Butler, conscience is not simply an instantiation of the state; 'on the contrary, it is the vanishing point of the state's authority, its psychic idealization, and, in that sense, its disappearance as an external object. The process of forming the subject renders the terrorizing power of the state invisible – and effective – as the ideality of conscience.'[77] Conscience, in other words, dissimulates state regulation. Through melancholia what is prescribed and prohibited, as well as (more importantly) the acts of prescribing and prohibiting, become an unavowable loss, the very lost objects of desire with which the self identifies. By producing unavowable losses and impossible love-objects, prescription and prohibition become libidinally charged: the subject will desire to be ruled and repressed.[78]

Perspectives as varied as that of Hegel on self-consciousness, Freud's melancholia and the birth of the ego ideal, or the epistemological and political analyses by Foucault and Althusser coincide in explaining how this redoubling of the self sets up the structure for the internalization of authority, whose political consequences both Althusser and Foucault denounce. When state or religious authority internalizes itself as a psychic operation, as happens in the case of the split unhappy consciousness or the ego–superego division, the ego is particularly predisposed to take authority in. By virtue of repeating the ego's basic structure, which allows the established power to dissimulate its authority as an impulse towards self-punishment, such power operates more efficiently than external coercion, while still managing to appear simply as a set of rules imposed from the outside.[79] Furthermore, internalization allows the source of social and political power to displace away from itself any responsibility for repressing and punishing the self and to appear instead as a benevolent regulator of social life.

Foucault explores the ways in which subjects become erotically attached to repressive power and to regulation in general, and stresses the crucial role that libidinal attachment to punishment plays in the process of *asujetissement*.[80] According to Foucault, subjectivation – the production of subjects – originates in the simultaneous ability of state power to subordinate and form subjects. 'There are two meanings of the word *subject*: subject to someone else by control and dependence, and tied to his own identity by a conscience or self-knowledge. Both meanings suggest a form of power which subjugates and subjectivizes (*une forme de pouvoir que subjugue et assujettit*).'[81] Becoming a subject thus entails being at once subjected to power ('subject to someone else by control and dependence') and constituted by it ('tied to his own identity by a conscience or self-knowledge').[82] In Butler's formulation, subjective agency presupposes 'its own subordination': 'the power that initiates the subject fails to remain continuous with the power that is the subject's agency. A significant and potentially enabling reversal occurs when power shifts from its status as a condition of agency to the subject's "own" agency.'[83] The subject does not perceive its agency as a transmutation of the initial subordinating power, but rather as its own voluntary and willed effect. I will presently return to the fact that agency depends on constraint because of its association with the illusion of the autonomous subject, after tracing this pattern in Althusser.

In his seminal essay 'Ideology and Ideological State Apparatuses' (1969), Althusser finds a similar redoubling of meaning in the ambiguous term 'subject', which he enumerates in reverse order: '(1) a free subjectivity, a centre of initiatives, author of and responsible for its actions; (2) a subjected being, who submits to a higher authority, and is therefore stripped of all freedom except that of freely accepting his submission.'[84] The double meaning of 'subject' suggests that agency is at once exerted on the subject and realized as the subject's willed effect. As an instance of the process of producing subjects, Althusser turns to analyse the interpellation realized by religious ideology, where God plays the role of the subject that calls subjects into being. The fact that the subject's only freedom consists in 'freely accepting his submission', he argues, 'gives us the meaning of this ambiguity, which is merely a reflection of the effect which produces it: the individual *is interpellated as a (free) subject in order that he shall submit freely to the commandments of the Subject, i.e., in order that he shall (freely) accept his subjection*, i.e., in order that he shall make the gestures and actions of his subjection "all by himself".'[85] This is yet another allusion to the fact that autonomy is born in heteronomy.

Althusser concludes that *'[t]here are no subjects except by and for their subjection'*,[86] stressing the exigencies of agency. Perceived by the self as its own initiative, subjective agency remains tied to the conditions of the self's emergence.[87] 'It therefore appears that the subject,' he writes, 'acts insofar as he is acted by the following system (set out in the order of its real determination): ideology existing in a material ideological apparatus, prescribing material practices governed by a material ritual, which practices exist in the material actions of a subject acting in all consciousness according to his belief.'[88] Here we can trace the influence in Althusser of the Pascalian idea that belief is not the reason for action, but rather is accomplished in action, through empty gestures, in 'material practices governed by a material ritual'. According to Pascal's idea of the necessity of the wager, even if one does not believe, one must make the gestures of belief (the gestures of religious piety, for example), and belief will happen 'quite naturally': 'You want to be cured of unbelief and you ask for the remedy: learn from those who were once bound like you and who now wager all they have. . . . They behaved just as if they did believe, taking holy water, having masses said, and so on. That will make you believe quite naturally, and will make you more docile.'[89] The relation between agency and constraint is, in other words, circular. Hence the site of agency's enactment must remain ambiguous, oscillating between the generative subjectivating power and the individual, who now perceives itself as the origin of its own agency, only to bounce back to the state when the subject unwittingly enacts state demands.

But how and why does one become a subject? On the point of the birth of the subject, most of the narratives examined here call upon a typically tragic pattern: one becomes a subject by assuming guilt for having trespassed a law whose content one ignores. One has always already transgressed an objective necessity whose ultimate command remains a secret. According to Althusser, one becomes a subject through a reprimand, a call one misrecognizes as addressing oneself, which resonates in the individual's conscience as a condemnation. When the pedestrian who turns to the policeman's hailing in Althusser's narrative is called as a suspect, he assumes the role of the one who has broken a law whose content he ignores, who is guilty beforehand, in the manner so well described by Kafka. 'You see, Wellem,' says one of the guards that have come to arrest Joseph K. in *The Trial*. 'He admits that he doesn't know the Law and yet he claims he's innocent.'[90] Joseph K. is not aware of having done anything wrong, yet he feels he has infringed some inscrutable law. 'There's been no mistake,' says one of the guards. 'After all, our department, as far as I know, and I know only the lowest level, doesn't seek out guilt among the general population, but, as the Law states, is attracted by guilt and has to send us guards out. That's the Law. What mistake could there be?'[91] Counter-intuitively, guilt comes before the Law. Because the Law is elusive, it produces a guilt detached from any cause, from any reprehensible action taken by the self, and therefore can neither be expiated nor absolved.[92] It is not that the self becomes guilty by committing a fault, but rather it first feels guilty and then attaches a content to that guilt.

However oppressive, then, guilt is productive of an intelligible self. By identifying with a set of rules one has always already transgressed, even without being aware of having committed a fault, the self hopes to achieve identity. 'This readiness to accept guilt to gain a purchase on identity,' writes Butler, 'is linked to a highly religious scenario of a nominating call that comes from God and that constitutes the subject by appealing to a need for the law, an original guilt that the law promises to assuage through the conferral of identity.'[93] It is by appropriating guilt, in sum, that one is inaugurated as a subject of law. By taking upon oneself a symbolic debt, one becomes a participant in an intelligible social order in which rules liberate the self from the responsibility of having to decide what is right and what is wrong.

Staying on *this side* of power or the subject's participation

That one can assume guilt, and thus become a subject of desire, depends, as in the tragic narrative, on an act of self-blinding to the origin of the transference of a defilement. One must avoid seeing that the initial transgression comes from an internally fractured source of authority. More exactly, it is the fact that authority is fractured that constitutes the transgression. As I argued in Chapter 1, tragic power must remain undifferentiated, so that the human self can blind itself to its monstrous source.[94] That source of power is itself a void structure that remains empty in spite of the attempts by competing and inconsistent claims to authority to fill it with substantial content. Referring to classical tragedy, Paul Ricoeur writes that language 'swings from one another among *daimon, theos, theoi, tuche* and *ate*. No doubt such an evasive theology cannot be worked out with precision, since, in order to express primordial incoherence, speech must become out of joint and obscured, as Plotinus says of the thought of non-being, of the "lying essence".'[95] The success of the tragic theology in producing subjects is thus grounded on its elusiveness, on its ability to allow the human self to recognize the evil inflicted on it while ignoring its divine origin. The self can now accept a transference of guilt, appropriate what it perceives as objective necessity, and 'redeem' the gods, the father or the past (all of them roles that will be assumed by the Law) from their evil effects.[96] In so doing, the self can become a subject produced by an abstract legality on the condition of not denominating the origin of its doom.

It is important to note that it is not exactly the case that the source of power is itself elusive. Rather, the origin of authority appears elusive only from the subject's limited perspective. This limited perspective enables the sublimity of Kantian Law, and thus the very enunciation of the categorical imperative.[97] In order for subjectivation to work, in order for the subject to be able to persist in itself, the self must restrict itself to the perspective from which its attachment to dependency – the acceptance of guilt that premises its birth – remains invisible. Hegel's unhappy consciousness must be unaware of the fact that its changeable and unchangeable parts are one and the same, an unawareness that allows for the confrontation of one part against the other. In Freud's account of melancholia, in turn, it is precisely invisibility or unconsciousness of loss that gives melancholia its central role in the formation of the ego. In so far as the lost object is foreclosed to consciousness, the individual will undergo a melancholic process formative of the ego, since an acknowledged loss is impossible to mourn.[98]

According to the narrative of melancholia, Foucault's regulating soul or Althusser's interpellation, then, the act of internalizing guilt must be invisible, in order that abstract law can wield its power. The self thus purchases its intelligibility, identity and agency at the price of obliterating its dependency on a superior power. Only thus will it internalize imperatives (henceforth perceived as self-imposed rules), turn against itself and achieve self-consciousness. The very possibility of becoming a subject depends, therefore, on the self's blindness to the facticity and requirements of subjectivity. This pattern works only if the subject's perspective remains restricted to *this side* of fate, to *this side* of the Law, which is the sublime origin of enabling gestures. Subjectivity must be perceived as *natural*, and the subject must experience itself as its own self-willed origin. There is a correlation between assuming guilt, blinding oneself to its origin and becoming a subject that wields a constrained agency perceived as potential freedom.

We begin to see how it would be inaccurate to place, on one side, control-wielding state power (or the Father, or destiny, or objective necessity), and on the other side the initially *innocent* subject on whom control is exerted. While in locating the origin of heteronomy in state power Althusser's and Foucault's descriptions do take into account the self's cooperation in its own subjection, it is perhaps Freud's narrative that makes it clearer how the ego needs to internalize external coercion in order to constitute itself. As Judith Butler points out in her conversation with Ernesto Laclau and Slavoj Žižek in *Contingency, Hegemony, Universality*, it is impossible to conceive of power without the participation of the subject.[99] This enabling intertwining of subject and source of control is instantiated in my reading of *Blood Wedding* as the dynamic interaction between a necessary and a fictional fate.[100] While Lorca's tragedy depicts an objective necessity that indeed usurps the agency of the characters, I will propose a coexisting reading of fate as constructed and essentialized (that is, 'made' and then 'made real', in Elaine Scarry's terms) by the characters themselves under the mystifying denomination of 'blood'. Here blood plays a double role, that of vehicle of transmission of an inherited defilement, and of embodiment of objective necessity, a destiny that is appropriated to the point of running through the characters' veins.

A question that arises when speaking about 'internalization' is whether one internalizes an 'external' coercion that exists out there, or whether one creates that source of control and then projects it onto the world. In fact, if seen from the perspective of Ernesto Laclau's conception of social antagonism, the opposition between external and internal does not really hold: it constitutes a suspended binary used in order to express the idea of the 'operator of dislocation'. The 'operator of dislocation' refers to the fact that the dividing line between the self and reality (the world), or between subject and object, cannot be located or frozen, but rather is in permanent displacement.[101] The inextricability of an essential and a constructed fate that we will find in Lorca provides an apt poetic description of that displacement.

Given the dislocation of the line that separates 'power' from the subject, it is now time to ask what is the 'power' to which these accounts (particularly by Althusser, Foucault and Butler) refer as the source of control that produces subjects. This question is crucial, for even though the goal of these narratives is to trace the ways in which subjectivity is constructed, they might attain the unintended effect of mystifying and essentializing 'power' as an abstract source of authority. Trying to steer clear of any mystification of power, Althusser refers to the source of subjectivation specifically as ideology and ideological state apparatuses. Foucault, in turn, strategically chooses to examine power indirectly by analysing the concrete struggles against different forms of power. The aim of these struggles alone, he argues, is particularly revealing of the concrete workings of power. Some of these struggles 'attack everything which separates the individual, breaks his links with others, splits up community life, forces the individual back on himself and ties him to his own identity in a constraining way'. Others oppose 'secrecy, deformation, and mystifying representations imposed on people'.[102] As Foucault's depiction of struggles against power suggests, the subject's initial turn to ideological power monopolizes the self's ability to relate to otherness, isolates individuals, ties them to a constraining identity and uproots them from the field of interhuman relations, as is also the case in tragedy. Although it is the state's task to regulate life in community, it often operates by destroying that life. In his attempt to de-essentialize power efficiently and explicitly, furthermore, Foucault claims that 'there is no such thing as an abstract power above the human', that 'something called Power, with or without a capital letter, which is assumed to exist universally in a concentrated or diffused form, does not exist'.[103] At least in a first moment this clarification seems liberating, if we bear in mind the tragic requirement that power be undifferentiated, so that the human self can blind itself to its monstrous source.[104]

Yet, in spite of Foucault's efforts to make power appear concrete, an attempt at demystification that Butler emphatically joins, the effect of most accounts of subjectivity, Foucault's and Butler's included, is to present the power that creates subjects as an impersonal force beyond the human. It would seem, in other words, that no account of the facticity of power can entirely liberate itself from what is described as power's inflexible design. Hence the need for acknowledging the constructedness of power time and again. While these accounts are instrumental in revealing that power is historical and contingent, while they aim at depriving power of its ontological character, after reading Foucault's and Butler's compelling explanations one cannot help feeling that there is indeed an intangible Power (with capital P) at work. It would seem that the elusiveness of the object of analysis pervades the analysis itself, however determined its effort to dissect the ways in which power operates. Or perhaps what is elusive, more accurately, is the effect that objective necessity has as source of subjectivation in the analyser, who is himself or herself also a subject (like myself) writing from a subjective position, and thus occupying an impossible gaze when writing about the subject in the third person. One is left to wonder whether mystification of power might not be due, in the end, to the fact that there is nothing outside the subject. Or is there?

By way of clarification, it may prove useful to examine power from the perspective of the objective necessity that tragic characters construct as the desire of the Other now understood in Lacanian terms as the symbolic order.[105] Objective necessity materializes the self's desire to presuppose the existence of the Other's desire, as I proposed in Chapter 2. It is the embodiment of the self's desire to be driven by the desire of the Other, to be given the opportunity to renounce its acts, and thus achieve through that desire a position in the framework of guilt. Objective necessity constitutes an empty structure that one invests with the power of containing what one perceives as the inscrutable desire of the Other. The source of authority is therefore a result of the subject's construction, but since it is precisely that construction that makes the subject a subject, it continues exerting its influence even when the subject becomes aware of its own part in creating it. In the next chapter I will examine the subject's participation in creating necessity from the viewpoint of the interplay between a necessary and a fictional fate. I will propose an understanding of agency as the effect of this tension between givenness (essentiality) and artificiality.

That one cooperates with the source of authority that inaugurates one as subject and enables subjective agency implies that resistance and opposition to power do not constitute a one-way action against power, but rather manifest one's own participation in it.[106] (This would explain the divergences of the different accounts of the subject when they address the subversive potential of resisting power.)[107] Acquaintance with the requirement that we blind ourselves to the origin of power may lead us to conclude that subjectivity would collapse if only the subject became aware of the conditions of its emergence. Though this was, admittedly, a hope that I entertained for a long time, such a conclusion is misleading. It is indeed tempting to ask whether in displaying the constructed nature of power, in defusing its aura and seeking for resistances to it, these accounts ultimately do not ultimately succeed in revising subjectivation and provoking opposition to it. Such a question, however, would miss the fact that the self's cooperation is inherent to the 'necessary facticity' of power. If 'we subjects' cooperate with power, it is because both 'subject' and 'objective necessity' bear the paradoxical status of 'necessary fictions'. They are fictions, we have constructed them, but we cannot do without them because they constitute what we are.

The cooperation between subject and power can be observed in the working of ideology. Again, it is not the case that power exists out there in the form of an external coercion that imposes itself upon the subject. If this were so, displaying the constructedness of power might help us dismiss it if that construction is not working well. But since power and the subject's cooperation exist in inextricable interaction, revealing the fictionality of power does not entail overcoming it. In fact, as Sloterdijk and Žižek convincingly argue, ideology achieves more support, proves more influential, and thus works at its best precisely when its constructedness or 'falsity' is revealed.[108] We will see, furthermore, that dominance requires opposition, that authority necessitates its 'other' to succeed. Tragedy instantiates this dynamic collaboration between 'external' control and subjective resistance as the subject's short-lived challenge to the fulfilment of fate. Upon creating the occasion for the re-enactment of the (traumatic) illusion of the world's collapse, the subject quickly cooperates with objective necessity, providing the opportunity for the symbolic order to reaffirm itself. It is as if in challenging fate the tragic subject (think of Racine's Phaedra) recoiled from the realization that there is something worse than tragic death. And there is, which is what makes tragic death so welcome as evasion, as escape.[109]

Precisely because our participation in power is enabling, it is not necessarily a bad thing. From the viewpoint of political action, becoming aware of the contingency of power, its dislocations and our own cooperation with it, is decisive, as we shall see in the last chapter. While the Law may remain elusive, the site of political power has agents and faces that it is vital to recognize.

*

The elusiveness of power seems safe, it will be preserved successfully, no matter how efficiently we manage to reveal its operations. Its mystification cannot be entirely dispelled because the subject is too invested in it. It is precisely because of the central position that the Enlightenment attributes to the autonomous rational subject, and not in spite of it, that the inscrutability of power must be preserved. After all, the sublimity of the Law that enunciates the categorical imperative depends on the subject's limited perspective on it. As we saw in Chapter 2, in the *Critique of Practical Reason* Kant stays on *this side* of the Sublime Law, overlooking the fact that such enabling sublimity is based on its obverse, monstrous *other side*. That one is able to perceive one side or the other – sublimity or monstrosity – is just a matter of perspective. If one were to come too close to the Sublime Law, the sight of its monstrosity would undo one as subject.[110]

This is what Kant intimates in 'On the Wisely Commensurate Proportion of the Human Being's Cognitive Powers to His Practical Vocation'. Kant initiates this section of the Second Critique wondering what would happen if nature had endowed us with the illumination and capacity for insight that we so much wish we possessed. In the first place, he writes, we would demand the satisfaction of our inclinations, causing the moral law to speak 'in order to keep the inclinations within their fitting limits and even to subject them, one and all, to a higher purpose that takes no account of any inclination'.[111] But then, the conflict between inclinations and moral duty would be suspended, since our new capacity for insight would give us unceasing access to God and eternity. Let me quote at length:

> But instead of the conflict that the moral attitude now has to carry on with the inclinations, in which – after some defeats – moral fortitude of soul is yet gradually to be acquired, God and eternity with

their dreadful majesty would lie unceasingly before our eyes (for, as regards certainty, what we can perfectly prove counts as much for us as what we assure ourselves of as manifest to the eye). Transgression of the law would indeed be avoided; what is commanded would be done. However, the attitude from which actions ought to be done cannot likewise be instilled by any command. . . . Therefore most lawful actions would be done from fear, only a few from hope, and none at all from duty; and the moral worth of actions – on which alone, after all, the worth of the person and even that of the world hinges in the eyes of the highest wisdom – would not exist at all. The conduct of human beings, as long as their nature remained as it is, would thus be converted into a mere mechanism, where, as in a puppet show, everything would gesticulate well but there would still be no life in the figures.[112]

As a consequence of having absolute knowledge of God and eternity (which would now 'lie unceasingly before our eyes'), and thus unhindered access to the site of enunciation of the Law, the 'respect devoid of self-interest' which 'the moral Law in us demands' would be lost. Having lost our transcendental freedom, we would become lifeless puppets which perform the right gestures mechanically, instead of in free acceptance of the duty imposed by the Law. We would lose, in a word, our ability to dedicate ourselves to the 'highest good' that Kant locates in the moral Law. Though the Law would be unfailingly obeyed, it would no longer be obeyed in fulfilment of our duty, but rather out of fear.

What is this fear, this terror? The fear of seeing God in the face to which Kant refers here is a metaphor for absolute certainty: 'for, as regards certainty, what we can perfectly prove counts as much for us as what we assure ourselves of as manifest to the eye.' Could we then venture that this is, in effect, a fear of knowing too much, the fear of trespassing the limited perspective that protects us from the vision of the other side of the sublime moral Law? Isn't this fear caused by the possibility of abolishing the distance that keeps the sublimity of the moral Law from turning into monstrosity? This suggests that inscrutability might be less a property inherent in the Law than the materialization of our own need to perceive it as such. For what could be the terror provoked by this access to the emptiness of the Law, if not the terror of losing the Big Interlocutor, the Law that orients all our social actions, including those aimed at transgressing its own limits?

Subjection for the sake of autonomy

We may thus agree with Lacan's idea that 'the limit of Enlightenment is in the Enlightenment itself',[113] in the caveat that Kant adds
to the activity of the autonomous subject of theoretical reflection ('the
scholar'): 'Reason about what you will and as much as you will – but
obey!'[114] Together with the right to 'reason autonomously', Kant would
seem to introduce a contradiction or fissure at the core of the project
of the Enlightenment: 'Obey!'[115] If considered carefully, though, the
injunction to obey constitutes less a fissure than the enabling feature of
Enlightenment.[116] It can be no coincidence that the very tragic art that
modernity recovers as the beginning of the Western tradition is inflected
by an injunction to follow a command. Perhaps this illuminates the
apparent historical paradox in institutional life in classical Greece,
where the time in which in the Greek *polis* human self-sufficiency
begins to prevail over mythical and heroic self-representations coincides
with the moment in which the first tragedians stage the self's unredeemable fall.[117] The commands dictated by objective necessity are
described by the tragic protagonists as a traumatic intrusion that
imposes itself violently on the human order of things. In Chapter 2 I
argued that although tragic characters initially lament the control of
destiny over their lives, in effect they construct objective necessity
as the desire of the Other. When in *Oedipus at Colonus* Antigone tells
Polynices that in attacking Thebes he is about to die at his brother's
hands, thus fulfilling Oedipus' prophecy, Polynices replies: 'True, /
that's his wish – but I, I can't give up.'[118]

What Polynices cannot give way on is his desire for the desire of the
Other. It is by virtue of becoming a desiring subject that the tragic self
achieves an inalienable position in the tragic framework of guilt, which
is why Oedipus wishes he were guilty: since when he committed his
crimes he ignored that he was fulfilling the prophecy, he was deprived
of the opportunity of desiring the objective necessity dictated by it.
Deprived of the possibility of becoming a desiring subject, Oedipus considers he is not guilty. Without desire and guilt he is denied the possibility of achieving a subjective position, and hence he refuses to die.
Sophocles' Oedipus suspends the tragic pattern of subjectivation
through death, and in so doing he constitutes the exception that testi-
fies to the desire for subjectivation and guilt: the very destiny that controls human action constitutes the self's object of the desire. It is this
desire, which Polynices expresses so vehemently and which Agamemnon qualifies as 'impassioned passion', which secures the self's position

in the framework of guilt through which subjectivity is achieved. Though Agamemnon initially laments that objective necessity forces him to make an impossible decision ('A heavy doom is disobedience, but heavy, too, if I shall rend my own child, the adornment of my house, polluting a father's hands with streams of slaughtered maiden's blood close by the altar'),[119] he immediately decides passionately to cooperate with it: 'For it is right and holy that *I should desire with exceedingly impassioned passion* the sacrifice staying the winds, the maiden's blood.'[120]

But how, exactly, does tragic subjectivation concern modern subjects? In the absence of a tragic destiny, what makes modern subjectivity traumatic is precisely the lack of an objective necessity with which one can cooperate. If in classical tragedy the irruption of objective necessity in human life creates a kind of trauma, says Lacan in his Seminar VIII, *Le transfert* (1960–61), the trauma in modern times is not destiny itself, but the fact that destiny no longer applies.

> We are no longer guilty just in virtue of a symbolic debt. . . . It is the debt itself in which we have our place that can be taken from us, and it is here that we can feel completely alienated from ourselves. The ancient *Ate* doubtless made us guilty of this debt, but to renounce it as we can now means that we are left with an even greater misfortune: destiny no longer applies.[121]

As Lacan remarks, in classical tragedy one becomes guilty by virtue of occupying a position in the scheme of destiny. In modern times, however, after the death of God or of a superior necessity that structures the social field, one runs the risk of having to do without guilt, without the refuge afforded by the awareness of being in debt. Since we are deeply identified with guilt, since it provides the division through which we become subjects, having to do without that symbolic debt precipitates us into uncharted territory: not even our identity – our identity least of all – can be experienced as a shelter. Without guilt we run the risk of losing, together with our position in the symbolic framework (and therefore in the ontological edifice of reality), the structure of meaning that liberated us from the responsibility of acting with no guarantee of success. Hence what Lacan calls 'an even greater misfortune'. Aside from providing the alibi that liberates us from responsibility by controlling our acts, destiny sustained the only side of ethical goals that we allowed ourselves to see, blocking our access to the other terrible side. Without a destiny that establishes our guilt in advance, we feel destitute and lost.

But are we indeed destitute, are we indeed without destiny? It would seem that we are not, since we have managed to transfer the traits of destiny as objective necessity onto other essentialized constructs, such as Power, the State or the Law. The modern need for objective necessity is exemplified in the libidinous attachment to conscience of Racine's Phaedra. As I argued above, the modern subject is in simultaneous subjection *and* cooperation with the power that produces it, caught in the very tension that defines the double bind of subjective agency.[122] It is precisely that cooperation that produces the self-conscious universal subject willing to submit to the law in exchange for civil liberties. It enables the social contract, life in community and modern subject-based politics, no less. So, to alter Lacan's words slightly, destiny does apply after all, since we seem to have succeeded in preserving guilt by creating 'necessary fictions' such as the Law. These essentialized constructs have an aporetic nature. Though not given or necessary but rather historically contingent, we cannot renounce them, not even repair them easily. Like (Aeschylean) tragic protagonists, we create objective necessity as the desire of the other; in desiring objective necessity we become desiring subjects, that is, subjects of guilt; the guilt that objective necessity instills in us then produces us as subjects. Though the constellation of guilt is circular, guilt is crucial. Without it, the ontological effect of reality attached to the social order in which we have a position would be lost.

Guilt is the last thing we would be willing to renounce.

Why?

First, depicting ourselves as victims allows us, (tragic) modern subjects, to invoke an inexorable fate as an alibi ('It was inevitable, I was acting under fate's control . . .'), thus disclaiming responsibility for our actions. Being responsible for one's actions implies being responsible before someone else, so that by denying our responsibility we also deny our accountability to other people. It is the receiving pole of action, the real people who suffer from our acts, that we blind ourselves to when we depict ourselves as victims. (In this sense, when we claim we are victims we create real victims.)

But beyond, and perhaps before, refusing responsibility, is the aspiration to preserve the social symbolic order that produces us as subjects. Why be subordinated to an impersonal Other instead of relating to an actual person? Perhaps because, as Levinas maintains, the human other is the only one who can indeed disrupt the self-centred world of the same. Only other people are real others who can question our way of life. Therefore, while the abstract otherness of fate, Law or the Father configures the self as an intelligible subject, real people, with their presence and needs, question the centrality of the self. Paradoxically, the eagerness to embrace subjection, even at the cost of death, responds to a fear of leaving ourselves, to an urge to preserve our integrity, and with it the preeminence of sameness that only a real person can disrupt. Hence the paradox of our *tragic* subjectivity: we represent ourselves as victims in order to preserve our autonomy.

Agency premised on constraint

Since modern subjectivity depends on the act of essentializing constructs such as the Law, what are the possibilities opened by the realization that essentialized coercive forces are contingent? Wouldn't the subject be the 'construct' that would benefit most from becoming aware of its fabricated nature? Is it possible to break with the subject's pattern of self-victimization and to restitute the possibility of agency?

As long as agency is contingent on the fiction of the modern subject, the answer seems to be no. Given its association with the autonomous self, itself a heteronomous construction, we must assume that human agency does not exist except when it is denied, at risk of imminent peril, in the face of constraint. Only this constrained idea of agency supplies the foundation for an acceptable self-representation as agent that leaves one's sense of autonomy intact.

Though the illusion of agency is associated with freedom (with freedom of decision and of action), though freedom is held to be the highest value, in fact freedom might not be so desirable after all, at least within subjective agency. The fact that the Kantian motto of the Enlightenment, 'think freely', must be qualified by 'but obey' attests to the undesirability of a freedom that exceeds the constraints of subjectivity. However desired and invoked, freedom is precisely what we want to escape by seeking the shelter provided by rules. As we shall see in the final chapter, deciding 'freely' – deciding how to fulfil one's duty or how to respond to the ethical demand – undoes, in a way, the self-conscious subject by depriving it of intelligibility and confirmation. This comes as a surprise, since it is reputedly in the search for the human break with external control, for man's emancipation from any unchosen determination, that modernity looks back to Greek tragedy. It would seem, at first view, that what modernity finds in tragedy is a break with what Levinas calls 'participation' or the self's dissolution in larger horizons of meaning (in this case, this is a break with the mythical, heroic and religious traditions).

Yet, we are beginning to see that is not the case. If modernity looks to tragedy, it is not only (or not primarily) in search of an incipient process of individual and political emancipation. Rather, it would seem that modernity seeks instances of internalization of external authority and of human cooperation with it, even at the risk of one's life. What modernity seems to find in tragedy is a model for making externally imposed actions appear voluntarily chosen, whereby human subjection to authority is ultimately occluded by the self's passionate cooperation with necessity. The very tragic sites in which we expect to find the gradual representation of the human self as agent, and thereby the human ability to change the conditions of existence, teach us that initiative must be relinquished in favour of identity. It is because of the insights it offers into the production of meaning or intelligibility that tragedy is still so relevant today. It provides the inspiration that allows modern theories of subjectivity to re-enact the tragic subjection to authority while appearing emancipatory. From this perspective, we could venture that modernity finds in tragedy a testing of the possibility of the world's collapse when its organizing principles (the tragic causality) are disturbed. As we saw in the analysis of Racine's *Phaedra*, however, ultimately it is not the symbolic order that might collapse, but rather one's identity, if one does not sacrifice oneself for saving the tragic world.

What tragedy seems to teach us is that agency resides in assuming as voluntarily chosen what was inevitable in the first place. Agency is thus not the same as acting. It consists in creating the framework for the interpretation of one's act as effective, that is, in creating the circumstances that will give meaning to the acts that one then inserts in the world (mechanically repeated, empty gestures, as described by Pascal and Althusser would be included here, since they create productive conditions or circumstances). It would seem, according to this, that the effectiveness of actions, their ability to incide in a particular context, is due less to a concrete act – what we would identify as an 'action' – than to the restructuring of the context in which the act is then inscribed.

The inextricability of agency and coercion belongs to the same constellation as the interdependency of the subject's cooperation and the 'external' sources of control. From this perspective, we may suggest that agency is premised on dying a tragic death, the kind of death that provides an escape from a responsibility that falls outside any subjectivating framework of guilt. The dependency of power on the subject's cooperation – or the reliance of agency on 'death-inflicting' 'external' coercion – imposes, within the scheme of modern subjectivity, the need to undergo a symbolic death (which in most tragedies is also literal) in order not to die to the symbolic.[123] In so doing, in dying symbolically, one 'saves' the social order, achieves or retains one's position as a subject, secures the subjectivity of all others by reaffirming its confer-ring source and achieves subjective agency.

The necessary interplay between 'inner' potential and the 'external' authority to which one must submit for the sake of autonomy is addressed by Hegel in the *Logic*.[124] Significantly, Hegel criticizes the duality that philosophies of essence establish between the self, on the one hand, and the external pressure that allows the self to realize itself, on the other. If the self's possibilities can be brought to fruition only by external coercion, he argues, it is because in self-realization inner poten-tial and the external conditions that allow for the actualization of that potential are inextricable; they are one and the same thing.[125] The self's potential is therefore premised on the embodiment of that potential as heteronomous coercion in the material world. '[T]he moment the subject is bereft of external obstacles which can be blamed for his failure, his subjective position will collapse on account of its inherent inauthenticity,' writes Žižek in his reading of Hegel's *Logic*.[126] Special-ized in gathering itself as same in the face of change, the self seems unable to achieve its coherence without (created) external obstacles. If that hindrance is removed, the self, left to the free deployment of its inner potentials, free to 'be itself', is destroyed.

The modern self feels insecure about its acts when those actions were individually chosen and so liable to judgment. Therefore, we construct social versions of objective necessity and exclude ourselves from 'the autonomous world . . . and its immanent law of creation'.[127] As Mikhail Bakhtin argues in *Toward a Philosophy of the Act* (1919–21), we act more confidently under necessity or social constraint, that is, 'only when we do so not as ourselves, but as those possessed by the immanent neces-sity of the meaning of some domain of culture', because those acts are not answerable, and so we do not feel individual responsibility for them.[128] Hence, in order to avoid responsibility, we tend to renounce what Bakhtin denominates the 'non-alibi of existence' in order to prove our 'alibi in Being'. 'It is only my non-alibi in being that transforms an empty possibility into an actual answerable act or deed.'[129] In a line of thinking that Levinas would later develop (without having had access to Bakhtin's text on action, which, though written between 1919 and 1921, was not discovered and rescued from decay until 1972), what

Bakhtin argues here is that I am the only one who can fulfil my responsibility, because 'my *obligative (ought-to-be) uniqueness*' makes me irreplaceable.[130]

Might it not be the case that all self-representations must rely on the inseparability of 'inner' potential from 'external' constraint? This seems plausible, for however repressive, constrained action liberates the actor from all responsibility, from the accountability inherent in actualizing one's 'free' initiative. The difference between being freed from responsibility by our faith in a destiny that controls our action and having to assume that responsibility in the absence of destiny is, according to Lacan, what separates classical and modern (post-Christian) tragedy. What defines classical tragedy, in Lacan's view, is that its protagonists believe in a substantial truth, a destiny or objective necessity, which is eventually replaced by faith in God. But after the death of God, we feel disoriented, without a destiny that gives us a position in the framework of guilt. Without the debt and guilt that guided our actions (as *Ate* did in Greek tragedy), we experience the vertigo of having to assume full responsibility for our decisions. The refuge provided by our investment in becoming guilty of a symbolic debt that can guide our steps is, according to Lacan, no longer within our reach.[131]

Is there an object of faith that can replace the lost 'truth' initially embodied by destiny and then by the Christian God? According to Lacan, the modern self is held 'hostage of the Word' (*l'otage du Verbe*, which also plays with the sense of Verb as God). The subject is now compelled to act in particular ways that testify to its faith, an absolute faith, not in the truth of any transcendent source of meaning, but rather in the semblance of truth in order to prevent the disintegration of 'the Word which guarantees the semblance of Meaning'.[132] As Althusser expresses it in his own Pascalian reading of the subject, the subject's belief is 'governed by a material ritual' and accomplished by 'a subject acting in all consciousness according to his belief'.[133] One does not pray out of belief, but rather one will eventually believe by virtue of regular prayer; it is in repeatedly performing the gestures of subjectivity (subjection, assumption of guilt, obedience, blindness, cooperation) 'all by oneself' that one becomes a subject. This is how ideology, itself an empty structure, functions and reaffirms itself: in the 'empty gestures' performed by precisely those who realizing that it is false, nevertheless continue 'believing' in it.[134]

What Lacan overlooks in his reading of classical tragedy is the fact that tragedy already denies the existence of any firm truth, a truth with substantial content, a Faith with an object. Already in Greek tragedy, the art of conferring sublime sense – that is, the ability to produce intelligibility (to posit an external transcendent principle that guarantees the sense of particular occurrences) – is enabled by a void. In fact, the classical tragic subject gives everything (even its life) in the attempt to legitimize the emptiness or lack of substance of an otherwise unforsakable faith. Perhaps it 'realizes' that the object of belief is empty, false. This would explain its efforts to preserve faith at all costs, as the only guarantee of the existence of the object of that faith, transcendent authority. The tragic subject would seem to recognize that objective necessity is based on a monstrous transcendent dimension which is unbearable. But this recognition must be repressed, lest it reveal the fact that the intelligibility provided by the law is purely formal: it offers no advice for acting well and no clue of what a good action is. All it offers is the certainty that every action will be doomed to fail. What tragedy expresses (indeed, what inflects the tragic plot), in sum, is the self's awareness of being in charge of an unpayable debt, and thus the impossibility of an agency that is not based on constraint. Hence the subject's passionate cooperation with necessity.

In tragedy objective necessity offers no legitimation of concrete action (in spite of encompassing divine commands and city rules, which can themselves be concrete), but neither does the categorical imperative or the sublime Law that sustains modern subjectivity. Though in 'What is Enlightenment?' the object of Kant's 'obey!' is social rules, in the *Critique of Practical Reason* the duty one must fulfil remains unspecified, unless the self dares fill it with substantial content, and act with no support or guarantee of success. Hence the vertigo that duty produces and the need to keep its initial emptiness, the formality to which one must give substance, out of the self's scope of vision as a forbidden 'other side'. Confronting the emptiness of the ethical goals is unbearable because the responsibility it places on the self is extreme. This responsibility is impossible to fulfil by definition, since it is not defined or evaluated or judged by a positive set of stipulated criteria. It is the vertigo of this responsibility that tragic death averts, when it usefully reaffirms the self's limited perspective (whose ultimate limit is fixed in tragic death), thus helping us avoid the empty 'other side' of destiny and the sublime Law. We now understand the intensity, indeed the despair, with which we aspire to remain intelligible, to occupy a position in a symbolic network – whether the tragic causality or the linguistic requirements to enter sociality in the post-classical world. And we also understand the usefulness of representing our experience as tragic, and of resorting to tragic death.

Beyond sublimation or worse than tragic

The impact of the emptiness of authority is thoroughly displayed in tragedy. In this display tragedy would seem to afford a worst-case scenario description of other situations of heteronomy that I will examine in the final chapter, such as the emptiness of ethical goals of which Kant speaks, Levinas's 'substitution', or Lacan's remarks on inserting an act outside of the symbolic. (Central to these different approaches is a faithfulness to desire, the need to keep the gap of desire open.) The abstract injunction that the self must translate into concrete obligations places the self in a situation of infinite responsibility – as results from Kant's formalism or the impossibility to interpret the injunction in Levinas, which opens the path to an ethics of misinterpretation.[135] The injunction would seem to resemble the decision that tragic necessity makes for the human self without counting on him or her. But the crucial difference between tragedy and ethical responsibility, as Kant, Levinas and Lacan understand it in different ways, is that the vertigo of emptiness in the absence of external confirmation that characterizes the latter is precisely what most tragic characters try to evade. One can go as far as suggesting that the very act of avoiding emptiness is what makes subjects specifically tragic – and it is from this perspective that Antigone, by acting in conformity with her desire and pursuing the death drive (according to Lacan's reading),[136] is not tragic.

I have already argued that tragedy creates a crisis in order to reaffirm intelligibility at its breaking point, and also that tragedy bears the traces of the emptiness of authority in the invisible form of the 'other side' of Destiny.[137] That monstrous emptiness, the void around which the tragic universe is structured, cannot be represented. It can be perceived only in the rejection it provokes, and it is this avoidance that tragedy suggests in its depiction of the human self's self-blinding and passionate cooperation with necessity.

What characterizes tragedy is not the threat that emptiness poses to the symbolic order it enables. It is, rather, the act whereby the self assumes a traumatic injunction dictated by objective necessity (in an attempt to fulfil the desire of the Other) in order to blind itself to the fact that the *other side* of objective necessity is empty, that it is supported by a void. 'Tragedy' is primarily defined neither by the threat posed by that void – the threat of suspension of meaning energizes any symbolic framework – nor by the confrontation of competing forces that precipitates the human self into an irredeemable struggle with transcendent authority. Tragedy is characterised, rather, by the act whereby the human subject blinds itself to the nothingness that supports meaning in order to preserve the integrity of the tragic order that bestows the self's identity. Because Antigone is not even seduced by an intelligibility that she refuses beforehand (she considers herself dead to the social order from the outset), she is not tragic, as I have argued above.

But a tragic play is larger than the objective necessity to which tragic characters restrict their vision. It also depicts in negative terms the *other side* of destiny to which tragic characters blind themselves. Hence another paradox of tragic subjectivation: in order to become tragic subjects, characters must *evade* the *other side* that enables the tragic symbolic order by narrowing their perspective. Tragedy, in other words, portrays a primordial heteronomous constellation (destiny's *other side*) that the tragic subject evades by passionately taking part in the heteronomous structure dictated by fate (objective necessity as *this side* of destiny). The primordial heteronomy evaded by tragic characters may be considered ethical, since it places all the weight of responsibility on the human self. In the absence of an objective necessity that predetermines the course of action to follow, the self must decide what its duty is and act on it without the support of any controlling and organizing transcendence. Since this ethical responsibility exceeds tragic sense, and therefore lies beyond sublimation, it may be considered more terrible than tragic. The injunction imposed by objective necessity, in turn, is not ethical, but rather tragic. By claiming that it is not in control of its action, that its agency has been usurped by a terrible Otherness, the self shields its intelligible and self-centred universe from the irruption of the very real persons who suffer the consequences of its acts.

In more concrete terms, tragic heteronomy is different from the heteronomy informed by Kant's duty to fulfil one's duty without taking one's duty as an excuse.[138] It is also different from heteronomy as Levinas understands it, as the desire for the absolute other for whom the self must respond and act in the void, without the support of any ontological horizon. Tragic heteronomy has a non-ethical sense of renouncing responsibility for the sake of intelligibility: I accept a transference of guilt to which I blind myself in order to preserve my identity.

What is it, then, that we fear so much as to prefer to become a victim? There is something even more terrifying than tragic death, and that is acting beyond the social rules that legitimate our actions.[139] It is daring to decide what our duty is, to give it substantial content, and then to act on it without any external confirmation or support. It is taking the risk of acting without the guarantee of success, expanding the space of political action beyond the safe realm of institutions and laws. When confronted with this infinite responsibility, this uncertainty that undoes us as intelligible subjects, the tragic death that reaffirms the symbolic order comes as a relief. Tragic death rescues us from the terror caused by the anarchic responsibility that suspends the self's intelligibility as self-conscious subject (and appeals the sensible self – embodied, experiential, sensitive – that in the process of subjectivation one had been compelled to renounce). Tragic death as evasion, as escape.

Subjectivity as *necessary fiction*

Now we can retake the question of the *necessity* of becoming an intelligible subject. In 'The Subject and Power' Foucault proposes a radical alternative to subjectivity by situating oneself outside, namely, to refuse identity and the kind of individuation spawned by the state. 'Maybe the target nowadays,' he writes, 'is not to discover what we are, but to refuse what we are. We have to imagine and to build up what we could be to get rid of this kind of political "double bind".'[140] But should we really be interested in escaping the ambivalence of being subordinated to social power as a condition for achieving subjectivity and agency? Would this not disqualify us, in Gillian Rose's words, 'from any understanding of the actualities of structure and authority, intrinsic to any conceivable social and political constitution',[141] making us leave those structures intact?

We cannot renounce subjectivity, for it is a necessary creation constitutive of who we are.[142] However problematic, this subject premised on assuming guilt and depicting itself as victim constitutes the basis of democratic politics, since it is the locus of the rational principles of universality and equality. Therefore, the very egalitarian principles that found democracy, enabling constitutions, the rule of law, and courts of human rights, may result, paradoxically, in an inability to reach out to others, if not in their suppression. (This is what I will refer to, in the last chapter, as the deadlock of ethics and politics.)

Were we to renounce subjectivity, with it we would give up agency (however precarious), the possibility of political struggle and of the rule of law (however imperfect). We would relinquish the very constitutional arrangements that secure the bodily inviolability of the other, as well as mine. By renouncing subjectivity we would give up ourselves, that is, the very position from which such a renunciation is made.

*

What is it, in sum, that modern philosophy ultimately finds in tragedy without explicitly denominating it 'tragic'? I would like to rehearse several possible reasons for the modern return to tragedy:

(1) To avert, through tragic death, the risk of the collapse of the symbolic order, and with it the risk of losing intelligibility.

(2) To learn about the birth of agency under constraint.

(3) But also to become aware of the fictional (though necessary) status of that birth, for might not tragedy, as a self-conscious fiction, be able to provide insight into the act of creating the tragic consciousness? It is not in its awareness of its fictionality that classical tragedy exceeds the (Lacanian) modern condition of being hostage to the Word, but rather in the open declaration of that awareness: tragedy *is* a work of art.

Here the widely acknowledged reasons to look to tragedy, namely, as birth of agency and of self-conscious fiction, meet. Because tragedy (1) enables subjectivation, (2) rehearses the birth of agency under constraint (the interpretation of this birth is complicated, as we shall see, by the interplay between a necessary and a fictional fate), and (3) provides insight into the process of constitution of the subject as a *necessary fiction*, the modern recovery of tragedy proves rather fruitful.

But perhaps the most important reasons to look at tragedy concern not so much what modern subjectivity inherits and preserves (such as the pattern of subjectivation or death as escape), as what it excludes.

(4) In order to be able to identify with universals, the modern autonomous subject denies its own sensibility and materiality and represses its conflicting desires. Though the tragic subject, in choosing to undergo tragic death, also renounces that which in the individual could have exceeded the subject, tragic plays favour conflicts between equally demanding loyalties in which emotions and desires play a central role. In inheriting only tragic death as escape, subjectivity excludes the possibility of a sensible subject and favours only a self-conscious self. This death (the kind of death undergone by Polynices or Phaedra, but also by the modern subject in the process of its constitution), a death that instead of annihilating the subject saves and produces it, requires the death of the sensible subject for the sake of the birth of the self-conscious self. (In the final chapter we will see that Levinas's theory of the subject is based precisely on the sensible self repressed by the modes of subjectivation studied here; the sensible self would also seem to play an important role in Lacan's idea that one must not give way on one's desire, or avoid absolute death.)

Finally, (5) tragedy exceeds tragic subjectivity by insinuating the void side of fate. The tragic subject blinds itself to this excess, thus *betraying* the tragedy. Tragedy insinuates the suspension of intelligibility and the infinite responsibility that tragic subjects die to avoid. By virtue of surpassing the tragic subject's restricted perspective, tragedy becomes the intersection of two different kinds of heteronomy.[143] On the one hand, it conjures up the heteronomy imposed by the objective necessity that commands the death of the character for the sake of subjectivation (a form of heteronomy that I will provisionally denominate *tragic*). On the other hand, tragedy comprises the unbearable heteronomy dictated by the emptiness of the other side of both destiny and the sublime Law (a form of heteronomy that we may tentatively denominate *ethical*).[144] Since (I will argue) these two forms of heteronomy respectively inflect *subject-based politics* and what I will call the *ethical demand*, tragedy might offer important insight into the difficult relation between ethics and politics.

4
The Fiction of Fate

Few spectators would deny that the end of Federico García Lorca's tragic plays is brought about by the workings of fate, as stipulated by the classical model they re-enact.[1] Lorca's characters express the sense of being controlled by an inexorable force. In *Bodas de sangre* (*Blood Wedding*) (1933) the Mother fears that her son, the Bridegroom, will be killed at the hands of a member of the Félix family, following the same fate as his father and his brother.[2] Meanwhile, the Bride decides to marry in the hope of being freed from the irresistible attraction she still feels for another man called Leonardo, himself a Félix, three years after the end of their relationship.[3] Both situations point to the characters' lack of control over their acts. The first demonstrates the problematic relationship between the tragic subject (here the Mother's son, the Bridegroom) and the Past, which has its origin in an inherited defilement, a form of guilt attached to the characters' ancestors. Blood in *Blood Wedding* is the channel for this irreversible transmission of guilt, and a diffuse version of fate that dissimulates its transcendent source.[4] Embodied in blood, fate now appears natural. Accordingly, both Leonardo and the Bride are compelled to 'follow the course of their blood',[5] while the Bridegroom, suddenly forgetting his desire to marry and secure the continuity of his lineage, inherits the fate of his 'casta de muertos en mitad de la calle' (*breed that dies in the middle of the street*),[6] and hastens to re-enact his father's and brother's death. '¿Ves este brazo?' (*See this arm?*), he says. 'Pues no es mi brazo. Es el brazo de mi hermano y el de mi padre y el de toda mi familia que está muerta' (*Well, it is not my arm. It is the arm of my brother and of my father and of everyone in my family who is dead*).[7] Unable to detach themselves from this inherited fault, an embodied fate, the characters can only expiate it through death.

The second situation is an example of deliberation without any actual choice. Although the Bride deliberates between yielding to the attraction of her ex-lover and building a relationship with her future husband,[8] the latter does not constitute a viable alternative, given the gripping power that Leonardo's image and voice have on her. This voice, she claims, 'me arrastra, y sé que me ahogo, pero voy detrás' (*it drags me, and I know that I am drowning, but I follow it*).[9] As the plays quickly reveal, the attempts of the characters to steer the course of their lives, to retain some agency over events, are utterly futile. The Bride will elope with Leonardo on her wedding night, and the two men will kill each other in the woods, once again re-enacting the feud between their families. As is true in Greek tragedy, the duration of *Blood Wedding* seems to be the time it takes fate to reassert itself.

In staging an inevitable inheritance of culpability, self-division in a performance of deliberation that consists of a dual structure without content, a narrative reversal by virtue of which human action turns into its contrary and recoils against its agent, and, most importantly, the self's act of self-blinding and of cooperating with the necessity he or she had initially refused; in reasserting, in short, the fate that had been temporarily delayed by human freedom – by human action – through the characters' imminent death, *Blood Wedding* re-enacts a tragic plot, the precise narrative structure within which Greek tragedy engenders tragic fate, the tragic causality and the tragic view of life.

The creation of destiny: Lorca's *Blood Wedding*

As tragedy traditionally presents human initiative ultimately destroyed by fate, it indirectly raises the question of human freedom. If the characters' acts were not driven by fate, what explanation would account for tragic death? What would be the status of human action if it were no longer measured against an inflexible causality and reduced to a moment of discordance within a superior order? Is fate indeed accountable for men's and women's lack of control?

This is the question that I want to explore here by proposing a shift in the understanding of fate. Side by side with a given and necessary fate that determines human acts, Lorca's dramas suggest a new understanding that renders the authority of fate contingent. While *Blood Wedding* does indeed posit a necessary fate that usurps human agency, it simultaneously questions that fate is necessary or inevitable by presenting the tragic events within a different framework. In contrast to the ways in which the characters depict their fate, this dramatic framework reveals that fate is not necessary, but rather constructed. This dif-

ferent interpretation casts light on the ethical consequences of the tragic mode of interpreting experience. If the protagonists experience their lives as predetermined by fate, it is because of their compulsion to repeat a narrative of the past, which they project into the present time of the play. When the Bride, the Mother and Leonardo in *Blood Wedding* insist on repeating the past, these characters relinquish, in effect, their ability to act and interact. *Blood Wedding* thus suggests that fate is a fiction that the characters create, in order to depict themselves as victims and disclaim responsibility for their acts. Let's see how this happens.

In *Blood Wedding* both Leonardo and the Bride are restricted to remembering the time when they were still lovers, a time of which the play offers no explicit information. Memory as a narrative can, like all narratives, be rearranged without ceasing to be perceived as a reliable record of past events. As George H. Mead indicates in 1932, 'We speak of the past as final and irrevocable. There is nothing that is less so. . . . [T]he past (or some meaningful structure of the past) is as hypothetical as the future.'[10] In order to achieve some credibility for itself, memory disguises its creative transformation of the past. There is a high degree of fictionality in what one remembers, but the fictionality of memory is forgotten. What prevails is a constructed version of the past, while, paradoxically, the 'historical event' vanishes.[11] Therefore, when Leonardo tells the Bride 'Abre y refresca tu recuerdo' (*Open and refresh your memory*),[12] communication between the two cannot exist because each of them follows their own individual version of what happened.[13]

(But, some spectators may ask, don't Lorca's characters follow the dictates of their own desire, instead of those of a tragic fate? Isn't their fate defined precisely by their faithfulness to their own desire, which drives them to defy social restrictions in a courageous exertion of human authenticity?)

Simultaneously, the Mother cannot cease to narrate the killings of her husband and elder son and to reveal her fear that her younger son may also be killed. When she states: 'Cien años que yo viviera no hablaría de otra cosa' (*If I lived a hundred years I would speak of nothing else*),[14] apart from confirming the presence of the past, she also announces her intention to project a narrative of death on the future, thus assuring, paradoxically, her younger son's future destiny.

If fate is not real but fictional, how can one be driven by it *only* by virtue of narrating? What makes the characters' imagining of the past so charged, and their depiction of fate so powerful, as to be taken as necessary? By projecting a narrative of the past into the present the characters interrupt the dialogue between present and past that characterizes the creative activity of memory. Memory in tragedy functions differently from memory in life, where the act of remembering is creative. A historical being, the person as it existed in a particular historical moment to which we have no access, should not be mistaken for the historical consciousness, the self-image constructed by the remembering self from the viewpoint of the present. '[E]very image of the past that is not recognized by the present as one of its own concerns threatens to disappear irretrievably', says Walter Benjamin in his *Fifth Thesis on the Philosophy of History*,[15] a fact that Funes the Memorious reverses in Borges' story. Funes' rare gift (and misfortune?) consists in reproducing the past exactly, second by second, in an indiscriminate act of remembrance that takes up all present time, precluding both the distance necessary for reflection and the possibility of new experience.[16] In our less extraordinary daily practice, we revise the past in accordance with present concerns and needs, permanently rearranging memory. The person who remembers is, in turn, influenced by that reorganized self-image, in a process where subject and object of remembrance mutually refashion their identities in a continuous dialogue between present and past.

It is this dialogue that tragedy interrupts. In *Blood Wedding* the image of the past is so powerful that it disrupts the mutual redefinition of past and present.[17] Tragedy freezes the moment when the characters are caught up in the self-image composed in remembrance or anticipation, an image that is then naturalized as the formula that will prevail. Plunged into inflexibility, the tragic protagonist is compelled to repeat a fixed narrative simultaneously as subject and object, as spectator and victim.[18]

The characters repeat a narrative at the expense of the present. Their act of bringing the past on the present seems to blind them to the present as the time in which they could act (shape and improve events) rather than simply narrate, and in which they could steer the course of their lives if they refrained from attributing it to fate. Under the influence of memory the characters lose their agency. Thus the Bride's complaint about 'cientos de pájaros que me impedían el andar' (*hundreds of birds that blocked my steps*).[19] The characters express their craving for agency, but they express it only by talking about it, or by means of gestures such as spitting or screaming, which are not aimed at transforming reality. The Mother says, for instance: 'Pero oigo eso de Félix y es lo mismo (*entre dientes*) Félix que llenárseme de cieno la boca (*escupe*) y tengo que escupir, tengo que escupir por no matar' (*But I just hear*

'Félix' (under her breath) and hearing 'Félix' is like having my mouth fill up with slime (she spits) and I have to spit, I have to spit, so I won't kill!).[20]

Moreover, as they narrate a story the characters also change their status as listening and speaking subjects. As Emile Benveniste observes, by not addressing an existing 'you' in conversation, refusing to participate in a dialogical situation that incorporates an 'I' and a 'you', the individual loses its capacity to posit itself as the subject of speech, a capacity generated in the reciprocity with another through dialogue where 'the linguistic basis of subjectivity is discovered'.[21] Lorca's characters complain about an aggression to their bodies of uncertain origin which affects their capacity for vision and for speech. 'Tienes una espina en cada ojo' (*You have a thorn in each eye*), says the Wife to Leonardo, intimating not only a rupture in the continuity, symbolically established by the eye, between inside and outside worlds, but also the two-directional nature of the thorn's piercing action.[22] The thorn seems at once to pierce Leonardo's eye from the outside, while the image of the thorn is born precisely from his eyes, piercing outwards towards the object of his gaze. A two-directional disintegration is similarly implied in Leonardo and the Bride's claim '¡Qué vidrios se me clavan en la lengua!' (*Glass splinters pierce my tongue!*) The violent interruption of speech inflicted from the outside (glass piercing the tongue) is counterbalanced by the syntactic structure of the sentence ('*se* me'). What would normally be understood as the grammatical subject ('I') is replaced by the object of the subject's action ('glass') in a shift that also emphasizes the passivity of the original subject.[23]

This double origin of violent action, both external and internal, characterizes an ambiguous state in which the characters do not consider themselves to be fully agents, nor do they feel completely controlled from the outside. It is as if Leonardo and the Bride postulated a middle point between agency (capacity for action) and subjection to external control (inability to act). In so doing they posit, perhaps unwittingly, a concept of fate that nevertheless carries the seed of human action, reflecting at the level of speech the rhetoric of agency at work in the play – that is, the oscillation between denying and affirming it, corresponding to each vision of fate. Significantly, the aggression that the characters lament affects their capacity to speak ('Glass splinters pierce my tongue'), which is, after all, the only event that usually takes place on the dramatic stage.[24]

If, as I argued in Chapter 3, tragedy and modern subjectivity aspire to produce intelligible selves, if, moreover, they are both based on obliterating, conceptualizing or consuming the other (as happens in Hegel's account of self-consciousness, in Freud's narrative of melancholia or in Lorca's tragedy *Blood Wedding*); if, finally, tragic and modern selves represent themselves as ineluctably controlled by an alien will – as victims – in order to prevent the irruption of others and thus preserve their centrality as self-same, why should the characters in *Blood Wedding* complain of losing their integrity (as suggested in claims such as 'Glass splinters pierce my tongue') precisely when they should be achieving it? Is it not, perhaps, because the operation by which the modern state confers subjective identity proves the more successful precisely when it seems to fail? I will come back to this.

The characters' inability to posit themselves as speaking and listening subjects destroys, in turn, their potential relationships to the other characters present onstage. By virtue of remembering – of picturing themselves in a past scenario that they narrate – the Mother and the Bride become primarily the theme of their own narratives, the *said*. Likewise, their potential interlocutor (the 'you' with whom the 'I' could be speaking) also shifts from the second to third person, becoming a narrated other or a fiction of the other. Unlike the first and second persons, which participate in dialogue in the interchangeable roles of speaker and listener, the third person refers to the object of discourse, of which a predicate is stated. The third person becomes what is spoken about, instead of the one who speaks, and therefore, according to Benveniste's study of subjectivity in language, or from the ethical perspective of Levinas's phenomenology of subjectivity, a non-person.[25] For example, in the first conversation between Leonardo and the Bride, she refers to herself, as well as to Leonardo, in the third person: 'Un hombre con su caballo sabe mucho y puede mucho para poder estrujar a una muchacha metida en un desierto' (*A man on his horse knows a lot, and he has the power to squeeze the life out of a lonely girl stranded in a desert*).[26] Even when they do use the pronouns 'I' and 'you', it is either to introduce verbs in the past tense ('¿Quién *he sido* yo para ti?' – What *have I been* for you?),[27] to presuppose predicates that characterize the other in accordance with the speaker's interpretation ('Tú, que *me conoces*, *sabes* que no la llevo;' 'tú *crees* que el tiempo cura y las paredes tapan y no es verdad, no es verdad' – You, *you know me* and *you know* that I have no second intentions; Because *you believe* that time can heal and walls can hide, but it's not true, it's not true),[28] or to end the conversation, preventing the other's voice from being heard. It is then scarcely surprising that the Bride's use of personal pronouns oscillates between the second and third person, intimating that she has refrained from addressing Leonardo while still speaking to him: 'No puedo oír*te*. No puedo oír *tu* voz. . . . Y sé que estoy loca, que tengo el pecho podrido de aguantar, y aquí estoy quieta por oír*lo*, por ver*lo* menear los brazos' (I can't listen to *you*. I can't listen to *your* voice. . . . And I know that I'm crazy, that my breast is rotting away with the suffering, and here I am, quietly listening *to him*, watching *him* move *his* arms).[29] Through this shift of personal pronouns from second to third person, the Bride stops positing Leonardo as a viable presence, imposing on him her own memory of Leonardo in what constitutes an interesting instance of absence *in praesentia*.[30]

Lorca's main characters reduce the other to an image or a fixed theme. This *no longer other*, a fiction that replaces the other present on stage, ceases to be the 'you' with whom the 'I' can communicate. Posited as a third person, the other is turned into a non-person, deprived of a voice and reduced to a fixed theme, which is as powerful as it is fictional. Hence Leonardo and the Bride describe each other as alienating forces, as non-persons who have become at once less and more powerful than a person. In the Bride's words, Leonardo is now 'un río oscuro, lleno de ramas, que acercaba a mí el rumor de sus juncos y su cantar entre dientes' (*a dark river filled with branches that brought close to me the whisper of its rushes and its murmuring song*).[31] The force of the person remembered is imposed upon the other who is present on stage, in this case the Bridegroom. Although the Bride tells the Bridegroom of her desire to hear only his voice ('no oír más voz que la tuya'), and to see only his eyes ('no ver más que tus ojos'), what is presupposed in the opposition established by the word 'only' is the voice and eyes of Leonardo, which deafen and blind her to any new voice. The Bridegroom's eyes and voice thus become desirable only by virtue of their potential to prevent the manifestation of Leonardo's voice and eyes. For were Leonardo to speak, his voice would be more compelling than the voice of the dead, even if the dead person speaking were her own mother: 'I wish you could hold me so tight,' she tells the Bridegroom, 'that even if my mother, who is dead, called me, I couldn't pull myself from you' (*Y que me abrazaras tan fuerte, que aunque me llamara mi madre, que está muerta, no me pudiera despegar de ti*).[32] The power of an imaginary 'other' thus displaces the *existing*, speaking person onstage.

By projecting a narrative of the past upon the present, the characters destroy their interaction with others, whose presence they negate ('silencio', 'basta', 'déjame', 'vete' – 'silence', 'enough', 'leave me alone', 'go away' – are among the most frequent utterances in these plays). They appear blinded to the present as the time in which they could interact with others rather than narrate them, in which they could act and shape events instead of suffering inevitable death. The result of the characters' confinement to their own narrative is a loss of the capacity to act creatively: they cease to have an influence on events and instead claim they are acted upon. Leonardo, the Bride and the Mother relinquish their agency. This loss of agency, and the subsequent lack of an agent who can be held responsible for their actions, lead them to construct an all-powerful otherness, fate, to which they attribute control over their lives.

This reading of Lorca's play thus suggests a different understanding of tragic conflict as a condition no longer provoked by *inexorable* fate, but rather by the *fiction* of fate, devised by the characters in order to account for an *acquired* inability to act and interact. They acquire this inability by displacing the other present on stage with a narrated one. It is this displacement that leads to the construction of inevitability, a fact that puts the common understanding of fate into question. Unlike the traditional interpretation of fate as an externally imposed will, I propose reading fate as a constructed – rather than given or necessary – force that the characters author in order to hold it responsible for their destructive acts.

Accordingly, tragic events are not unleashed by impersonal fate, but rather dictated by the characters themselves in their narrative. Since as narrators they restrict the alternatives available to them, the only way of taking agency that they conceive is to re-enact, time and again, the fixed role patterns they have fashioned for themselves. In so doing they bring about the fate they have constructed and insert a tragic drama into the play's present.

If fate may be read as a fiction that both conceals and legitimates the characters' abdication of agency, this suggests that their loss of the capacity to act and their claim that they are acted upon could be avoided. The characters re-enact tragic events within a dramatic framework that functions as the counterpoint to their experience of fate. In *Blood Wedding* that framework comes to view again in the last scene, where after the men's death each woman in the play recounts the tragic events from her own perspective.[33]

In framing the tragic events, emphasizing once again the departure from action and interaction that triggers them, this last scene suggests that death was perhaps avoidable, even if none of the actual interpretations offered is explicit about alternatives to death. Death appears inevitable when one clings to only one meaning and is blinded to others, that is, when one obliterates the multiplicity of meanings and possibilities, as characters do in this play. But when the possible interpretations expand in multiple perspectives that render a range of diverse, even conflicting views of the world, death may appear simply as one option among others.[34]

This does not mean that fate is cancelled – abolishing fate would be the obverse, and thus equivalent, of affirming it – but rather that death is not the only alternative.[35] At stake here is a change in emphasis and intensity. Moving beyond the sweeping 'I exist – I shall die', Raymond Williams invites us to understand 'we exist' as a permanently alternative statement, one that suggests that if 'we exist – we shall not die'.[36] As soon as we imagine alternatives to fate, the possibility of acting responsibly comes to the foreground. By suggesting the positive vision denied to the characters, the dramatic framework in *Blood Wedding* permits us to understand tragedy *also* as an affirmative, even reparative, event. Unlike the tragic character, the audience is permitted to realize that tragedy, the spectacle of fate, is not necessarily fatal.

Exiting death

> Yet over a very wide range we see [individual death] transcended in tragedy. Life does come, life ends the play, again and again. And the fact that life does come back, that its meanings are reaffirmed and restored, after so much suffering and after so important a death, has been, quite commonly, the tragic action.
>
> Raymond Williams, *Modern Tragedy*

Tragedies generally do not end with the death of the protagonist. Although from our individual viewpoint we tend to construe individual death as a conclusion, tragedy is neither about the individual nor even about character, but rather about action (as Aristotle insists in the *Poetics*), and action continues after death. In *Blood Wedding*, once the tragedy configured by the enactment of the two narratives of memory reaches its climax with the men's death, the dramatic framework in which it was originated comes into focus once again. Those who did not die – all the female characters – come back to tell the story in the last scene, marking with their return the limits of the tragic play-within-the-play. Appropriately, the stage direction depicts an indeterminate and monumental space painted white, with no shades of grey to indicate perspective.

> *Habitación blanca con arcos y gruesos muros. A la derecha y a la izquierda escaleras blancas. Gran arco al fondo y pared del mismo color. El suelo será también de un blanco reluciente. Esta habitación simple tendrá un*

sentido monumental de iglesia. No habrá ni un gris, ni una sombra, ni siquiera lo preciso para la perspectiva.[37]

A room with arches and thick walls. At left and right, white stairways. Upstage, a very large arch, and a wall the same colour. Even the floor is shining white. This unadorned room has the monumental feeling of a church. There must not be a single grey, a single shadow – not even if required for perspective.

The stage has become 'blanco', a blank space or screen on which anything new, fresh, can be written. This blank space is like the backdrop on which transference can begin. Now that the tragedy is over and the tragic stage has disappeared, the blank stage seems to effect the return to the present and erasing of the past, of the past discourse that has constituted the word and the silence of the play. At this point the reconstruction of meaning can begin. But what meaning is reconstructed, and what significance given, constitutes a variable choice. Indeed, the fact that in this space there are neither shades of grey – no nuances – nor a defined perspective already suggests a particular kind of significance. In this last scene, where all the characters are women, the *blood wedding* itself becomes the object of manifold acts of narration, where each woman recounts the tragic events using different poetic forms that range from classical to popular verse. In telling the same story in a variety of ways these female voices not only propose different modes of dealing with the past, but also set forth different (and conflicting) strategies for reading the play.

Here I want to concentrate on two of these narrations. The first, the Beggar-woman's account of the killings and the little girl's response, exemplifies the coexistence of 'elevated' poetry in eleven-syllable verse and popular shorter verse, with no transition between the two:

Mendiga:	Yo los vi; pronto llegan: dos torrentes
	quietos al fin entre las piedras grandes,
	dos hombres en las patas del caballo.
	Muertos en la hermosura de la noche.
	(*Con delectación*)
	Muertos, sí, muertos.
Muchacha 1:	¡Calla, vieja, calla!
Mendiga:	Flores rotas los ojos, y sus dientes
	dos puñados de nieve endurecida.
	Los dos cayeron, y la novia vuelve
	teñida en sangre falda y cabellera.

Cubiertos con dos mantas ellos vienen
sobre los hombros de los mozos altos.
Así fue, nada más. Era lo justo.
Sobre la flor del oro, sucia arena.

(*Se va. Las Muchachas inclinan las cabezas y rítmicamente van saliendo.*)

Muchacha 1: Sucia arena.
Muchacha 2: Sobre la flor del oro.
Niña: Sobre la flor del oro
            traen a los muertos del arroyo.
            Morenito el uno,
            morenito el otro.
            ¡Qué ruiseñor de sombra vuela y gime
            sobre la flor del oro!³⁸

Beggar woman. *I saw them. They'll soon be here. Two torrents, / Still at last among the boulders. / Two men at the feet of the horse. / Dead in the splendour of the night. / (Savouring it) Dead! Yes, dead!*

First girl. *Quiet, old woman!*

Beggar woman. *Their eyes are broken flowers. Their teeth / Are just two handfuls of frozen snow. / They both fell dead. The bride returns / With bloodstains on her skirt and hair. / Covered with blankets, the bodies come, / Come on the shoulders of tall young men. / That's how it was. Nothing more. It was just. / Over the golden flower – filthy sand.*

(*She leaves. The Girls bow their heads and start to exit, rhythmically*)

First girl. *Filthy sand.*

Second girl. *Over the golden flower.*

Little girl. *Over the golden flower. / They bring the dead from the stream. / Young and dark, the one. / Young and dark, the other. / The nightingale of shadow / Soars and grieves / Over the golden flower!*

'That's how it was. Nothing more. It was just,' says the Beggar-woman (a character who, in the previous scene, cooperated with the blood-thirsty Moon in bringing about the men's deaths), asserting the inevitable. The use of eleven-syllable verse lends her account solemnity and pathos, as if declaimed by a Greek Chorus, and unites the story with the elevated themes of *poesía grave*. Furthermore, her appreciation of the beauty of death suggested by 'Over the golden flower, filthy sand', as well as by the stage direction 'Con delectación' (*Savouring it*), suspends any ethical concern. On the other hand, the little girl's use of popular verse ('Morenito el uno, / morenito el otro') rescues the events from classical tradition.³⁹ Incorporated into a folkloric tradition, the events of *Blood Wedding* are reinscribed into a wider context of human experience, but this is an experience interpreted and fixed – folkloric repetition halts the possibility of interpreting events otherwise.

The now popular form of the story seems to promise its transmission from generation to generation. Rendered in accordance to pre-existing folkloric formulae, the tragic events transcend the limits of the play. The Wife's narration of Leonardo ('Era hermoso jinete / y ahora montón de nieve. / Corrió ferias y montes / y brazos de mujeres. / Ahora, musgo de noche / le corona la frente' – *He was a handsome horseman / And now he's a bank of snow. / He rode through the fairs and mountains / And into the arms of love. / And now the moss of night / Is a crown around his forehead*),[40] for instance, combines the motif of the passional hero with that of the horserider's imminent death, so frequent in Lorca's own *Poem of the Deep Song* and *Gypsy Ballads*, while the account by the group of women invokes religious imagery ('Dulces clavos, / dulce cruz, / dulce nombre / de Jesús.' *Sweet nails, / Sweet Cross, / Sweet Name / – Jesus*).[41] Aside from having recourse to pre-existing roles and patterns, the women here construct fatality in language, furthermore, by displacing agency from persons to things, in what constitutes one of the most frequent strategies in the play. In the last and most definitive of those displacements, the Mother and the Bride shift the burden of responsibility from the persons involved in the tragedy to 'a little knife' ('Y apenas cabe en la mano, / pero que penetra frío / por las carnes asombradas / y allí se para, en el sitio / donde tiembla enmarañada / la oscura raíz del grito.' *And it scarcely fits the hand, / But penetrates so coldly / Through the astonished flesh, / And stops there – at the place / Where, trembling and entangled, / Lies the dark root of the scream*).[42] With these words the play concludes.

What should not be overlooked in these women's act of reading is the element of convention, that is, the process of selecting, isolating and reframing events from the viewpoint of a closure that characterizes narrative. Narrative creates sense by means of a plot, a work of synthesis that integrates isolated events within a refashioned context, an intelligible whole or system in relation to which subjects acquire significance. What makes a narrative specifically tragic, beyond the strategies of emplotment, is its aspiration to create only one kind of meaning, a sense of the inexorable and irreparable, by instituting fate as the cause of all suffering. This process of abstracting and generalizing fate as transcendent evil entails detaching oneself from the ongoing action and its agents, and denying any concrete experience,[43] as the women do in this last scene by isolating the tragedy from its causes, when they recast Leonardo and the Bridegroom as heroes. Although having recourse to abstraction and breaking up with experience always exacts a high price from the self, tragic interpretations offer the immediate advantage of purifying and exalting human suffering by offering a sense that renders the past intelligible and safe. Since suffering is accepted for the sake of meaning, of an intelligible causality that simultaneously becomes the origin of responsibility and confers intelligibility on the tragic self, attributing suffering to fate suspends the need for further scrutiny. But doesn't positing fate as an ultimate meaning foreclose, in effect, the possibility of any meaning?[44]

The women paradoxically erase experience by recasting it as memory. In their repetition of the tragic dénouement there is therefore both a tendency to remember and a tendency to forget. While the events are remembered, the original cause, the characters' responsibility for re-enacting the tragic drama, is forgotten. Memory is key in the configuration of *Blood Wedding* in that the characters, limited to remember, insert the repetitive time of tragedy into the linear time of the play. But memory also configures the play in yet another crucial sense: by including popular songs, sayings, proverbs and other poetic structures, the drama itself becomes a remembrance of those forms. However, the supremacy of memory in *Blood Wedding* is paradoxically achieved at the price of forgetting. What is ultimately forgotten is that human suffering is a consequence of human action, and that the capacity for responsible action transcends all constructions of fatality.

But the causes for the tragedy should not be forgotten. In her own confession after the men's death, the Bride reveals a marked tension between her intention to build a future with the Bridegroom and the inexorable force that, in preventing her from acting constructively, constitutes her fate (incarnated in her image of Leonardo). Unlike the rest of the narrations in this scene, which only record the dénouement in the preterit, the Bride reflects upon the context and development of the events in imperfect tense, accounting for the action in progress.

¡Porque me fui con el otro, me fui! (*con angustia*). Tú también te hubieras ido. Yo era una mujer quemada, llena de llagas por dentro y por fuera, y tu hijo era un poquito de agua de la que yo esperaba hijos, tierra, salud; pero el otro era un río oscuro, lleno de ramas, que acercaba a mí el rumor de sus juncos y su cantar entre dientes. Y yo corría con tu hijo que era como un niñito de agua fría y el otro me mandaba cientos de pájaros que me impedían el andar y que dejaban escarcha sobre mis heridas de pobre mujer marchita, de muchacha acariciada por el fuego. Yo no quería, ¡óyelo bien!, yo no quería. ¡Tu hijo era mi fin y yo no lo he engañado, pero el brazo del otro me arrastró como un golpe de mar, como la cabezada de un mulo, y me hubiera arrastrado siempre, siempre, aunque hubiera sido vieja y todos los hijos de tu hijo me hubieran agarrado de los cabellos![45]

Because I ran away with another man, I ran away! (Anguished) You would have gone, too! I was a woman consumed by fire, covered with open sores inside and out, and your son was a little bit of water from whom I hoped for children, land, health! But the other was a dark river filled with branches that brought close to me the whisper of its rushes and its murmuring song. And I would go with your son, who was like a little boy made of cold water, and the other would send hundreds of birds that blocked my way and left frost on the wounds of this poor, wasted woman, a girl caressed by fire! I didn't want to – listen to me! – I didn't want to. Your son was what I wanted, and I have not deceived him. But the arm of the other dragged me like the surge of the sea, like a mule butting me with his head, and would have dragged me always, always, even if I had been old and all the children of your son had held me by the hair!

The Bride's extraordinary narrative appears to conjure up fate's power – 'Yo no quería' (*I didn't want to*), 'cientos de pájaros que me impedían el andar' (*hundreds of birds blocked by way*), 'el brazo del otro me arrastró como un golpe de mar' (*the arm of the other dragged me like the surge of the sea*), as well as the extension of fate's control into the future: 'y me hubiera arrastrado siempre, siempre, aunque hubiera sido vieja y todos los hijos de tus hijos me hubieran agarrado de los cabellos' (*and would have dragged me always, always, even if I were old and all the sons of your son held me by the hair*). In attending, none the less, to the process and its duration, and in omitting the events that constitute the tragic plot, the Bride's words display the act of abstracting the other as fate that lead to the deaths. However passionately she invokes inevitable constraint, that compulsion now acquires texture and a human face, Leonardo, whom the Bride desires. Because of her reluctance to act on it, the Bride's desire is recast as an implacable, fatal nature out of control – a galloping horse, the bloodthirsty moon, 'a dark river filled with branches', 'hundreds of birds that blocked my way', 'the surge of the sea' – which victimizes the self, allowing the self, in fact, to follow its desire without taking responsibility for it. Unlike the rest of the women, who interpret the tragedy as a dramatization and recognition of abstract evil, the Bride conjures up images of concrete action. Though she disowns responsibility by denying that she intended her acts ('I didn't want to,' she tells the Mother; 'You would have gone with him, too'), she confronts the listener with the concreteness of lived experience, avoiding the impulse to abstract and generalize that shapes the rest of the versions. In so doing, in revealing what the other women had repressed, her account opens the way for a potential revision of human responsibility. Rather than accounting for the men's deaths, she describes her subjection to the power of Leonardo's image, a power fuelled by her own unacknowledged desire, which she refashions as fate. Her confession reminds the audience that the tragedy was not an arbitrary act of an external will, but rather a consequence of replacing ongoing experience with fixed memory, of reenacting the past by refusing action and interaction, by projecting a fictional image of the others and of herself.

In presenting the audience with at least two ways of interpreting the tragedy, the women in the last scene of *Blood Wedding* make explicit the two modes of understanding necessity that coexist in the play.[46] The first consists of an inexorable chain of tragic events. This interpretation, constructed by recontextualizing selected events from the viewpoint of the closure (creating the illusion of causal sequence and intelligibility), could perhaps provide a conclusion that might enable the characters to overcome the past and resume life. But this can be done only at the terrible cost of naturalizing suffering, instituting fate and projecting it into a future time in which fate may again usurp human agency, provoking a new tragedy. The Bride's own version, by contrast, suggests that the tragedy was ultimately brought on by the characters' act of replacing the other characters present on stage with imaginary ones. It is most remarkable that this second interpretation, itself tragic, should suggest alternatives to death.

'A particular evil, in a tragic action, can be at once experienced and lived through. In the process of living through it, and in a real action seeing its moving relations with other capacities and other men, we come not so much to the recognition of evil as transcendent but to its recognition as actual and indeed negotiable.'[47] Unlike those traditional readings that seem satisfied with recognizing fatality, it is possible to read tragic actions, suggests Raymond Williams, as conflicts that were not, but may have been and thus might be, lived otherwise.[48] Denying that events may have been different implies isolating suffering from human agency, that is, from the human interests, decisions or omissions that provoked that suffering. This act of denial, responsible for the alienation of a large part of human experience, is not politically innocent. When a lived order is made abstract and universals invoked to justify suffering, a breach opens between social life and ethical control. Those responsible now have an alibi (fate, God) that forecloses the possibility, and ignores the actual work, of concrete struggles to make a better world. Hence the importance of discerning the political agenda that is behind those interpretations indifferent to suffering and oblivious of human efforts, especially when they present themselves as absolute – every interpretation is, intrinsically, historically conditioned. Against the tragic reading of life as the inheritance of an irreparable past, Levinas remarks: 'Fate does not precede history; it follows it. Historiography . . . recounts enslavement, forgetting the life that struggles against slavery.'[49] To read a life from the viewpoint of death is a choice, and not an innocent one.[50] Interestingly, the separation of ethical responsibility from life does not mean, as one would expect, that the part primarily affected is the neglected and suffering other, at least not in tragedy. Although obliterating the other in *Blood Wedding* shapes the structure that produces the tragic events (rather than standing as one trait among others in the depiction of character and conflict), eliciting sympathy for the persons disregarded does not constitute the play's primary purpose. The neglected or obliterated other does not disappear *in* itself, it disappears *from* the world of the self. Thus, without denying the ethical implications of failing to recognize the other, what this play underscores is the consequences that obliterating the other has for the self: loss of agency, construction of fate, self-representation as victim, tragic death.

Of the tragic determination to die, and intimating that the viewpoint of the hero, who is obsessed with death, does not necessarily coincide with that of the spectator or reader – who attributes the tragedy not to death but obsession – Benjamin writes: 'Just as in the ordinary creature the activity of life is all-embracing, so, in the tragic hero, is the process of dying, and tragic irony always arises whenever the hero – with profound but unsuspected justification – begins to speak of the circumstances of his death as if they were the circumstances of life.'[51] He then quotes Lukács, who observes that 'the dying heroes of tragedy . . . have already been long dead before they actually die'.[52]

However deep tragedy's influence in modern identity models, tragic art's alliance is not with fate or death, but rather with action in progress and lived through. Here tragedy, the very cradle of the tragic vision that shapes modern subjectivities, can perhaps help us shift the focus from the heteronomous practices it so seductively depicts through fate's victory, to action. It invites us to a scrutiny of human action, of the human decision to act in certain ways, and the human inability to act, as *Blood Wedding* does. By deploying tragic crisis in terms of loss of human interaction provoked by the allegiance to a transcendent fictional force, the framing act in *Blood Wedding*, visible to the spectator, reorients the self towards the other and potentially relocates the initiative, which fate seemed to have usurped, into human hands.

Tragedy has been traditionally understood as a confirmation of necessity. But if we agree that action is shaped by the protagonist's narrow vision; if, moreover, at least two moments of tragedy (the poetic moments of emplotment and staging) disturb the tragic narrative, it can be argued that rather than simply confirming destiny, Lorca's tragedy also overcomes it. Rather than celebrating inexorable death, Lorca's play portrays the protagonists' illusion of fate, and poetically laments their inability to envision life. Here, from the spectator's viewpoint at least, the death of the character was not inevitable.

Affirming a sense of life in the midst of failure, however, is not enough. Indeed, the awareness of a simple opening for action may produce sentiments of liberation but not concrete action, foreclosing through complacency the disruptive and political potential of this new tragic consciousness. Beyond opening a potential for agency, then, shouldn't the awareness that fate is fictional lead to concrete action, commitment and involvement? The reading of tragedy I propose here intimates that the characters' death was perhaps avoidable but was not avoided, affirming that inevitability constitutes one interpretation among others. But the work of tragic art on behalf of human action must be more radical.[53] By locating the cause for loss of agency in obliteration of the other, this perspective on Lorca's plays establishes the other as mediation between the self's potency and act. In redescribing the self's relation to otherness by shifting the emphasis from fate to living people, this reading of tragedy would seem to incite spectators and readers alike to assume responsibility for their actions and influence the conditions in which they live.

In terms of subjectivity, realizing that the source of control that produces us as subjects is constructed entails recognizing our own co-operation in the processes that subject us. That the subject is not necessary but contingent, yet subjectivity cannot be renounced, ultimately implies that the subject is invested as an infinitely responsible agent. As we shall see in Chapter 5, the subject is called to take high risks, such as acting in the absence of any external support. It must decide how to respond to others in a relation that is asymmetrical and non-reciprocal, and how to act on their needs, beyond any legitimizing paradigm, radically exposing itself. What politics may learn from this new reading of tragedy is how to expand itself to respond to situations that are more terrible than tragic. To act politically in this sense would mean to assume responsibility for decisions and actions that can no longer be attributed to a transcendent source of authority, not even to the obedience of rules. This expanded political space must resist the allure of sublime tragic sense.

From self-victimization to responsibility

As Lorca's theatre reconfigures the tragic to reopen the possibility of human agency, it becomes a privileged site for examining the human capacity to act, a capacity associated, as these plays suggest, with the ability to inter*act*. As Ricoeur notes, the link between interaction and action is embodied in the concept of goodness, a concept that in many languages defines 'at one and the same time the ethical quality of the aims of action and the orientation of the person towards others, as though an action could not be held to be good unless it were done on behalf of others, out of *regard* for others'.[54] It is precisely a new emphasis on the need to recognize the presence of others, their suffering and needs, that constitutes, in my view, the main contribution of my reading to a poetic understanding of the tragic fable. I see Lorca's plays as dramatizing two crucial moments. The moment where they repeat the tragic narrative concerns primarily the relationship between a transcendent Otherness and the human self, where the latter is destroyed. The moment of reconfiguration, by contrast, may be called ethical in a double sense, first because it opens up a space for action, and second because it defines this opening as an entry into the realm of human relations. In short, this reconfiguration of the tragic reformulates the question of otherness by shifting the emphasis from a person's relation with the divine to the realm of intersubjective relationships. The result of this detour away from the human other, and then back to it via the transcendent, is a reshuffling of responsibilities. Now the deficiency of the protagonists as agents can no longer be attributed to divine control. The misery of the tragic subject thus consists, in Peter Sloterdijk's words, 'not so much in one's sufferings as in the inability to be responsible for them'.[55]

If tragedy is ultimately concerned with intersubjective relations, why cannot Lorca's plays stay within the realm of the human without having recourse to the transcendent? Likewise, if these plays reinstate the human capacity for action, why present such a capacity only at the point at which it is threatened and ultimately denied, instead of depicting concrete instances of acting? A reading informed by these questions reveals that Lorca's tragedy does not *first* repeat and *then* disturb the tragic fable. Rather, the moment of repetition (that is, of fate's victory) and the moment of disturbance (that is, of fate's fictionality), which symmetrically prevent or permit action, occur simultaneously and are intertwined. The coexistence of these two moments is precisely what facilitates the unique depiction of human action by virtue of which the art of tragedy may cast light on subjective agency.

Perhaps now we can suggest why it might be that Lorca's play, though ultimately concerned with intersubjective relations (as I have claimed), returns to them only after having recourse to the transcendent. If in order to reinstate the human capacity for action tragedy presents such a capacity only at the point of self-destruction, it may be because the threat of failure is itself a condition for acting. Every voluntary act can fail. An ethical action does not depend, therefore, on the agent's good intentions (tragic characters 'have' good intentions), the ability to make the 'right' decision (which often does not exist),[56] or the action's successful results (for whom?). Rather, as this play suggests, acting ethically is premised on the agents' ability to be responsible for their acts.

However reassuring it may be to conclude that the clearing for action afforded by the realization that objective necessity is constructed solves the problem of tragic conflict and of human agency in general, this opening remains ambiguous in so far as it depends on the self's infinite responsibility for others. The responsible self is vulnerable and uncertain, as Levinas indicates. Levinas's ethical thought might prove helpful here, because it understands conceptualizing the other (as Lorca's characters do) as an act of abolishing alterity altogether. According to Levinas, the self is constituted as a subject in a primordial and anarchic dimension by being faced by the other, who speaks.[57] The manifestation of the other's face, however, does not presuppose a symmetrical act of apprehension or assimilation on the self's part. Rather, the face of the other 'at once gives and conceals the other [in a] situation in which an event happens to a subject who does not assume it'.[58] By exposing itself, the face does not become 'visible' or 'comprehensible' in so far as seeing and comprehending imply grasping, picturing or mapping. Any attempt to conceptualize the other – to turn it into a theme, a 'said' (*le Dit*) – would suppress the otherness of 'saying', and therefore annihilate the other altogether. In order to be able to manifest itself, says Levinas, the other must be acknowledged by the self as 'saying' (*le Dire*), that is, as the one who speaks.[59] By speaking, the other obliges the self to respond and to justify itself, calling the self to responsibility. In Levinas's own words, 'language accomplishes a relation such that the terms are not limited within this relation, such that the other, despite the relationship with the same, remains transcendent to the same'.[60] It is precisely because the other transcends the same that the ethical relation is nonsymmetrical: 'I am responsible for the Other without waiting for reciprocity, were I to die for it. Reciprocity is his affair.'[61] (A question that will be raised in the last chapter is whether this non-reciprocal relation would not create, as in tragedy, a heteronomous situation. If for Levinas responsibility for the other constitutes the self's freedom, is there any difference between being enjoined by the other's injunction, subjected to abstract law, and victimized by tragic fate?)

The fact that action is linked with the other constitutes at once its limitation and its promise. While the call for responsibility places the self in an ambiguous and vulnerable position, it simultaneously concentrates the initiative – how to act for the other? – in the self's hands. If the other's initiative in demanding responsibility from me did not in turn free my own initiative, allowing me to respond to his or her call and to act creatively upon that call, asks Ricoeur, would not the call go unheard?[62] How is responsibility for the other to be assumed, if not by acting on the other's needs?[63] If in the summons to responsibility the initiative comes from the other, in responding to the suffering other the initiative comes from the self.[64] Thus, the other's injunction inaugurates the 'I' it calls upon as an agent, but it does so, paradoxically, by bringing the self's action, the spontaneous movement of the self's all-encompassing conscience, to a halt. The opening for action here is first a closing, a denial of the egotistical initiative of the self, in order that a reinscribed initiative is invested by the other. This different kind of agency thus emerges from a radical passivity, the passivity of a self whose self-interested impulses have been revealed as egotistical by the other's naked face, to which the self has become receptive. In so far as the self 'is not free to ignore the meaningful world into which the face of the other has introduced it' and cannot refuse responsibility, the epiphany of the other limits the self's freedom. But 'the will is free to assume this responsibility in whatever sense it likes'.[65]

It is particularly important to underscore a problem that affects Levinas's own philosophical reasoning, namely, the impossibility of thinking the 'saying'.[66] As Levinas himself describes it, philosophical inquiry constitutes a search for truth instead of the ethical opening to what is radically other than the self. Philosophical speculation is intrinsically a thematizing activity that must turn every act of saying into a 'said', into an idea that belongs to the thinking I and that depends on the self's interpretation. In which ways does the other's unrepresentability, as well as that of its demand, affect the self who must respond? For even supposing that the self is willing to act on that command, how can it respond to the other's needs without first interpreting what those needs are? Although the other presents itself by speaking, its demand that I care for its needs, calling me to responsibility, is unspoken – expressed by the other's irreducible presence, rather than articulated through words – and therefore radical.[67]

If I cannot interpret the demand, how can I determine how I should act on my responsibility? I could attend to it according to the way in which I interpret it, but this leaves me without knowing if my interpretation was correct, and therefore with the anguish of not being solicitous enough. Furthermore, isn't interpreting the other's needs already a way of picturing the other, of creating my own version of what those needs may be? If I am left to my own resources to decide what is best for the other, do I not run the risk of imposing on the other what I think would suit him or her best, thus ultimately establishing a relationship of power? The call to responsibility, which demands that the self be permanently ready to respond to the other's unarticulated injunction, places the self in an uncertain and vulnerable position, always wondering if it is acting well enough. And, what is perhaps more unbearable, it places the self outside of the tragic dimension in which it becomes intelligible by assuming a symbolic debt.

The ambiguity of the ethical relation, which I have initially approached here through Levinas, is linked with the paradox of a self-denying creativity: subjective agency is based on constraint.[68] Tragedy reveals the constitutive constraints of agency when it places the agent in a situation of subjugation to a transcendent force that victimizes the self. In any case, the vulnerability inherent in action surpasses the boundaries of the self, because it springs from the self's commitment to the other, on which action hinges. This inextricable link between interaction and action, by which the other determines my acts if I care for him or her, but also suffers from my acts to the extreme of *dying of them* if I ignore his or her needs, accounts for the difficulty of acting well, or, in Martha Nussbaum's formulation, for the 'fragility of goodness'.[69]

Awareness of fictionality

The vulnerability unleashed at the core of action by its association with the other is thus related to another trace of fragility. Creation (or 'making') inscribes into itself the possibility of its own denial by including among its products destructive fictions (such as fate, certain laws and some gods) that inhibit human initiative. But does this self-denial of Western creativity bring about the end of creation, or does it represent, rather, an achievement of creativity? Rather than precluding action, it would seem, this self-denial of action secures the very impulse that drives it and attests to its creative potential. We could indeed argue that the more powerful a god or fate (that is, the more successful its ability to influence human life), the more vigorously it attests to the success of the human imagination, since these forms are themselves the imagination's products and projections.[70] Following this argument, we could even propose that if the power of these *artefacts* is perceived as hostile to the creative power of the human imagination, it may be because of the imagination's own tendency to efface its activity. As Elaine Scarry explains, 'a god can much better work to recreate its people if its ability to recreate them is not recognized as only an extension of their own projective actions – if, that is, the god is not recognized as a fiction or made thing'.[71] It would seem, then, that the imagination erases the traces of fictionality from the things it creates in order that the now freestanding artefact can perform its function better, without troubling us with questions about its origin.[72]

But what happens when an artefact, shedding the traces of its artificiality and appearing now natural and given, takes up the form of an authoritative external will that usurps human agency? How can an artefact, a freestanding record of human creativity, deny the very possibility of creating? It is indeed extraordinary that action should realize its full potential by carrying the seeds of its own denial. Perhaps the imagination can permit itself such an extreme activity because of its invention of yet another kind of artefact, the work of art, where fictionality (the signature of its human author), as Scarry points out, is not only evident, but also self-announcing.[73] In acting as a reminder of artificiality – in reminding us of the possibility of reassessing or repairing those things that fail us – art carries a promise of reparation.

As a work of art, tragedy openly displays its fictionality, allowing for a potential recovery of the fictionality of other artefacts in need of reassessment[74] – especially of those constructs that appear essential and

alienate the human self. Aside from standing as an emblem of the imagination's activity, tragedy enhances its work on behalf of human action
by depicting instances of the power that imagining fate has over the
human self. The display of fate's fictionality in Lorca's tragedies intimates that if some fictions (laws, fate, gods) present themselves as
authoritative entities ruling over the human self, it is because they have
emancipated themselves from their human origin by eroding the site of
their own creation. It reminds us that these artefacts might be repaired,
so that they perform their function better, or dismissed so that human
beings can create again.

Or is this not so?

In displaying the oscillation between an origin of agency that is at
times external (as embodied in the knife) and at times internal (blood),
Blood Wedding re-enacts the tension between two competing versions of
fate: destiny as objective necessity and destiny as a fiction. The contribution of this reading of *Blood Wedding* to the discussion of tragic and
subjective agency consists in displaying the presence of both versions
of fate – one inexorable, the other invented – in interaction, without
allowing one to prevail. Becoming aware that fate, or the Father, or the
law are fictional, in other words, does not cancel their ability to alienate. These essentialized sources of control are structured by a productive tension between artificiality and essentiality which makes them
appear at once fictional and necessary. And the modern subject is precisely one of those paradoxical concepts that we have denominated,
with Judith Butler, 'necessary fictions'.[75]

To explain this through the instance of fate, however much a fictional
fate (as well as the potential liberation implicit in the awareness that
fate is constructed) may be conditioned by its interplay with fate's
victory, this second interpretation inserts into objective necessity the
seed of its own denial, affirming the possibility of human agency against
fate's control. Then again, the human agency restituted through the
awareness of fate's fabricated nature is rendered fragile by the presence
of fate. The coexistence of fate's fictionality with fate's victory intimates
that however responsible and well intended human action may be,
however effective it may appear at times, it is primarily vulnerable,
fragile and potentially destructive.[76]

Now we can repose the question of whether becoming aware of fate's
fictionality would prove liberating. It was the initial purpose of my work
on tragedy to discern the trace of the human hand in the constitution
of essential-appearing fictions such as tragic fate, the Father or the Law,
particularly when those fictions become oppressive and alienate the

human self. My aporetic reading of *Blood Wedding* was initially motivated by the hope that displaying the role human creativity plays in the construction of objective necessity (if I may express myself in paradoxical terms) would prove liberating. Inspired by Scarry's study of the internal structure of artefacts, I thought that becoming aware of the fictionality of all mystified sources of authority would reinstate human agency by revealing that those artifacts that undergo an essentializing process, erase the trace of the human hand and become oppressive – those fictions, that is, which are beginning to fail us – may be reshaped so that they fulfil their function better, or dismissed and replaced by others.[77] Wouldn't the awareness that fate is fictional break up the pattern of self-victimization and restitute the possibility of agency?

But the fact that artificiality exists in tension with essentiality complicates this question. How does this tension within fate, as well as within other sources of control, affect the subjectivities it informs? While agency might be liberated by the awareness that fate is also fictional, an infinite responsibility is now placed on the self, who becomes accountable for the results of its actions. Since in the process of becoming a subject renouncing agency is inseparable from disowning responsibility, and both of these refusals premise the possibility of becoming intelligible, recovering one's initiative (the so-called freedom of action), however attractive in principle, may not be so desirable after all.

Essentialized sources of control are fruitful. This fact puts into question that becoming aware of the fabricated nature of these forms of authority entails defeating their power. Indeed, according to Sloterdijk's idea of cynical reason, an established set of values needs people who do not believe in them in order to survive.[78] Ideology, that is, is reinforced by those who, realizing that it is false, nevertheless continue to support it. This is brilliantly exemplified in tragedy. By acting, the tragic subject delays the fulfilment of the tragic causality, but this temporary delay introduced by human initiative is necessitated by tragic causality in order to be able to reassert itself, to re-emerge energized after having been challenged. All symbolic orders welcome resistance, since it is by incorporating it that they can assure their continuity and success. That continuity is necessitated by the subject, and hence its participation in it.

On the other hand, efforts towards this potential restitution of human initiative cannot take the origin and conditions of agency for granted. It may well be the case that human agency does not exist except when it is denied, at risk of imminent peril, in the face of constraint. It may happen that it supplies the foundation for an acceptable self-representation as agent that leaves one's sense of autonomy intact. From this perspective, we should ask whether the characters' act of constructing fate does not respond to an impulse, inherent in tragic and contemporary selves alike – and beyond any desire to deny the presence and needs of others – to base agency upon constraint in order to avert the vertigo of acting in the void, without the support of the social order.

The interplay between a necessary and a fictional fate thus speaks of the possible failure of every act, underscoring the immense responsibility every action entails. In making a decision whose coordinates are not confirmed by any objective source of meaning, in the absence of destiny, I risk my position in the social order which legitimized my actions, rendering them intelligible. The symbolic framework which produced tragic meaning depends on objective necessity. When tragic intelligibility is challenged by the possibility that fate is fictional, any symbolic framework which determines the validity of one's action in advance, even the content of one's duty, no longer applies. But this is the very reason why we are not likely to renounce the guilt that enables our subjectivity. For even supposing that we could, that renunciation would entail a loss of an intelligibility that we cannot do without. Precisely because subjectivity is so constraining, its productivity is vital to us, and it is that very productivity that the paradox of tragic self-depiction (depicting oneself as a victim paradoxically in order to achieve autonomy) preserves. Without the illusion of a symbolic system to which to attribute control over my acts, my responsibility is radical, it becomes infinite and impossible to fulfil. Deprived of the guilt that gives me a position in the scheme of destiny, I must face the vertigo of having to decide what my duty is. I must run the risk of making a decision and taking an action in the absence of any ontological support, without the guarantee of legitimation, in a void.

The tension between responsibility and guilt is acknowledged in the interplay between two representations of fate. (In Chapter 5 I will read these interpretations as belonging to two different modes of intelligibility, based on different understandings of heteronomy.) On the one hand, the power of fate may be neutralized by displaying its fictionality and consequently reopening the possibility for action. On the other, the threat of failure is reintroduced in the core of action, accounting for a fragility whose obliteration would imply negating action itself.

For us, spectators and subjects alike,[79] this double gesture constitutes an invitation to political responsibility, a call to assume the infinite vulnerability inherent in all human acts without relinquishing the initiative to the seductions of fate.

5
Tragic Autonomy Meets Ethical Heteronomy

> The order of responsibility, where the gravity of ineluctable being freezes all laugher, is also the order where freedom is ineluctably invoked. It is thus the irremissible weight of being that gives rise to my freedom. The ineluctable has no longer the inhumanity of the fateful, but the severe seriousness of goodness.
>
> Emmanuel Levinas, *Totality and Infinity*

> I find the order in my response itself, which, as a sign given to the neighbour, as a 'here I am', brings me out of invisibility, out of the shadow in which my responsibility could have been evaded.
>
> Emmanuel Levinas, *Otherwise than Being*

This book has been in conversation with two different modes of intelligibility. On the one hand, it has outlined the aspiration to intelligibility that underlies modern *tragic* subjectivity. On the other, it has intimated the presence, prior to any process of subjectivation, of an ethical demand coming from another which obligates the self to respond. Whether expressed in terms of an imperative to fulfil one's duty that dares the self to posit that duty (Kant), of a responsibility that increases the more it is fulfilled (Levinas), of fidelity to one's desire and the crack it opens in the ontological edifice (Lacan),[1] the ethical demand has always already taken place, and compels the self to act in a space that exceeds social regulation. As Levinas understands it in *Otherwise than Being*, this ethical demand has always already and unconditionally traumatized the self, obligated the self to respond for the other (*autrui*), to assume responsibility even for that for which the other is responsible. And it is only when it finds itself responding that the self becomes aware of the demand.

What I would like to do here, in the form of an initial and tentative exploration, is stage the beginnings of a conversation *between* the tragic subjectivity that premises the order of political rationality and the unconditional ethical demand. In order to do so, it will become necessary to trace the structure of demand and the ways in which the addressee (the subject) receives it and responds to it.[2]

The first idea I want to advance is that tragic subjectivity and the ethical demand are based respectively on what would appear to be two different ways of experiencing heteronomy. Though these two manifestations of heteronomy might turn out to refer to different perspectives on the same experience, I will separate them conceptually in order to explore how they function and intersect. To put it briefly, the heteronomy that constitutes tragic subjectivity as examined in the previous chapters consists in the apparent alienation of the self's ability to decide freely, derived from the necessity to act according to the inexorable dictates of objective necessity (destiny, the gods, the Father, the state, the Law). This loss of agency and freedom, however, would not succeed without the self's willingness to take upon itself a debt, and its eagerness to cooperate in its own subjection (Oedipus and Antigone, I argued, are exceptions to this). Since *objective necessity* denominates an internally inconsistent and ultimately empty source of coercion, the self's cooperation may be explained in Lacanian terms as the self's desire for the unknowable desire of the Other. Though subjectivation is premised on some kind of death, which in tragedy is brought about by a necessary fate, it should be noted that tragic heteronomy is extremely fruitful. It produces subjective identity, the illusion of autonomy, the fiction of the autonomous subject, social intelligibility and recognition, duties determined and action legitimized by the social order, symmetrical and reciprocal intersubjective relations, the social equalities enabled by universal principles, and subject-based liberal politics. This fruitfulness is often premised, however, on the self's deposition of responsibility and obliteration of others, paradoxically by assuming guilt.

Ethical heteronomy, in turn, inflects an unconditional ethical demand that I will trace in Kant and Levinas. In tragedy this demand becomes perceptible negatively through the suggestion that fate (that is, the impositions of objective necessity) is fictional, a construct that allows the subject to protest that it is controlled by someone or something other, and thus to displace responsibility away from itself.[3] The demand also can be sensed, still negatively, in the strong reaction of avoidance that it provokes in the characters, who avoid an extreme responsibility perceived as worse than tragic by complying with tragic subjectivation and death. Related to ethical heteronomy are the inauguration of subjective action as infinite responsibility, a way of acting without any ontological support or social legitimation, a shift from guilt to responsibility, lack of confirmation that one is fulfilling one's duty well, asymmetrical and non-reciprocal relations, the self's exposure to the disruption of others to the point of substituting itself for them, the suspension of a certain kind of intelligibility, extreme vulnerability and uncertainty.

Although these two forms of heteronomy interrelate in various ways, in Chapters 2 and 3 I suggested that tragic heteronomy allows the self to avoid the ethical demand, to deny approval of the obligation to respond and justify itself. Tragic heteronomy, or the subject's cooperation with objective necessity as a condition for becoming intelligible, permits the subject to evade ethical heteronomy, that is, the infinite responsibility imposed by others. By evading this responsibility which is impossible to fulfil, what is ultimately avoided is the vertigo of having to give substantial content to one's duty without any external confirmation, the risks of acting without the support of the social institutional order, and the fact that one becomes responsible the more one responds. Against the colloquial connotations of the word *tragic*, I therefore maintain that the tragic death that inaugurates tragic subjectivity is not the worst kind of death. In effect, it constitutes the space for evasion from something even more terrifying, an unconditional responsibility which in addition to suspending autonomy and freedom (such as they are understood in post-Kantian ethics), only increases the more it is fulfilled.

Since tragic heteronomy constituted the main focus of Chapters 1–3, here I will concentrate on the ethical heteronomy that underlay those analyses but was explicitly addressed only in Chapter 4. Then I will examine the apparent conflict between this way of understanding the ethical demand and the order of political rationality, that is, the tension between ethics and politics. My claim here will be that what has been perceived as a hiatus in need to be bridged, or as an 'existential drama' (Gillian Rose's words), constitutes a tension within an expanded political space that exceeds institutions and rules. I will thus recast this apparent disencounter between ethics and politics as a tension within the political. True to this tension, political action must attend to the irreducible ethical responsibility upon which it rests.

A difficult question that will gape at us throughout, and that I welcome as a challenge, is whether these two kinds of heteronomy, which I tentatively call *tragic* and *ethical*, can ultimately be conceptually separated, whether there is not, beyond an area in which they intersect, a point where they ultimately coincide. I would also like to clarify that I have extricated a tragic and an ethical kind of heteronomy for the sake of conceptual analysis. In experience they are inseparable, they coexist in interaction and shape subjectivity in different ways. The interaction between these two forms of heteronomy was depicted in Chapter 4 as the dynamic interplay of a necessary and a fictional fate. Like the tragic protagonist and against the expectations created by the modern supremacy of reason, on the other hand, the modern self depicted in the various philosophical versions studied above desperately *aspires* to become tragic, to compensate for the unbearable expulsion from the constellation of guilt (or, more exactly, for the irrelevance of that constellation) which follows the claim that God is dead.[4]

If our existence as obligated subjects is potentially *worse than* tragic in the classical sense, it is not because a tragic destiny still controls our actions – *that* would be typically tragic – but rather because destiny no longer exists. Since objective necessity provided the framework of debt in which we have our place, without it we may find ourselves unconstituted, undone, as Lacan points out.[5] Hence the modern subject might be said to avoid that loss by essentializing constructs, such as the Law, which adopt the status of necessary fictions. But however essentialized, the Law does not determine in advance the coordinates of our action, it neither dictates nor legitimizes the concrete content of our duty. Though it is determined by reason, in the end it has more in common with the *other side* to which the tragic subject blinds itself than with the *this side of destiny* with which it cooperates. The Kantian moral Law that grounds modern subjectivity does not offer any ultimate assurance or confirmation, unless we blind ourselves to that monstrous emptiness, which is why the modern subject is configured by the act of self-blinding and the turn against itself that sets in motion the tragic fall. The constitutive act of self-blinding is precisely what brings about tragic death, a kind of death we desire because it averts something worse.

The *something* that from the limited perspective of the tragic subject appears *worse* than tragic constitutes the focus of this chapter. It will begin by raising the question of the relation between the two kinds of heteronomy and Kant's moral Law. If the Law is incomprehensible, as Kant intimates at the end of the *Grounding for the Metaphysics of Morals*, if it is, moreover, supported by a terrible void which plays a similar role as the *other side* of destiny that tragic subjects die to avert, might tragic destiny (with its power to usurp human agency) and Kant's sublime Law (the very universal law that coincides with the self's freedom) be considered to belong to the same constellation?

The enigma of Kant's ethics

One of the main initial differences between Kantian and Levinasian ethics is that Kant asserts the primacy of autonomy, whereas for Levinas moral and social life is inflected by heteronomy. But is this really a difference? What exactly does it mean, in the context of Kant's practical reason, that the subject is autonomous? Kant's philosophy has been considered by a number of thinkers to formulate a 'tragic' kind of heteronomy. A conflict of tragic nature arises, for example, in the breach that Kant opens between theoretical and practical reason, that is, from the difficulty to reconcile the mechanistically determined causality of nature and the causality of human freedom.[6] Moreover, as I argued above, the modern rational subject depicts itself in forms that are typically tragic: it represents itself as a victim, assumes guilt, and repeats the externally imposed gestures of subjectivity (Pascal, Althusser) in order to become a subject. Ultimately, modern subjectivity is death-bound, it is propelled by a constitutive constraint that the emergence of subjective agency replicates. Without the pressure under which the subject's 'free potential' realizes itself, that potential would dissolve, and perhaps with it the subject . . .

The frequently raised question, then, is whether Kant's idea of autonomy is not fundamentally dependent on heteronomy, whether the constitutive illusion of autonomy that allows the rational subject to conceive of itself as self-ruled and free is not inflected by heteronomy. In the *Grounding for the Metaphysics of Morals* (1785) and subsequent writings, Kant repeatedly affirms that morality emerges from the coincidence of obedience to the moral law and the autonomy of the will, where one comes to will one's duty. In defining autonomy as 'that property that itself wills to be its own law', he establishes the identity of the Law and the law of the subject: the will.[7] The will of the autonomous subject takes itself for the Law.

That the autonomous subject must freely obey the Law means that duty and the subject's will must coincide, that the subject must come to will the obligation imposed by the moral law. This is a perplexing assertion required for the sake of the principle of autonomy, one which is nevertheless not distant from the self's willing cooperation with an imposed necessity that enables tragic subjectivation. Submitting to the Law and obeying one's duty is, in fact, even more important than life.

As Kant expresses it rather boldly in the chapter on 'Incentives of Pure Practical Reason' of the *Critique of Practical Reason*, the tranquility that pervades the subject when it obeys its duty 'is the effect of a respect for *something entirely different from life, something in comparison and contrast to which life* with all its agreeableness has, rather, *no worth at all*. He now lives only because it is his duty, not because he has the slightest taste for living'.[8] In the end, not only does the Kantian rational subject presuppose a tragic kind of heteronomy, the kind of heteronomy that sets tragic subjectivity in motion. Furthermore, if we focus specifically on Kant's definition of moral duty, the freedom of the autonomous subject consists in voluntarily choosing what has been determined as necessary, that is, what has passed the test of universality. The free rational subject must come to will and desire the unconditional moral Law, and act in response to it.

Kant's assertion that the self must will its duty would seem to imply that it must desire its obligation and fulfil it in response to that desire. But this desire for duty, he emphasizes, is incompatible with a 'taste for living'. Could this willingness to assume one's duty and live because of it be understood as desiring the desire of another, the obligation imposed by the other? Here the perplexing coincidence of duty and will that configures Kant's idea of autonomy again comes close to what we described as tragic heteronomy. The tragic subject experiences objective necessity as an unconditional obligation imposed from the outside, which it willingly assumes as its duty by cooperating with it. In this sense, Agamemnon's act of desiring 'with exceedingly impassioned passion' the sacrifice of his daughter Iphigenia commanded by Artemis may be interpreted as a desire for guilt, the guilt that according to Hegel is the last thing tragic protagonists would be willing to renounce.[9] Ultimately, then, this desire for objective necessity may be read, at least from a Lacanian perspective, as the self's desire for the unknowable desire of the Other.[10]

An objection that might be raised at this point is that heteronomy presupposes obedience to the command of another, whereas the Kantian moral duty is dictated by reason, and is therefore self-imposed. If by a free act of reason I bind myself to the moral Law, a duty that is defined by reason alone, and that I give myself, how can I be considered to be involved in heteronomy, ruled by another? That duty is self-imposed, however, does not necessarily imply that the alterity of the Law is neutralized. The self-giving of the Law does not exclude the possibility that one's obligation comes from another, for might not that other be an other within the self towards which the ethical subject is disposed? Such is the nature of the obligation imposed by what Levinas calls 'the other within the same' which is not reducible to the same, as he formulates it in *Otherwise than Being*. Levinas's insistence here that the other that commands me is an other within me marks a departure from the emphasis in *Totality and Infinity* that the absolutely other (*autrui*) is exterior to the self.

Let us look more closely to Kant's definition of autonomy as 'that property that itself wills to be its own law'. Such definition presupposes the identity between the Law and the law of the subject, whereby the will takes itself as the Law. The question that arises at this point is whether the autonomy of the Law (what Kant calls 'the autonomy of the principle of morality') coincides with the autonomy of the will. In raising this question, Jacob Rogozinski perceives a trace of excess in a formal Law that does not necessarily aim at any pre-established notion of the Good, an ethical Law that seems to differ from Rousseau's idea of self-legislation, where freedom is defined as obedience to the Law that the subject's will gives itself (a Law, that is, prescribed by oneself). Rather than giving itself the Law, the subject receives it from elsewhere, and it is the alterity of the Law that constitutes its subjectivity.[11] If the Law is not authored by the self-legislating subject, but rather comes from elsewhere, if it contains an element of alterity, of inhuman foreignness, wouldn't this affect the coherence of Kant's *oeuvre*? The possibility that the Law is not given by the subject, that the Law comes from elsewhere, would seem to threaten the internal coherence of practical reason. It also has the potential to jeopardize any smooth connection between pure and practical reason, 'between the auto-affection of I think (*Je pense*) and the autonomy of I must (*Je dois*)' (interestingly, in French *devoir* has the double sense of obligation – of being under the necessity of something – and of owing something, of debt).[12] That the Law comes from elsewhere would imply that rather than dictating its own law, the will receives it. If that were the case, how could the inextricability of submission to the Law and freedom be justified? We could no longer assert, it seems, that the subject's submission to the Law constitutes the very free act that informs the concept of freedom, unless we are ready to admit that freedom is not based on absolute autonomy.

So does the idea of freedom involve a certain heteronomy? In the section on the kingdom of ends in the *Grounding for the Metaphysics of Morals*, Kant posits the existence of a sovereign will that legislates, that gives the Law, without being its author.[13] Then, in the *Critique of Practical Reason*, he specifies: 'We are indeed legislating members of a kingdom of morals possible through freedom and presented to us by practical reason for our respect; but we are at the same time subjects of this kingdom, not its sovereign, and . . . [our] attitude of refusal toward the authority of the holy law – is already a defection from the law in spirit, even if its letter were fulfilled.'[14] It is therefore difficult to understand how this subject excluded from the legislating sovereignty remains nevertheless subjected to the Law, that is, the Subject of the Law, 'legislator in a kingdom of ends'.[15] In order to get out of this loop, Kant has recourse to the distinction between the legislator and the author of the Law. As Rogozinski puts it:

> Autonomy, in the authentic Kantian sense, would not be the absolute autonomy of a sovereign Subject creator of the Law (a hypothesis which is strictly impossible, according to Kant), but a *heteronomous* autonomy, the auto-heteronomy of a subject submitting to a Law of which he is not the author, which he has not created, which he receives and makes his as if it were its own Law.[16]

Although the human subject does not author the Law, it receives the Law and obeys it as if it did, as if it had given itself the Law. The self is therefore legislator not in Rousseau's sense of a sovereign people that authors the law through a shared decision, but in a sense more in line of Kantian politics, where the self 'must submit without reservation to the absolute authority of the "Sovereign of the State", obeying his laws as if he were himself their author'.[17] Here we find the echo of Kant's otherwise puzzling dictum in 'What is Enlightenment?' – 'Reason freely, but obey!' – in which the autonomy that reason achieves in self-legislation is undercut by heteronomous obedience.

The alterity of the Law reaches direct expression in Kant's *Philosophy of Religion*, where he speaks about God as 'so to speak, the moral Law itself, but thought of as personified',[18] that is, as a symbol for the Law. As Rogozinski remarks, this personification of the Law constitutes an attempt to express the symbolic alterity of the Law, that is, the fact that the Law appeals to us as the voice of a stranger which comes 'from Outside and from the Other'.[19] Thus, writes Kant, 'the concept of God is the concept of a subject which obligates outside of me'.[20] When we think of ethical obligation or moral constraint, we think of the will of another, and though we might call this alterity 'God', 'this duty regarding God (actually regarding the idea we make of such a being) is a duty of man to himself'.[21]

How are we to understand this paradoxical structure of heteronomy in autonomy, where the self-donation of the law by the subject and the alterity of the Law coincide? The enigma of Kant's ethical law is that the Law and the self are simultaneously identical and different. The Law is at the same time 'other' (it appears as the Law of the Other) and 'same' (it gives itself to the subject as the subject's Law), transcendent and immanent. How does the Law manage to impose itself on the subject both as the same and as its other? Indeed, it could not do so unless the Law is that which already constitutes the subject. [22]

The Law is therefore the support of the subject, the *subjecto* (that which is placed below the subject and sustains it) of the *subjectum* (subject) (*le 'sujet' du sujet*): it brings about the subject and sustains the subject in being.[23] It is not the case, then, that a fully constituted subject freely chooses to submit to the Law. All the subject can choose is whether or not to obey it, but it cannot choose its submission, which is a constitutive fact. The subject has always already submitted to the Law because it has been constituted by it, because without the Law, the subject would not exist. The subjection (or constitution or grounding) of the subject *by* the Law and the subject's subjection or submission to the Law coincide. In short, 'subject' means unconditionally submitted to a Law of which one is not the author (it is in this sense that it comes from the Other), which one does not understand, and yet must experience as its own Law, as that which configures the subject and by virtue of which it remains in itself.[24] This subject simultaneously submitted and constituted by an agency that it then experiences as its own willed effect grounds the subjects to which Freud, Foucault and Althusser refer.[25]

The Kantian subject is thus caught in what Rogozinski calls the enigma of auto-*heteronomy*, that is, in the paradoxical situation in which it is neither absolutely autonomous nor absolutely heteronomous. Understanding autonomy and heteronomy as absolutes would ultimately betray Kant's conception of the moral Law and of ethics. An absolute heteronomy would foreclose the possibility of ethics, that is, of an ethical subject who acts freely in accordance to universal laws. An absolute autonomy would, in turn, efface the alterity of the Law.[26] However much emphasis Kant places on autonomy, and however critical he is of heteronomy, autonomy and heteronomy are inextricably linked in his conception of practical reason, of the subject that submits freely to the moral Law.

Having reached the inseparability of autonomy and heteronomy, I would like to focus briefly on heteronomy, since that is precisely the part of the equation that Kant does not pursue, even while unequivocally affirming the alterity or foreignness of the Law. This alterity becomes more explicit in later texts such as the *Metaphysical Principles of Virtue* (1797), the *Philosophy of Religion* or *Opus Postumum*, where Kant repeatedly emphasizes that the self does not give itself the Law, but rather receives it from another. Heteronomy, however, inflects autonomy in Kant's writing much earlier than his explicit recognition of it. In fact, even the first time the principle of autonomy is enunciated (in the *Grounding for the Metaphysics of Morals*, 1785), it is already constituted by an essential heteronomy that leads to the concept of the Sovereign in the kingdom of ends, which is then further developed in the Second Critique (1788), and which represents the 'complete determination' of the categorical imperative.[27]

'It could be said, in effect, that far from constituting its "unique principle", the doctrine of *autonomy serves to conceal another experience of ethical obligation*, which, moreover, it does not manage to efface entirely, which consistently returns in the *oeuvre* as a mark of an irreducible heteronomy of the Law of autonomy.'[28] Or, to reformulate Rogozinski's words in the terms I used in the previous chapters, any attempt on the part of the subject to affirm its autonomy must be accomplished through heteronomy, through a recognition of the heteronomous investment of one's freedom, which the tragic subject manifests by representing itself as inevitably controlled by another. But the point I am making here is that the tragic subject actually evades that primordial heteronomy in favour of a tragic kind of heteronomy that will produce it as intelligible subject. Hence the need to create the illusion of objective necessity that takes the form of tragic destiny or, after Kant, of the Law. In tragic subjectivity intelligibility takes precedence over the primordial responsibility that heteronomously constitutes the subject. Hence what I call the paradox of tragic subjectivity, whereby the self represents itself as inexorably subjected to another paradoxically in order to achieve, reaffirm and preserve its integrity as an autonomous self-same.

But my inquiry into heteronomy remains still unsatisfied after the present exploration of heteronomy in Kant. The (ethical) heteronomy beyond heteronomy that I am trying to trace is not reducible to the quasi-heteronomy presupposed in quasi-autonomy. Rather, if we can sense that radical heteronomy, it is in the negative reaction it produces in tragic and modern subjects. We can perceive this rejection of ethical heteronomy negatively in the passionate determination with which tragic and modern subjects avoid it by clinging to the commands of objective necessity or the Law. This radical heteronomy is precisely what the subject seeks to evade by heteronomously submitting to the law of destiny.

The heteronomy that the tragic subject tends to avoid is already present, at least in small measure, in the very donation of the Law in Kant, whereby the subject is simultaneously constituted by the Law of an Other and made autonomous by a free act of giving itself the law. Here heteronomy is dissimulated, and the alterity of the Law concealed, by means of the very free act through which the self adheres to it. If the subject did not blind itself to the moment of its constitution in submission, the otherness of the Law would be revealed, perhaps jeopardizing the self's perception of itself as autonomous subject.

But beyond the element of foreignness inherent in the Law, the Law represents an even more unbearable kind of heteronomy, a heteronomy that we might call monstrous. This unbearable heteronomy manifests itself only very partially in the unsettling and incalculable consequences of the fact that the very Law to which the subject submits, the Law that constitutes the subject, is incomprehensible. This unknowability must be understood not so much in the sense of lacking content, as in that of existing outside of the constellation of content. As we shall see presently, the very principle of subjective intelligibility is itself unintelligible, or, more exactly, it exceeds the constellation governed by the intelligible, the unintelligible, and all their gradations. Could this radical heteronomy constitute 'another experience of ethical obligation', the 'irreducible heteronomy' which the doctrine of autonomy seeks, but ultimately fails, to efface? [29]

Or to approach this matter from a slightly different angle, what exactly is the ethical law and what role does it play in determining the substance of our actions, in giving concrete content to the ways in which our capacity for action should be actualized? The moral Law, which the subject gives itself as its own law even though it comes from another, is a law that the subject does not even understand. In the concluding remark of the *Grounding for the Metaphysics of Morals*, where Kant insists that an ethics based on freedom leads to an absolute necessity (the necessity of the unconditional law), he initially reproaches to human reason its inability to render comprehensible the necessity of what should happen, of 'an unconditional practical law (such as the categorical imperative must be)'.[30] Yet, he goes on to affirm, reason should not be blamed for not willing to explain the condition of the Law, because the condition of the Law lies beyond its reach. It is the moral Law itself that is incomprehensible, for otherwise it 'would no longer be moral, i.e., a supreme law of freedom'.[31] Kant's association of the moral Law with the concept of freedom is therefore premised on the incomprehensibility of the Law: 'And so even though we do not indeed grasp the practical unconditional necessity of the moral imperative, we do nevertheless grasp its *incomprehensibility*. This is all that can be fairly asked of a philosophy which strives in its principles to reach the very limit of human reason.'[32] This inconceivability is irrevocable, because it does not refer to a zero degree of knowability. If it were unknowable, the Law would still belong to the constellation of knowledge, in the same way as one reaffirms its subjection to the Law even (or precisely) when one transgresses it. More exactly than lacking content, the Law lies outside the constellation of content. Kant's moral Law, in other words, exceeds the boundary of human reason and its ability to synthesize and comprehend. It neither provides us with any substantial content that dictates our duty, nor offers any coordinates for our action that might legitimate it in advance.

From this apparent emptiness of the Law it follows that Kantian ethics effects a rupture with an ethics of the good, with what Lacan calls 'the service of goods' (*le service des biens*), in which the content of the good is determined in advance. As in Levinas, where the fact that I am irreplaceable in my responsibility means that I am the only one who can decide what the good is, in Kant acting ethically no longer involves acting well in any kind of pre-established or socially sanctioned sense. Ethical obligation – what is 'done in conformity to duty *and* only because of duty' – is an excess, a surplus of what he defines as legal – of what is 'done in conformity to duty'.[33] For Kant, as for Levinas and for Lacan (despite the important differences among them), acting in accordance with prescriptions and norms has nothing to do with a radical kind of ethics where the self must give substantial content to its duty, and act on it. This is revolutionary, and at the same time, by excluding an absolute measure against which to judge one's action, it transposes that infinity to the duty itself (as in the mathematical antinomy, where the infinite, which is no longer an external measure, parasitizes the finite, as Lacan's reading of Sygne's 'no' instantiates; see Chapter 2).

The fact that the Law cannot be comprehended would seem to introduce a further tension at the heart of autonomy, at the core of the subject's perception of itself as the author of a moral Law it has received. For how can the subject give itself a moral Law whose content it cannot comprehend? Indeed, how is the subject supposed to act on that law, to follow it? What is the status of freedom vis-à-vis a Law which is incomprehensible? On what basis can the subject be said to be acting freely by following the Law, if the Law does not offer any indication as to how to act? It would seem that the incomprehensibility of the Law complicates even more the notion of a free subject based on 'auto-heteronomy', bringing it closer to the uncertain and vulnerable addressee of Levinas's ethical demand. While in theory Kant's categorical imperative provides the basis for a conception of a free subject who comes to will its duty (a subject that becomes the cornerstone of liberal politics), in practice this subject is confronted with the formality of the imperative, that is, with the terrifying fact that the Law lacks content.

Kant would seem to shy from developing the ultimate consequences of that terrifying emptiness by having recourse to a Sovereign of the kingdom of ends, as we saw above. This sovereign dictates concrete laws for all subjects,[34] liberating them from the extreme responsibility of having to determine their duty in the absence of any coordinates that legitimate it in advance. It would thus seem that practical reason, based on the (formal) categorical imperative, works in theory, but what happens in practice? As Kant's 'What is Enlightenment?' intimates, one may reason as much as one likes because in practice others will dictate the rules ('but obey'), getting the subject off the hook of ethical excess. Although the sovereign whose rules one must obey represents an important moment of heteronomy in Kant's practical philosophy, this legislating 'other' should not be confused with the alterity of the Law. Far from embodying that alterity, the sovereign, an enabling intermediary, serves further to occlude the unbearable foreignness of the Law that already lies outside of the subject's field of vision. If the alterity of the Law consists in its emptiness and monstrosity, in the unbearable responsibility that it places on the self, then that responsibility is averted by means of the rules that the sovereign dictates. It is the obligation to obey those concrete rules that allows the subject to evade the abyssal and impossible responsibility ultimately imposed by the imperative to fulfil one's duty.

To conclude, from the viewpoint of Kantian ethics the self's freedom consists in willing to fulfil its duty. Since that duty is, however, undefined, it corresponds to the self to give it substantial content. Unlike following concrete rules, daring to posit one's duty constitutes a vertiginous act, for the decision with which one fills up the empty category of duty will remain suspended in an abyss, unconfirmed. There would seem to be two different kinds of heteronomy at play here, a tragic-like desire for one's obligation as established by the law, and the (perhaps much less desirable) infinite responsibility to make one's duty concrete in an act of radical exposure. But is it really possible to differentiate between these two kinds of heteronomy, or do they ultimately collapse? This question will prove crucial for reading Levinas, since the first (tragic) kind of heteronomy is one of the aspects he critiques in what he calls the ontological tradition. Levinas would denominate this kind of heteronomy 'participation', meaning that the self accepts to take part in a drama of which it is not the author.[35] The second kind of heteronomy is the heteronomy in which an unknowable ethical imperative that exists prior to the distinction between incomprehensible and comprehensible places the self in a situation of asymmetrical and endless faithfulness to duty. The self that accepts this demand, that commits and binds itself to it, seems akin to the self of which Levinas speaks, a self constituted by the impossible task of responding to the order of obligation imposed by the other within itself.

If the distinction between a 'tragic' and an 'ethical' heteronomy ultimately holds, then it will become necessary to compare the claims each of them places on the subject and examine whether there is a relation of equality or of priority between them. But if the two heteronomies collapsed into one, the implication would be that there is no *outside of* subjectivity, in which case it would be indispensable to keep in mind that not all subjectivity is tragic. Whatever the answer, its consequences will be political. If the two heteronomies, as well as the different modes of intelligibility they presuppose, were ultimately to coincide, then the rational political order, the systems of human rights and the rule of law, which are based on the (ultimately tragic) idea of autonomy, would remain unaffected by any prior and anarchic ethical demand. But if the two heteronomies were indeed separable, or if they afford different perspectives on a similar experience, then we would be called to conceive of a political space structured by the tension between two radically different ways of understanding obligation, activity, responsibility and justice.

Levinas and the ethical demand

We have begun to see how the very notions of autonomy and freedom that serve to create ethical duty in Kant ultimately reaffirm the self in its sameness. The self must believe it has given itself the Law, but the Law that constitutes the subject originates elsewhere, and thus represents a received, rather than self-given, obligation. This tension between autonomy and heteronomy serves, as I said above, a double function. An absolute heteronomy would foreclose the possibility of ethics (of the promise of freedom and the self's responsibility for its actions), while an absolute autonomy would negate the alterity of the Law. Constituted by this tension, the subject needs to believe that the Law is self-given in order to preserve the illusion of autonomy. The moment in which the subject could have given itself the Law, however, does not exist, because there is no subject prior to that obligation. This is, nevertheless, the tension that allows Kant's practical reason to make concrete the transcendental idea of freedom (enabled by the solution of the third antinomy of pure reason) as the idea of the free will that voluntarily adheres to the Law.

Levinas proposes an apparently similar structure. Like Kant's subject of moral Law, the self has been called by an other, and constituted as subject. Though in Kant the demand is placed by a fact of reason, and in Levinas by the face of the other, both accounts of the constitution of the subject through the imposition of a demand belong to a similar constellation.[36] What disturbs that parallel is that for Levinas the face of the other questions the self precisely *as* Kantian subject, as the self-conscious and autonomous subject of the Law. We could think of Levinas's sensible subject, in this sense, as a subject prior to the subject. Though the constitution of both subjects is initiated by a call from another (a heteronomous moment), the Levinasian subject stays in heteronomy, and if it achieves a certain sense of autonomy (which is central to this subject's political dimension), this autonomy rests on a constitutive heteronomy that is primordial and unconcealed. The Kantian subject, on the other hand, strives for an autonomy that I qualified, following Rogozinski, as a quasi-autonomy. Autonomy is achieved, as I argued in Chapter 3, by having recourse to a heteronomous source of obligation (objective necessity, the Law) designed to preserve autonomy by preventing the irruption of human others. It is in representing itself as a victim, in assuming a debt, that the self becomes what I have called a tragic subject, a tradition to which Kant's subject may ultimately be considered to belong.

It is this self who believes itself autonomous but *dissolves* in a transcendent horizon of reason that Levinas's ethics puts into question. Freedom, in Levinas's view, is promoted by the 'I think', by the monologue of a self that strives towards universalization by turning every exterior thing into an idea that can be possessed. What is lost in this process of abstraction and assimilation of every other is the self's ability to be in contact with what in *Totality and Infinity* (1961) he envisages as the really exterior, 'with a reality that does not fit into any a priori idea, which overflows all of them'.[37]

If the free act of the Kantian subject, an act in which the ethical demand and the self's will must coincide, defines the freedom that for Levinas must be put into question, what is an ethical subject for him, and how does it come into being? What is the difference between the approval of the categorical imperative realized by the Kantian autonomous subject, and the approval of the demand and response to it that in Levinas's *Otherwise than Being* (1974) constitutes the subject as subject? Let us begin by examining briefly how the structure of demand and response takes place in Levinas.

For Levinas, the demand comes from what he calls the face of the other. The face escapes comprehension, it is outside of representation, beyond essence (thus exceeding the object of ontology). The relation it establishes, one in which neither self nor other is comprehended or reduced to knowledge, takes place in language. I'm called by the other, I listen to the other, I speak, exposing myself in my acts of saying. In *Otherwise than Being* Levinas differentiates the act of speaking (Saying, *Dire*) from the language that represents and the thing represented (Said, *Dit*), in order to distinguish this relation of exposure from the relation of comprehension that prevails in the Western philosophical tradition.[38]

According to Levinas's account in *Totality and Infinity*, the face of a living other, which is here described as an absolutely exterior being, speaks to me.[39] The face speaks, but what it says cannot be deciphered or read – interpreting the face with a will to coherence would amount to missing its expression. In the act of looking at me, of speaking, the human other, my neighbour (*mon prochain*) obligates me to respond. Its command, 'thou shall not kill', is expressed without words in an injunction that takes place prior to my interpretation of his or her actual words. The irruption of the face in my existence does not constitute one event among others that happens to me. Rather, the ethical interruption has always already happened, in an immemorial past or primordial dimension that is prior to my existence and that of the world. 'Thou shall not kill': in enjoining me to respect its otherness and its separation from me, the other brings my all-encompassing impulses to a halt, putting into question my freedom, which now perceives itself as unjust.[40] 'A new situation is created; consciousness's presence to itself acquires a different modality; its positions collapse.'[41] This collapse of consciousness – or good conscience – when the radical other puts it into question does not mean that the spontaneous self now knows itself 'to be, *in addition*, guilty'.[42] This would constitute only one more attribute of the self's contented consciousness. That the other questions the self's freedom, that the other disrupts the self's world, means that such a world will never be the same, that the self will never 'find again its priority over the other'. The movement that turns every other into the same comes to an end.[43]

Let us pause for a moment to ask about the addressee of the ethical demand. Who is 'me'? The ethical demand addresses me (*moi*), the self, which Levinas distinguishes from the Ego (*le moi*). Who the self is, or who I am when I receive the call, however, changes from Levinas's earlier work to *Otherwise than Being*. I will address these differences briefly because they are relevant to the task of understanding the relation of Levinas's ethics to politics, as well as much of the criticism that his work has provoked in that respect. They will also play an important role in clarifying the structure of demand and response as we are examining it here in relation to Kant's practical philosophy, as regards the question of freedom. While in *Totality and Infinity* the self is an already constituted subject whose freedom the demand puts into question, in *Otherwise than Being* the subject is constituted by the very demand, which is experienced as an originary trauma.[44] And while the face was that of an exterior being (*Totality and Infinity* is subtitled 'An Essay on Exteriority'), in the later work the other is an other within the self, but irreducible to the same. This constitutes a significant change, one that Levinas introduces partially in response to Derrida's criticism in 'Violence and Metaphysics' (1967) that the other cannot be entirely exterior to the self.[45] Though already in 1957 Levinas's idea of the experience of absolute otherness within oneself was inspired in the idea of the infinity in me in Descartes' third *Meditation*,[46] in *Otherwise than Being* the other is definitely and other within me but irreducible to me. As a consequence of this shift, the self no longer tends towards the other through desire ('the lack in a being which is completely'[47]) as was the case in *Totality and Infinity*. The self is now traumatized and obsessed by the demand.

The fact that the self can no longer adopt a distance from itself, that it is obsessed, affects the idea of separation, which played a crucial role in *Totality and Infinity*. In the earlier work, the self is described as a sensible (not self-conscious) subject enjoying the world, and because it already exists as the centre of an economy, it can remain separated from the other at the same time as it relates to the other.[48] Thus, both self and other are able to absolve themselves from the relation, an idea we need to keep in mind in order to understand many of the apparent paradoxes of Levinas's work. The self, in other words, simultaneously inhabits two different dimensions which are inseparable in experience, that of interiority or separation and that of relation. As separated from the other, the self who is at home in the world acquires autonomous substantiality and gathers itself in its sameness.[49] Levinas presents the self's work towards reinstating its sameness in its alterations, towards identifying itself,[50] as a positive movement, since without it the heterogeneity of both other and self would be compromised: 'The alterity, the radical heterogeneity of the other, is possible only if the other is other with respect to a term whose essence is to remain at the point of departure, to serve as *entry* into the relation, to be the same not relatively but absolutely. *A term can remain absolutely at the point of departure of the relationship only* as I.'[51] As related to the other, however, the self transcends itself in the desire awakened by the other, a desire that does not objectify the desired. Instead of offering satisfaction, the desired other responds to the self's desire with an endless task, the self's responsibility for all the human others that it meets. The self would be totalized by the other and unable to take action on its behalf were it not because by calling the self to responsibility, by enjoining the self, the other also attests the self as an I. Without being independent, without having 'a concrete existence of its own', a pleasure-seeking body and hands to comfort the other, this sensible subject would not be able to respond to the other's call.

This structure of simultaneous inhabitation in two different dimensions is complicated in *Otherwise than Being*, where 'subjectivity is the other in the same'.[52] While here the self remains an atheist, which is Levinas's way of expressing that it does not dissolve or *participate* in larger structures (whether in religious or mythical participation or in the modern structures of rational mediation and self-identification of the self-conscious subject), it is no longer entirely separated from the other. But because in *Otherwise than Being* the self has never had the experience of separation, or any other experience previous to the disruption or trauma created by the other's demand, the self can no longer establish the distance from itself that would allow it to achieve a certain separation from itself, to *represent* itself. Now the self is constituted by a traumatic demand that comes from an other within the same. The subject is obsessed, responsible even for that for which the other is responsible, persecuted and hostage to the other, ready to substitute itself for him or her. *Otherwise than Being* thus makes clear something that *Totality and Infinity* had already insinuated in 'present[ing] itself as a defence of subjectivity',[53] of a subjectivity where the self's moral initiative, its 'attention to the Other as unicity and face . . . can be produced only in the unicity of the I':[54] that Levinas's ethical thought constitutes less an account of the other than a theory of the subject, as Lingis, Bernasconi and Critchley have rightly insisted.[55] In order to be able to respond to the other one must be a subject, 'Alterity is possible only starting from me.'[56] 'I am I in the sole measure that I am responsible, a non-interchangeable I. I can substitute myself for everyone, but no one can substitute himself for me. Such is my inalienable identity of subject.'[57]

Levinas, however, seeks to 'apprehend the subjectivity not at the level of its purely egoist protestation against totality, nor in its anguish before death',[58] as he affirms in the preface to *Totality and Infinity*. The subject of which Levinas offers a theory is no longer exclusively the self-conscious subject that dissolves in abstraction and is based on death – no longer the *tragic* subject that prevails in the philosophical accounts examined in Chapter 3 – but rather a sensible subject. Unlike the self-conscious subject, which following Hegel's unhappy consciousness must deny bodily experience in order to identify with the essential, in Levinas's subjectivity the duality between body and thought no longer holds: it is with its body, with its hands, that the self can ease the needs of the other in concrete ways, and suffering or dying for the other means that the I is attached to the material existence of which it is being deprived.[59]

What makes me a subject is my irreplaceablility, the fact that the demand is addressed to me and only to me, that I can substitute myself for everyone but no one can substitute me in my responsibility. In *Totality and Infinity* Levinas refers to the curvature of intersubjective space in which 'I welcome the On High'.[60] The appearance of the face subordinates my freedom to the other,[61] placing me in an asymmetrical relationship that is called 'substitution' in *Otherwise than Being*. I am irreplaceable, and yet, that I substitute myself for the other does not imply that the other substitutes herself for me: 'the substitution of the one for the other [of myself for the other] does not signify the substitution of the other for the one'.[62]

A freedom ineluctably invoked

What is the freedom that ethics puts into question? Is it in any way close to Kant's conception of freedom? The freedom that the demand puts into question initiates as a break with what Levinas calls participation or dissolution, which is how he refers to being made intelligible by a wider order of signification with which one has to identify. By displaying the impulse to act on the part of the tragic protagonists, which reflects the incipient initiative of a rational being who dares challenge religious and mythical power, tragedy, and with it the beginning of rational philosophy, might be considered to have initiated a break with participation in those powers. Levinas, however, charges the Western philosophical tradition (by which he means the tradition that starts in

Parmenides and culminates in Heidegger) with fostering new kinds of participation. Ontology understands the transcendent as the real from which everything obtains its being. In the descriptions of subjectivity studied in Chapter 3, this real or source of identity takes up the varied forms of objective necessity or God, later replaced by language, the Law, ethical imperatives or, more diffusely, 'power'. These sites of transcendence, themselves unintelligible, fulfil the two interrelated functions of providing intelligibility and enabling an agency which is extremely constrained. The self is now split between its sensible and its self-conscious part, or between its materiality and its essentiality. But however compelling this self-division (materialized in the pangs of conscience), '[t]he folding back of being upon itself, and the self formed by this fold, where the reflection of being remains correlative with being, does not go either to the crux of subjectivity,' writes Levinas.[63] The ultimate function of these sources of intelligibility and subjectivation, I proposed, is to preserve sameness by enabling the self to represent itself on the verge of self-disintegration, at risk of imminent peril. Whether the self attributes the disintegration of its own autonomy to a victimization by fate, a doubly-bound agency or a necessary submission to ethical imperatives and laws, the very subordination to an alienating Other allows the self to preclude the irruption of real persons.

Thus, although philosophy, according to Levinas, has the merit of having broken with participation, that is, with the self's magical dissolution in mythical forces (a break initially aided by tragedy as the artistic representation of the self's impulse towards self-sufficiency), it has created new ways of self-dissolution. Philosophy seeks to establish totalities or intelligible wholes that demand the self's identification with abstraction, dissolve the self's individuality and make it play roles in which it does not recognize itself. By representing and conceiving of totalities of being (universals, God) that engulf particulars, contends Levinas, philosophy fosters new forms of participation that converge with the very mythical and magic traditions with which it initially had to break in order to be able to emerge.[64] Hence the break with mythical participation enacted by philosophy must again be interrupted.[65] It would seem that this radical break, which happens outside of time, should interrupt freedom and do away with the illusion of autonomy, as well as with the tragic heteronomy on which that illusion is based.

It is another person who interrupts my freedom. It is not the case, though, that the other's face defeats my powers by counteracting them by force – by inscribing *real*, instead of ethical, resistance, and waging war. Rather, the face presents itself in all its weakness, in all the nakedness and destitution it suffers in its exile from the world in which I reign. If the face's resistance were real, if it constituted a phenomenal event, it wouldn't be a resistance, but actual coercion and control. But when faced by the living expression of the other, which is not plastic, visible or representable, 'I am no longer able to have power' (*Je ne peux pouvoir*).[66] The other's silent command not to kill, the call to responsibility that his or her expression addresses to me, reverses the structure of my freedom. My freedom is no longer the spontaneous freedom of my all-encompassing conscience, despite the fact that such self-centred freedom may already include respect for altruistic values and norms; it is the inclination of my freedom before the other, not before facts, that reveals it to be unjust. When I measure myself against the infinite other, my freedom, discovering its 'murderous and usurpatory' exercise, feels *shame* of itself.[67]

Paradoxically, this very divestiture of the freedom to which the self feels entitled *invests the self's freedom*. 'The presence of the Other, a privileged heteronomy, does not clash with freedom but invests it.'[68] 'This investiture of freedom constitutes moral life itself, which is through and through a heteronomy.'[69] But what does it *exactly* mean that the other invests my freedom by obligating me? Surely, if I am heteronomously obliged by the other's injunction, I cannot consider myself free. How can I, furthermore, perceive myself as an acting being if 'I am no longer able to have power', *to be able*, if my initiative is denied? And yet Levinas insists that the other 'does not limit but promotes my freedom'.[70]

A freedom invested by the other means that the self's free will is cancelled, and this happens in a primordial plane in which my violence has always already been called into question. It is in this sense that the I becomes passive before the other, enacting a passivity that precedes all activity or rather, that precedes any division between passivity and activity. Levinas writes: 'The term welcome of the Other expresses a simultaneity of activity and passivity which places the relation with the other outside of the dichotomies valid for things: the a priori and the a posteriori, activity and passivity.'[71] This 'passivity beyond passivity' of a self who has always already been made responsible by the other, where 'freedom is ineluctably invoked', refers to the suspension of the self's egoism – its self-contented freedom – rather than to the self's immobility or lack of action. Only by becoming passive at this primordial level, prior to my being in the world, am I invested as an agent and as a freedom, and given a task.[72] The other's ethical opposition to my egoism inaugurates my initiative, understood in the ethical sense that

Levinas gives to the term. In 1953, he writes: 'this opposition is not revealed by its coming up against my freedom; it is an opposition prior to my freedom, which *puts my freedom into action*.'[73] Then, in 1957, he writes: 'freedom is put into *question*',[74] equating a freedom put into question (the inauguration of ethical initiative) with a freedom put into action.

It is because the appropriating impulse of the self turns into passivity when questioned by the other that from this passivity emerges an 'activity beyond activity'. (I borrow the term from Gillian Rose, who uses it to restate the risks of political action.)[75] What is to be responsible for the other if not to act for the other, 'to respond to this essential destitution of the other, finding resources for myself'?[76] The other demands 'a response to the being who in a face speaks to the subject and tolerates only a personal response, that is, an ethical act'.[77] My freedom is no longer based on the question 'what can I hope for?', referring to what we can expect or extract from the world, but rather on 'what must I do?'[78] 'what am I to do'?[79]

And indeed, what am I to do? I must take action, but what kind of creative act that might be, and how it should be realized, is only for me to decide. 'The will is free to assume this responsibility in whatever sense it likes; it is not free to refuse this responsibility itself.'[80] As the relation to the other, which is a first philosophy, cannot be conceptualized or reduced to knowledge, neither can the demand. Hence, the self must respond (in *Otherwise than Being* the self has already responded) while assuming the responsibility of deciding how to respond, of daring to posit its duty in the absence of any external legitimation. The fact that the demand that takes place in 'saying' is not representable creates problems at the moment of grasping this process from the viewpoint of logic. How then should I act, how is this *ethical* initiative that the interruption of the other reinscribes? In important ways, for Levinas ethical action consists in *not* understanding, in 'doing before understanding',[81] a formulation that undoes the priority of theory over practice.[82] The language of the face is performative, not readable, and as we shall see, I respond to the demand even before becoming aware that the demand has been placed on me. The impossibility of interpreting the demand is aggravated by the fact that my response may only meet ingratitude from the other, because the relation is non-reciprocal.[83] Hence the unsatisfiedness of responsibility of which Levinas speaks. Rather than filling or fulfilling, the self's goodness is a hollowing out where responsibility increases in the measure that it is assumed: 'duties become greater in the measure that they are accomplished. The better I accomplish my duty the fewer rights I have; the more I am just the more guilty I am.'[84] It is no wonder that responsibility may feel like persecution.

Or am I already reading, and thus misreading, the face? The fact that the relation has always already taken place in an immemorial past, the fact that it does not belong in the existing world – that it is not ontic – does not shield it from our ontic perspective. It is precisely from this perspective that the relation between self and other flips over into persecution: from the viewpoint of worldly rules, the asymmetry and non-reversibility of the relation appears incomprehensible and suspicious. Hence our inclination to read, and in reading, misread the face.[85] 'Resenting its self-dispossession,' writes Robbins, 'the I blames the other, feels persecuted by the other. Responsibility feels like persecution, if it is not ethics.'[86] When the self, protesting against passivity and trying to repossess itself, does not respond (and this is not ethics), responsibility *feels* like persecution.

Levinas's work is full of apparent paradoxes that seem to contradict the will to coherence and the temporality of the world: a relation whose terms remain absolute (and *absolving* themselves), an activity that rests on a passivity beyond passivity, an initiative invested by bringing subjective agency to a halt, a freedom ineluctably invoked, a responsibility that feels like persecution, or an ethical demand that has always already taken place, and to which I have always already responded. This 'always already' indicates a structure prior to logic. Levinas uses 'anachronism' to refer to a situation that is diachronic and can never become synchronic, that cannot be mastered by coherence and logic (temporal terms such as anachrony, diachrony and synchrony, do not express temporality, but rather a *prior* to time and logic). These double binds should be thought of as taking place in two different dimensions, an ontic and a primordial one. Furthermore, the elements of each pair are not complementary; the link between them is governed by the profound asymmetry between self and other. Thus the distinction between primordial and ontic, or that between relation and separation, passivity and activity or saying and said, does not constitute a dichotomy; in each case, the two elements are inextricably linked, rather than opposed and more than simply interdependent. All these distinctions belong in the interaction between a non-temporal and a temporal dimension whereby, though appearing simultaneous from an ontic viewpoint – for the sake of the requirements of our logic, coherent thought – the non-temporal one has always already taken place.

Authoring the other's decision

If the free act of the Kantian subject, the act in which the moral Law and the self's will become identical, defines the freedom that for Levinas must be put into question, what is an ethical subject for him, and how does that subject come into being? What is the difference between the approval of the categorical imperative realized by the Kantian autonomous subject and the approval of the demand and response to it that in *Otherwise than Being* constitutes the subject as subject? In Kant the subject does not choose its submission to the Law – it can choose to obey or disobey the Law, but it cannot avoid being already submitted to it.[87] What is the relation, for Levinas, between the heteronomous order of obedience – the demand – and the self's way of receiving? Does the self respond to it on approving of it, that is, can the self *choose* to respond? Let us look closely at a passage from *Otherwise than Being*, where Levinas speaks of the 'witnessing' and 'inspiration' that take place as the self 'receives' the command. I quote at length:

> That the way the Infinite passes the finite and passes itself has an ethical meaning is not something that results from a project to construct the 'transcendental foundation' of 'ethical experience'. The ethical is the field outlined by the paradox of an Infinite in relationship with the finite without being belied in this relationship. Ethics is the breakup of the originary unity of transcendental apperception, that is, it is the beyond of experience. Witnessed, and not thematized, in the sign given to the other, the Infinite signifies out of responsibility for the other, out of the-one-for-the-other, a subject supporting everything, subject to everything, that is, suffering for everyone, but charged with everything, without having had to decide for this taking charge, which is gloriously amplified in the measure that it is imposed. Obedience precedes any hearing of the command. The possibility of finding, anachronously, the order in the obedience itself, and of receiving the order out of oneself, this reverting of heteronomy into autonomy [*ce retournement de l'hétéronomie en autonomie*], is the very way the Infinite passes itself. The metaphor of the inscription of the law in consciousness [*conscience*] expresses this in a remarkable way, reconciling autonomy and heteronomy. It does so in an ambivalence whose diachrony is the signification itself, an ambivalence which, in the present, is an ambiguity. The inscription of the order in the *for-the-other* of obedience is an anarchic being affected, which slips into me 'like a thief' through the outstretched

nets of *consciousness* [*conscience*]. This trauma [*traumatisme*] has surprised me completely; the order *has never been represented*, for it has never presented itself, not even in the past coming in memory, to the point that it is I that only says, and after the event, this unheard-of obligation. This ambivalence is the exception and subjectivity of the subject, its very psyche, a possibility of inspiration. It is the possibility of being the author of what had been breathed *unbeknownst to me*, of having received, one knows not from where, that of which I am author. In the responsibility for the other we are at the heart of the ambiguity of inspiration. The unheard-of saying is enigmatically in the anarchic response, in my responsibility for the other. The trace of infinity is this ambiguity in the subject, in turns beginning and intermediary [*commencement et truchement*], a diachronic ambivalence which ethics makes possible.[88]

I would like to approach Levinas's extraordinary words by asking three questions: How does the self receive the demand? How does the self respond? And in what sense is the self constituted as a subject?

How do I receive the demand?

I receive the demand from an other who relates to me in a way in which its otherness, its infinity, is not belied by its relation to me. Thus, I do not receive it as the Kantian transcendental subject would. Kant's idea of apperception is that all my syntheses of phenomena, and thus all my representations, are inflected by my act of thinking them, by the structure of my thought. For Levinas, in turn, I cannot thematize or conceptualize the demand because it is unheard of and unheard, it does not come to me as something reducible to knowledge. Instead, I witness it. Witnessing for Levinas does not mean being present and then reporting an event. The event that takes place here is not the demand, which occurs outside of action or inaction, but rather my act of responding.

What is it that I witness, and how? To witness, says Levinas, is to be inspired in a sense initially suggested by the common usage of the word. Being inspired means finding in myself something that was not in me before. What I find in myself comes from elsewhere, it does not originate in me, yet I can consider myself its origin or author. Inspiration is 'the possibility of being the author of what had been breathed *unbeknownst to me*, of having received, one knows not from where, that of which I am author'. Without even being aware that I was receiving it (since it has been 'breathed *unbeknownst to me*') I find in myself an order of obedience that I receive from elsewhere. I am heteronomously obligated, obligated by another, but since I find the command in myself, I can consider myself the author of what has been heteronomously imposed. This order, which has been 'breathed' without me being aware of it, which has 'slipped in me "like a thief"', sneaking through my consciousness but also through my conscience (*conscience* in French has both meanings, which Levinas exploits), has affected me to the point of inscribing itself in me like a trauma. But I don't become aware of the order in any sense related to knowledge, I don't even come to intuit it in its traumatic way of shattering me. It is only in so far as I am already responding – in so far as I find myself asking what it is I am responding to – that I realize that a demand has been placed on me. Only the event of my response makes me aware that a command precedes it. Since the order is inscribed 'in the for-the-other of obedience', in my disposition to obey – in my being disposed towards the other, in my response – I have not even been given the chance to choose whether or not to respond. Rather, I have found myself already responding. In fact, I have been constituted as *me*, as a self, in my responding. The trauma of the order has constituted me, prior to my awareness, to my self-consciousness (indeed, anarchically), as the one who responds, who is already responding, who has always already responded.

How do I respond?

This traumatism, this order, has caught me by surprise. Yet, I am the only one who can 'say' this obligation. In fact, 'it is I that only says' (*c'est moi qui dit seulement*): I can *only* 'say' it, I have no alternative but saying it, and I can do nothing else (my ability to act freely has collapsed). My saying it can only happen retrospectively, after the event of my act of responding, which takes place before my becoming aware of receiving the order. That I can only 'say' the unheard-of [unprecedented, *inouïe*] and unheard obligation does not mean that I can formulate it, that I can describe it, but rather that I can attest to the fact that is has taken place, and that act of witnessing is the only thing I can do, and all I can do. So what is it I do? In 'saying' I expose myself to the order – I expose myself to the other, who can now dispose of me. Perhaps, I even act on the order – I act for the other, whether or not I succeed, and even if my acting can never fulfil the order.

In what sense have I been constituted as a subject?

'This ambivalence is the exception and subjectivity of the subject, its very psyche, a possibility of inspiration.' I am constituted as the one-for-the-other, as a subject, by the exception ('exception to the rule of being',[89] i.e. that which constitutes the subject as otherwise than being) in the ambivalence 'of having received, one knows not from where, that of which I am author'. Being constituted as a subject means that I am simultaneously subjected to the other and supporting the other, 'a subject supporting everything, subject to everything'. Here Levinas exploits the double meaning of the word *sujet* in French, *sujet* as subject and *sujet* as support.[90] Being a subject in the double sense of being subordinated and supporting entails 'suffering for everyone, but charged with everything, without having had to decide for this taking charge, which is gloriously amplified in the measure that it is imposed'. Notice that any reference to freedom is absent here. I support the other, I suffer for the other but I am responsible for everything without choosing to become so, and the order is only 'amplified in the measure that it is imposed', which implies that my unchosen responsibility only increases the more it is fulfilled.

I have found the other, the order, in me. Subjectivity is 'a possibility of inspiration, the possibility of being the author of what had been breathed *unbeknownst to me*, of having received, one knows not from where, that of which I am author'. Levinas returns to this ambivalence of the subject, who authors what it receives, at the end of the paragraph, where he says that the subject is 'in turns origin and intermediary [*commencement et truchement*]'.[91] Does not this sound like the paradox of Kant's moral Law, where I give myself what I have received from elsewhere, and experience it as self-given? Indeed, the demand for the self's approval of a heteronomously imposed duty, which in Kant takes the form of self-legislation – of the necessary coincidence of one's duty with one's will – seems to belong to a similar constellation as Levinas's account of the constitution of the subject by a traumatic order of obedience in *Otherwise than Being*. Moreover, Levinas goes as far as recognizing that in inspiration autonomy and heteronomy are reconciled, or autonomy reverts into heteronomy. What does Levinas mean here by saying that heteronomy, the core of his understanding of ethics as first philosophy, reverts into autonomy, and 'this is the very way the Infinite passes itself'? Does he imply that the very autonomy that is questioned by the heteronomous demand is also the result of the demand? How should we understand that '[t]he metaphor of the inscription of the law in consciousness expresses this in a remarkable way, reconciling autonomy and heteronomy'?

The limited perspective of autonomy

Levinas's reformulation of the subject as constituted by the demand has a lot in common with that tension between autonomy and heteronomy in Kant, for whom the self gives itself the Law as an act of freedom, but then the Law is not self-given but rather received. This is, nevertheless, the tension in practical reason that Kant cannot be strictly said to pursue, for wouldn't the act of freely accepting as self-given what is in fact given by another ultimately undermine the act of freedom it defines? In making its will coincide with its duty, with the Law, the Kantian subject may be considered to approve of the demand, but only in so far as the alterity of the demand is recast as self-given. Only thus can the self's approval of the demand coincide with its act of freedom. The self's initial act of freedom must always prevail, even if that involves forgetting that heteronomy inflects autonomy in order that one's self-perception as autonomous remains intact.

The existence of the demand becomes evident to the Kantian subject only in its act of approving it, as happens in Levinas.[92] Though this could potentially pose problems to Kant's idea of freedom, it does not pose problems for Levinas, because Levinas is not concerned with the same concept of freedom. In fact, it is Kant's idea of freedom and his investment in integrating the alterity of the law within the principle of autonomy that Levinas might be said to contest. Rather than being involved in demonstrating that the self is free, Levinas has ethics question the self's freedom. And because he is not concerned with the concept of autonomy, he can directly describe freedom not as depending on a free act of the subject, but rather as 'ineluctably invoked'.[93] It is heteronomy that is first philosophy for Levinas.

The heteronomy to which Levinas refers is, however, non-alienating. It is not the heteronomy in which tragic subjects are involved, a heteronomy that returns the self to itself by splitting it, by causing the internal division that premises identity as identification. This is precisely what Levinas criticizes as the self's dissolution, as its playing part in a drama of which it is not the author.[94] As described in *Otherwise than Being*, Levinas's self cannot even adopt the distance from itself that would permit the realization of self-division. Rather than returning the self to itself, rather than reaffirming the self in its economy of being, the otherwise than being of heteronomy is a radical exposure to the other that takes place in the act of saying.

Far from betraying the centrality of heteronomy as first philosophy, then, in referring to the 'reverting of heteronomy into autonomy' Levinas throws unprecedented light on Kant's idea of autonomy. Levinas's point is that *although the self is indeed heteronomously obligated in a primordial or anarchic way, autonomy emerges as the effect of looking at oneself from the viewpoint of consciousness*. Autonomy manifests itself only to reason, not to ethical experience. Therefore, the reconciliation of autonomy and heteronomy, or our illusion that they coincide, only takes place once we find ourselves responding to a heteronomous order of obedience. Before the response there is no conscious decision, no conscious approval of the demand or awareness that the demand exists. For Levinas autonomy is not and cannot be a primordial experience: the illusion of autonomy takes place only upon reflection, it exists only at the level of consciousness, which, he writes, is inaugurated by the entry of the third person in the primordial face-to-face relation.[95] In this primordial dimension, the dimension of a sensible – not self-conscious – subject, it is impossible to adopt the distance from oneself that would permit the illusion of autonomy. The moment of inspiration, of autonomy – the realization that I author what comes from elsewhere – only comes *anachronistically*, once I have already responded.

Autonomy is only a moment of recognition, of finding in oneself what someone else has put in there without the self being aware or self-conscious of it. In this respect, autonomy may be considered to be secondary to heteronomy, indeed it comes *after* it, as a way of perceiving it, of finding the order of the other in oneself. Because this discovery takes place only in the act of responding to the demand, one has not had the chance of choosing that responsibility, one's initiative is absent from the response. This paradox of the absence of initiative in the self's act of responding is precisely what Levinas calls passivity, the passivity that premises all activity. Activity is now the act of responding, and passivity refers to the suspension of every action which is not the self's obedience, that is, of every action taken from a position of autonomy that has forgotten the heteronomy it comes from. Passivity, we may speculate, would not be entirely unfamiliar to the Kantian subject whose will and duty must coincide. In order to identify with the demand that constitutes it, the subject, it would appear, would need to suspend or renounce any action that does not conform to the moral Law.

Could we then not affirm that the Levinasian paradox of autonomy and the paradox of autonomy we found in Kant are the same? The discovery of one's autonomy, whereby one finds the demand in oneself, already presupposes forgetting the demand's foreign origin, its alterity in the case of Kant, and also the alterity that has placed it in one in Levinas. The discovery of that order of obedience in oneself inaugurates self-consciousness and the illusion of autonomy. And isn't this conditioned inauguration of autonomy what philosophical accounts of self-consciousness must have caught a glimpse at, when they premise subjective constitution on the idea of guilt or debt, on an originary or congenital subordination? If this is right, autonomy, which I have argued is an effect of tragic heteronomy in modern subjectivity, seems a faithful description of the birth of self-consciousness. The autonomy whose primacy modern philosophy affirms is the effect of tragic heteronomy in so far as representing itself as subjected to an alienating force, as victim of objective necessity or fate, allows the self to preserve its economy or sense of autonomy intact, by preventing the irruption of real people in its world. The problem is that tragic heteronomy, as well as the illusion of autonomy it enables, confer on autonomy the status of founding principle at the price of foreclosing to consciousness (indeed, of excluding from conscience) the initial and constitutive (ethical) heteronomy.

To my mind, the primacy of heteronomous obligation that Levinas emphasizes as first philosophy configures Kant's moral theory but is not pursued by Kant himself. Even where Kant and Levinas might be said to be catching sight of the same structure, the heteronomous demand that inflects autonomy, there is a crucial difference between them. While Levinas emphasizes the heteronomous character of responsibility, Kant leaves aside the heteronomous determination that inflects the self's act of willing the Law, and instead develops the doctrine of autonomy as the principle of practical reason. It is too tempting to wonder what would have happened if Kant had given a more prominent position to the heteronomy that constitutes the subject of Law. Perhaps this subject would not have been tragic in the end. But then, affirming the primacy of heteronomy might have posed unsurpassable difficulties to the notions of freedom and autonomy. Thus, although Kant has a glimpse into that constitutive heteronomy (and that is perhaps what makes Levinas 'feel particularly close' to him),[96] the primacy of freedom and autonomy in his account of subjectivity make his subject ultimately tragic.

At the beginning of the chapter I proposed that tragic death provides an evasion from something worse than tragic, by which I meant infinite ethical responsibility. The question that I would like to entertain at this moment is whether tragic alienation and ethical responsibility, despite their differences, might not end up producing a similar effect on the self. Let us think, for example, of the other crucial point of coincidence between Kant and Levinas (in addition to the paradox of autonomy): the fact that the demand is incomprehensible, that it lies outside of content. Just consider, then, the anguish that the incommensurability of the demand may provoke in the self. If the other is invisible and unknowable, if the demand coming from it is radical and my responsibility infinite; if, furthermore, I have to assume full responsibility for the responsibilities of the other, would not the other of which Levinas speaks seem to come ultimately close to the objective necessity that alienates tragic subjects? In what sense, then, would the responsibility of the I that substitutes itself for the other be different from the tragic assumption of transcendent culpability, of a debt that produces guilty, but not responsible, tragic subjects?[97] Could ethical responsibility not be confused with the guilt of the self-conscious subject who has always already infringed a law of elusive content (think, for instance, of Althusser's subject of ideology)? What is the ultimate difference, in short, between the tragic acceptance of a transference of alien guilt and the self's substitution for the other as Levinas accounts for it? Expelled from my position of welcoming host, obsessed by my endless responsibility for the other to the point of substituting myself for him or her, I am reduced to the position of hostage. It is true that Levinas affirms that the heteronomy imposed by the other is non-alienating, but if the self does only receive ingratitude as a response to its acts, if it feels persecuted and a hostage, who assures that the other that enjoins the self, despite the impossibility of representing it, will not be essentialized and perceived, once again, as fate?

Does this mean that Levinas's ethical subject and the very free self-conscious subject of Western philosophy, a subject that ethics puts into question and that I consider tragic, ultimately come to coincide? If so, how can it be that the ethical subject who exposes itself to the other instead of comprehending it, who is not configured by the idea of freedom or the fiction of autonomy, who does not evade ethical responsibility, may end up experiencing an oppression or 'external control' similar to that lamented by the tragic subject who cooperates for the sake of intelligibility, who believes itself autonomous, who dies in order to avert the very call for responsibility (or the very emptiness of the Law) that configures the ethical subject? How can the tragic subject who dissolves for the sake of intelligibility and dies to evade responsibility come anywhere close to the sensible subject who is constituted precisely by that responsibility and lack of intelligibility?

These reservations, which are formulated from the perspective of autonomy, instantiate precisely the limits of that perspective. It is when one looks at the extreme ethical demand from the viewpoint of autonomy, of self-consciousness, that ethics appears worse than tragic. Ethics suspends my intelligibility as autonomous subject, an intelligibility that I could purchase at the price of a tragic death which is no longer available to me, because nothing can liberate me from a responsibility that belongs only to me. Thus, my point here is that the tragic heteronomy that post-Kantian philosophy ultimately espouses by not pursuing the heteronomous determination that informs autonomy constitutes an evasion from what I have called ethical heteronomy, from a primordial and radical ethical demand. If considered from the limited perspective of autonomy, this extreme order of obedience may indeed appear more terrible than tragic.

Tragic heteronomy and *ethical* heteronomy

Now we can return, in the end, to our initial question concerning the relation between the two heteronomies studied in this chapter. What is the rapport between tragic heteronomy and ethical heteronomy? Are they ultimately separable, do they coincide at any point? The relation is neither one of opposition, nor one of exact coincidence. Rather, they account for a similar experience from two different perspectives. *The tragic heteronomy on which autonomy is based*, generally taken as the worst heteronomy possible, *constitutes only a partial account of the heteronomy that enables autonomy, of the ethical heteronomy that it contributes to occlude*. Tragic heteronomy and the tragic subjectivity it founds account for the self's subordination only from the perspective of autonomy, and in so doing, they overlook the fact that the opposition or resistance that the other has always already offered to my self-consciousness is not violent, that it does not happen by force. Ethical heteronomy, in other words, is recast as tragic heteronomy from the viewpoint of autonomy. For this reason, tragic heteronomy affords important insights into ethical heteronomy in so far as it describes the act in which the self cooperates with an unchosen command placed by another (by objective necessity in the case of tragedy), a cooperation or approval that becomes evident only to the self as it is already responding. This might explain why they may become confused at some point.

But the pathos of a human being destroyed by an inexorable Other is so compelling, and its purported heroism so seductive, that the tragic view essentializes that Other as terrible, blinding the self to the primordial heteronomous structure of which it otherwise catches sight.

Far from rejecting the philosophical tradition of autonomy, then, Levinas offers important insights into it. Autonomy has a long and venerable history to which Levinas gives its due. One of the merits of classical philosophy, as well as of tragedy, was to enable a break with the mythical and religious determination that required the *participation* of an alienated human self. The autonomy made possible by that break, which reaches its peak with Kant's doctrine (itself a revolutionary break with the break with participation), however, has recourse to what Levinas calls new forms of participation or dissolution, which I have summed up under the rubric of tragic subjectivity. Because of its need for intelligibility, for achieving a position within the paradigm of debt, subjectivity creates modern versions of objective necessity (of an alienating otherness or fate), sacrificing ethical responsibility. What the initial break with heteronomy championed by the doctrine of autonomy ultimately conceals, in effect, is an avoidance of ethical obligation. Autonomy allows the subject to reject precisely what inflects it, namely, the very anarchic heteronomy with which an order coming from elsewhere slips into me 'like a thief'. As I see it, what Levinas's ethical thought suggests is that the fear of the Western self to have its (egotistical) freedom limited is a consequence of looking at ethical heteronomy and ethics from the limited angle of autonomy.[98]

Not unlike Kant's practical reason, tragic subjectivity might be imagined to recognize a primordial heteronomy that it eludes. While the attention that modern philosophy devotes to tragedy attests to the centrality of that heteronomy, what has been displaced (by means of creating modern versions of objective necessity) is its true source. According to Levinas, the source of heteronomy is a demand coming from the face of a living other, a demand that a self alienated by any version of objective necessity (fate, the Father, the Past, the Law) can only perceive as a threat. Hence Levinas's insistence on the need for the self to be an atheist, to remain separated from any subjectivating otherness, so that it can also remain unencompassed by the infinite that obligates it.

The non-atheist self-conscious subject evades what could have been ethical responsibility in favour of guilt or bad conscience. Bad conscience is generated in the impulse to escape responsibility that also produces the self-division that inaugurates self-consciousness. However tortured and poignant, bad conscience is narcissistic, according to Levinas. To this it might be objected that Levinas is keen on quoting 'Each of us is guilty before everyone for everyone, and I more than the others' from Dostoievsky's *Karamazov Brothers*.[99] But what seems a praise of guilt *per se* becomes, in light of Levinas's other allusions to guilt, an apology of guilt as the revelation of the collapse of egoist freedom. Guilt, in other words, represents neither the ultimate effect of ethical obligation, nor its goal. Rather than commending guilt as an end, Levinas envisages it as the condition that leads to the passivity or suspension of free activity that premises responsibility. But guilt is still self-serving, it still belongs in the framework of autonomy, and thus it must raise to responsibility. As long as we cling to our guilt, we are constituted by the paradigm of debt. In assuming guilt, what we ultimately do is cultivate the alienating relationship with a terrible Otherness that will allow us to preserve our self-centred world from the irruption of other people. If the paradigm of guilt is so alluring, it is because it ultimately reaffirms the sameness of the same, as I have argued in this book.[100]

When one is guilty, one does not *respond*. Thus, although the questioning of my freedom by the other may initially be experienced as guilt, guilt must rise to responsibility. 'Freedom is then inhibited not as countered by a resistance, but as arbitrary, guilty, timid; but in it guilt rises to responsibility.'[101] According to *Otherwise than Being* I have already responded before I even realize I am guilty. The realization of my guilt is now a trauma that constitutes me as one who has already acted on its guilt and responded, one who must justify itself by bringing on justice. The shift from guilt to responsibility is also the shift from tragic subjectivity to ethics, or from the intelligibility of self-consciousness to its suspension. With this suspension a new intelligibility comes forward, an intelligibility prior to consciousness and created in my act of responding.

Guilt is instrumental to the intelligibility of the self-conscious subject constituted by the moral Law, and it is in relation to intelligibility that we can trace a final important difference between the self-conscious subject and the sensible subject constituted by the ethical demand. However uncertain the situation in which the Law places the self, it constitutes the self as an intelligible being and gives it a position in the social symbolic order. As I argued in Chapter 3, though the subject's intelligibility is achieved by assuming guilt, by taking a position within the framework of debt, it affords the subject a self-perception as agent, however precarious and conditioned that agency may be. The demand from the face, in turn, produces a self whose intelligibility is suspended, who should not wait for reciprocity, and whose response and action do not offer the satisfaction of a task fulfilled, but rather aggravate the other's exigencies on the self. The agency of the subject in Levinas is no longer conferred by a larger horizon of being, but rather given a task by the other's demand. How to respond is only for me to decide, but my response must exceed the idea of intelligibility with which I am familiar. Even if I want to welcome the other (as the self does in *Totality and Infinity*), in *Otherwise than Being* the words 'welcoming' and 'hospitality' become problematic. As a welcoming host I would *be otherwise*, but as *otherwise than being* I become hostage, ready to substitute myself for the other.[102] It is no longer for me to decide that I am the one who *is* here, who *belongs* here, and who is *able* to receive someone who comes from elsewhere. Do I have that right to say 'welcome'? asks Derrida in his 'Word of Welcome' at the colloquium organized at the Collège International de Philosophie in December 1996 to mark the first anniversary of Levinas's death. 'Would what comes down to me in this way still be a decision? Do we have the right to give the name "decision" to a purely autonomous movement, even if it is one of welcoming or hospitality, that would proceed only from me, by me, and would simply deploy the possibilities of a subjectivity that is mine?'[103] With the reversion of my free action into passivity and thus into activity beyond activity, a different kind of intelligibility might be said to arise in my creative response to *the other's decision in me*.[104]

A politics beyond commitment

My creative response to the other who 'orders me by my own voice' is political, and Levinas is explicit about this. Politics is precisely 'the reverting of heteronomy into autonomy', that is, 'the possibility of finding, anachronously, the order in the obedience itself'. But we should not lose sight of the fact that the reconciliation of autonomy and heteronomy happens 'in an ambivalence whose diachrony is the signification itself'. I am heteronomously obligated in a primordial and anarchic way, but I believe myself autonomous when I believe myself the author of a decision made in me. According to the ambivalence of inspiration, autonomy is the illusion that inaugurates my perspective as self-conscious being. If '*the other's decision is made in me*, a decision made but with regard to which I am passive',[105] how does the consciousness enabled by my perception of myself as authoring what I have received allow me to act? I find the order only in my act of obeying, but how does my obedience, my action, unfold in the world in which I live?

'Consciousness is born as the presence of a third party.' Thus, the third party is 'the birth of the question: What do I have to do with justice? A question of consciousness.'[106] If the command obliged me only to the other, the question of life in community and politics would not arise, because neither consciousness nor self-consciousness would have emerged. But since my other is also the other of others, for whom he or she is responsible, the order makes me responsible for every third person. Our asymmetrical relation of proximity is *troubled* by the entry of the third party. 'The third party looks at me in the eyes of the other . . . [T]he epiphany of the face . . . attests the presence of the third party, the whole of humanity, in the eyes that look at me.'[107] The third is not an empirical fact, but rather a structure of the other, and thus the self's responsibility for the third party does not impose itself by force. It has always already been there, in my relation to the face, a face that demands justice not only for itself, but also for the rest of humanity.[108]

Yet, with its presence, the third party already 'introduces a contradiction in the saying', in the non-totalizing relation between the self and the other.[109] This contradiction is 'without equal and without precedent,' says Derrida, 'the terrible contradiction of the Saying by the Saying, Contra-Diction itself.'[110] As your other, the one for whom you are infinitely responsible, the third has always already been present. The third's presence introduces an equality that did not exist in my asymmetrical relation with you: we are both accountable for a second person. Hence the entry of the third requires the mediating activity of institutions.[111] It universalizes the intimacy between you and me, inaugurating the dimension of justice.[112] The third demands comparison of those who are incomparable,[113] equality of the unequal, substitution of the non-substitutable, fixation of the saying in the said, and 'outside from anarchy, the search for a principle'.[114] In the end, the entry of the third requires 'the latent birth of representation, logos, consciousness, work, the neutral notion of being'.[115] Very importantly, the irruption of the third brings on the birth of consciousness, it is 'the very fact of consciousness', because it provides the distance from which you and I become elements of a panoramic and can be represented.[116] 'It is thus that the neighbour becomes visible, and, looked at, presents himself. . . . The saying is fixed in a said, is written, becomes a book, law and science.'[117] Since the third makes me equal to the other, with whom I am now contemporaneous in the order of justice, 'there is also justice for me'.[118]

The third, in short, corrects the asymmetry between you and me: 'The relationship with the third party is an incessant correction of the asymmetry of proximity in which the face is looked at. . . . There is a betrayal of my anarchic relation with illeity, but also a new relationship with it.'[119] At first view, this 'betrayal' would seem a disloyalty to the other's height, for what happens then with the radicality of the order it places on me? But the 'new relationship' that emerges with consciousness, and which takes place in the dimension of politics, is the embodiment of the most radical obedience yet to the command. Which is why Levinas can affirm that justice is not 'a degradation of obsession . . . a limitation of anarchic responsibility, a neutralization of the glory of the Infinite. . . . The equality of all is borne by my inequality, the surplus of my duties over my rights.'[120] Levinas conceives the rational political order as emerging from the asymmetrical relation between the self and the other.[121] Although justice requires *being-with-the-others*, that is, representation, contemporaneity and contiguity, it is given meaning by my *being-for-the-other*.[122] Consequently, the possibility of an 'egalitarian and just state' rests upon 'the irreducible responsibility of the one for all'.[123] Politics is not born from rational necessity, but rather from the face-to-face. And if the relation between ethics and politics appears *ambiguous*, it appears so from the perspective of the self-conscious subject who, forgetting the primordial demand from another that constitutes it, believes itself autonomous. This happens diachronously, in 'an ambivalence which, in the present, is an *ambiguity*'.[124]

In what concerns the rapport between ethics and politics, Levinas's thought frequently meets two interrelated objections. It is either criticized for betraying the primacy of heteronomy (that is, the self's infinite obligation towards the other) in its discourse on politics, or for not providing a convincing passage between ethics and political life (that is, for placing 'ethics beyond the world of being and politics').[125] What these critiques overlook, in my opinion, is the fact that Levinas's ethical thought does not present itself as an alternative to subjectivity (if it did, ethics and politics would necessarily be at odds), but rather as a theory of the subject. Levinas does not indict the self-conscious subject, as I hope to have shown. Instead, he takes a step back to underscore that self-consciousness rests on the heteronomous responsibility of a subject constituted by an ethical demand. What these objections ultimately miss, in other words, is precisely Levinas's proximity to Kant. The heteronomous determination of autonomy that Levinas privileges also informs Kant's practical philosophy, but must be left aside for the sake of the primacy of autonomy which is the ground of his ethical theory. Critical emphasis on the lack of rapport between ethics and politics is the price that Levinas must pay for privileging the insight that Kant does not pursue.

The inextricable link between ethics and politics is dictated by the fact that I find myself infinitely obligated by an other within me. That I have been constituted by an order from another, but I perceive myself as autonomous from the perspective of consciousness, means that the inseparability of ethics and politics has always already been realized within the subject, within me. 'What has to be acknowledged,' remarks Critchley, 'is the irreducibly heteronomous opening of autonomy (which does not at all mean that autonomy is abandoned), the unconditional priority of the other (which does not mean at all that the economy of the same can be done without).'[126] Politics understood in the broadest sense is already ethical, already demanded in the demand. And because the tension between ethics and politics is placed in the subject since its very constitution, the question of politics has always already been asked. When Levinas affirms that the way from proximity to the rational order of justice 'leads from responsibility to problems',[127] these 'problems' do not primarily refer to the logical challenge that Levinas's deliberate use of anachronism poses to theoretical consciousness (the limited perspective from which Levinas's understanding of the rapport between ethics and politics appears inconsistent). The one who has problems, who is in trouble, is none other than the subject, me. Politics becomes *my problem* as self-conscious subject, a problem that I have already undertaken with my responsibility for the other, as obedience to the other. If I am a political subject at all, it is because I am already obeying a demand to which I did not choose to respond, because I am acting on the decision that another has made in me.

The problem is not how to bridge ethics and politics, for ethics is already political, and it exists for the sake of the political.[128] My problem is, rather, how to make the ethical demand inflect every political act in each singular context, beyond socially sanctioned normativity. This would be a politics that exceeds the political space of reciprocity and representation. It would be a politics beyond theoretical consciousness and even beyond commitment, because in committing I can still assume what I take up as my duty.[129] How might we create a politics that rests on heteronomous obligation without dictating the itinerary of the response (yet without falling into a vaporous ethics of generous imaginings)?[130] How can I remain faithful to the vertigo of acting without assurance, while being aware that my action betrays the demand? How am I to act on the decision made anew in me, which renders me more responsible as I respond?

Notes

Introduction

1. The words I quote are from Ernesto Laclau, in 'Ethics, Politics and Radical Democracy: A Response to Simon Critchley'. *Cultural Machine*, 4 (2002), the Ethico-Political Issue, which in my opinion convey the gist of Critchley's initial essay, 'Ethics, Politics and Radical Democracy: The History of a Disagreement' (in the same issue of *Cultural Machine*).
2. Jacques Derrida, *Adieu to Emmanuel Levinas*, trans. Pascale-Anne Brault and Michael Naas (Stanford: Stanford University Press, 1999), p. 117, translation slightly altered. Derrida refers here to Levinas's view on the political.
3. Walter Benjamin, *The Origin of German Tragic Drama*, trans. John Osborne (London: Verso, 1985), p. 115.
4. Martha Nussbaum, *The Fragility of Goodness: Luck and Ethics in Greek Tragedy and Philosophy* (Cambridge: Cambridge University Press, 1986), p. 127.
5. Here I am inspired by Roland Barthes, *On Racine*, trans. Richard Howard (Berkeley and Los Angeles: University of California Press, 1992), pp. 44–7 and Paul Ricoeur, *The Symbolism of Evil*, trans. Emerson Buchanan (Boston: Beacon Press, 1967), pp. 212–20.
6. See Barthes, *On Racine*, pp. 44–7.
7. See, for example, G. W. F. Hegel's *Aesthetics: Lectures on Fine Art*, trans. T. M. Knox (Oxford: Clarendon Press, 1975), vol. 2, p. 1215.
8. See description of Chapter 3 above.
9. Emmanuel Levinas, *Otherwise than Being*, trans. Alphonso Lingis (Pittsburgh: Duquesne University Press, 1998), p. 157.

Chapter 1

1. Samir Amin, 'Imperialism and Globalization', *Monthly Review* 53.2 (June 2001), pp. 6–24.
2. See Paul Ricoeur, *The Symbolism of Evil*, trans. Emerson Buchanan (Boston: Beacon Press, 1993), pp. 118 and 120–1.
3. Jean-Pierre Vernant, *Myth and Tragedy in Ancient Greece*, trans. Janet Lloyd (New York: Zone Books, 1988), pp. 46–7 and 77.
4. Ibid., pp. 26–7.
5. Ibid., p. 89.
6. Ibid., p. 33. See also Benjamin, *The Origins of German Tragic Drama*, pp. 115–16.
7. Martha Nussbaum, *The Fragility of Goodness. Luck and Ethics in Greek Tragedy and Philosophy* (Cambridge: Cambridge University Press, 1986), p. 126.
8. See Vernant, *Myth and Tragedy in Ancient Greece*, p. 89.
9. Ibid., p. 90.

10. See ibid., p. 31.
11. Raymond Williams, *Modern Tragedy* (Stanford: Stanford University Press, 1987), pp. 51–2.
12. Ibid., p. 53.
13. Ibid., pp. 52–3.
14. On the precariousness of will in Greek tragedy and society, see Vernant, pp. 49–84. On the ambiguity of tragic action, see pp. 27 and 83.
15. Speaking about the 'madness' of Eteocles as simultaneously inflicted from the outside and originating inside, Vernant writes: 'The murderous madness that henceforth characterizes his *ethos* is not simply a human emotion; it is a daemonic power in every way beyond him. It envelops him in the dark cloud of *ate*, penetrating him as a god takes possession of whomever he has decided to bring low, *from within*, in a form of mania, a lussa, a delirium that breeds criminal acts of hubris. The madness of Eteocles *is present within him, but that does not prevent it also appearing as extraneous and exterior to him.* It is identified with the malignant power of defilement that, once engendered by ancient crimes, is transmitted from one generation to the next right down the Labdacid line.' Ibid., p. 35, my italics.
16. *Antigone*, in Sophocles, *The Three Theban Plays. Antigone, Oedipus the King, Oedipus at Colonus*, trans. Robert Fagles (Harmondsworth: Penguin Classics, 1984), p. 77.
17. The opacity of language replicates these ambiguities by expressing both the contradictions in the realm of authority and the hero's oscillation between self-determination and submission through several, contradictory layers of meaning. See Vernant, *Myth and Tragedy in Ancient Greece*, p. 114.
18. On the irony of self-control, see Charles Segal, *Interpreting Greek Tragedy* (Ithaca and London: Cornell University Press, 1986), p. 147.
19. Vernant, in *Myth and Tragedy in Ancient Greece*, p. 77.
20. Ibid., p. 27.
21. Ibid., p. 47.
22. 'Everything one says about Greek religion must always be tempered by the following consideration: there was never one Greek theology, but an overlapping not only of cults properly so called, but also of diverse religious syntheses attempted by reformers, poets, and religious propagandists, none of which ever succeeded in bringing the others into a single system. There is the authority of Delphi and there is the 'telestic madness' of Dionysus; the latter invades the domain of the former; but Apollo restrains Dionysus and embraces him by legislating for his cult and moderating his ecstasy' (Ricoeur, *The Symbolism of Evil*, p. 230). See also Williams, *Modern Tragedy*, pp. 17–18.
23. Ricoeur, *The Symbolism of Evil*, p. 220.
24. This questioning is not radical, since the cult of Dionysus takes place within the Apollonian institutional framework.
25. For other instances of inconsistencies in the divine world, see Ricoeur, *The Symbolism of Evil*, p. 220 and Vernant, *Myth and Tragedy in Ancient Greece*, pp. 39–40.
26. 'Here is the dilemma. Whether I let them stay or drive / them off, it is a hard course and will hurt. Then, since / the burden of the case is here, and rests on me, / I shall select judges of manslaughter, and swear / them in,

establish a court into all time to come / . . . They shall swear to make no judgment that is not / just, and make clear where in this action the truth lies.' *The Eumenides* in Aeschylus, *Oresteia*, eds David Greene and Richmond Lattimore, trans. Richmond Lattimore (Chicago: The University of Chicago Press, 1953), p. 152. See also Lattimore's 'Introduction', p. 7. Since I will be referring to two different translations of *The Eumenides*, I will specify the translator in each citation.

27. Ricoeur, *The Symbolism of Evil*, pp. 215–16.
28. *The Eumenides*, trans. Lattimore, p. 152. See Walter Benjamin, *The Origin of German Tragic Drama*, trans. John Osborne (London: Verso, 1992), pp. 116–19 and Vernant, *Myth and Tragedy in Ancient Greece*, p. 83.
29. Vernant, *Myth and Tragedy in Ancient Greece*, p. 38.
30. Ibid., p. 38.
31. Benjamin, *The Origin of German Tragic Drama*, p. 115.
32. See Ricoeur, *The Symbolism of Evil*, p. 230.
33. Louis Althusser, 'Ideology and Ideological State Apparatuses', in *Lenin and Philosophy*, trans. Ben Brewster (New York: Monthly Review Press, 1971), pp. 177–83. See Chapter 3 below.
34. *Oedipus at Colonus*, in Sophocles, *Oedipus the King. Oedipus at Colonus. Antigone*, eds David Greene and Richmond Lattimore, trans. David Greene, Robert Fitzgerald and Elizabeth Wyckoff (Chicago: University of Chicago Press, 1954), p. 122.
35. Ibid., p. 125.
36. Ibid., p. 121.
37. Ibid., p. 139. Interestingly, it is current practice with critics writing on *Oedipus at Colonus* (Ricoeur among them) to refer to Oedipus as a wise old man. It is in this play, however, that Oedipus curses his sons, and appears furious with Polynices and Creon, displaying an anger about which even the Chorus makes a remark. See Chapter 2 below.
38. There are, however, some instances in which the oracles of the gods are considered contingent, at least temporarily. In *Oedipus at Colonus* Antigone tries to persuade Polynices not to take action and thus not to follow the oracle of Apollo and his father's curse: 'Withdraw your troops to Argos as soon as you can. / Do not go to your own death and your city's!' (p. 141). Later, when Polynices refuses to renounce his plan of invading Thebes, Antigone adds: 'But see how you fulfil his [Oedipus's] prophecies! / Did he not cry that you should kill each other?' (p. 141). Polynices, however, offers inconsistent reasons as to why he cannot renounce his plan. At first he cannot back off because, although he recognizes that 'It is shameful to run' (p. 141), 'it is also shameful / To be a laughing-stock to a younger brother' (p. 141). Eventually Polynices disclaims his own agency, attributing it to the gods: 'All that / Rests with the powers that are over us, – / Whether it must be so or otherwise' (p. 142). Similarly, in the play *Antigone*, Tiresias gives Creon the opportunity to revoke his decision: 'All men may err / but error once committed, he's no fool / not yet unfortunate, who gives up his stiffness / and cures the trouble he has fallen in. / Stubbornness and stupidity are twins. / Yield to the dead. Why goad him where he lies? / What use to kill the dead a second time?' (*Antigone*, trans. Elizabeth Wyckoff, p. 193). But when Creon reaffirms his decree in spite of the seer's warning,

Tiresias moves on to announce the almost immediate extinction of Creon's kin as prophesied by the Oracle ('You'll bring me to speak the unspeakable, very soon', p. 195). Significantly, it is not until Tiresias speaks the prophecy of the gods that the prophecy is fulfilled. When Creon repents upon hearing it, it is already too late.

39. *Antigone*, trans. Elizabeth Wyckoff, p. 183.
40. A little earlier in the play, the Chorus tells Creon: 'We think – unless our age is cheating us – / that what you say is sensible and right' (p. 182). The equation of speaking well and being right also operates in *Oedipus at Colonus*, where the Chorus tells Oedipus: 'Old man / This argument of yours compels our wonder. / It was not feebly worded. I am content / that higher authorities should judge this matter' (p. 92), and then makes a case for Oedipus before Theseus: 'My lord, our friend is worthy; he has had / Disastrous fortune; yet he deserves our comfort' (p. 125). This same play again confirms the importance given to speech when both Theseus and the Chorus ask Oedipus to grant his estranged son Polynices, at least, the right to speak (pp. 131 ff.).
41. *The Eumenides*, in Aeschylus, *The Oresteia. Agamemnon, The Libation Bearers, The Eumenides*, trans. Robert Fagles (London: Penguin Books, 1977) p. 253.
42. Vernant, *Myth and Tragedy in Ancient Greece*, p. 81.
43. *The Eumenides*, trans. Lattimore, p. 150.
44. *Seven against Thebes* offers another instance of this oscillation in the figure of Eteocles. Eteocles appears one time as a rational statesman, and the next as the passionate murderer of his brother, following Oedipus' curse. See Vernant, *Myth and Tragedy in Ancient Greece*, p. 36.
45. Although in the first half of the play Creon presents himself as a statesman fulfilling his duty to the city, as soon as Tiresias spells out the prophecy against him, Creon undergoes a 'change of character': he identifies his rules with his own desire and necessity is no longer dictated by his own authority, but rather by the externally imposed will of the gods: 'How hard, abandonment of my desire. / but I can fight necessity no more' (p. 196). On the protagonist's desire for objective necessity, see Chapter 2 below.
46. 'There I shall hide her in a hollowed cave / living, and leave her just so much to eat / as clears the city from the guilt of death' (trans. Wyckoff, p. 184). 'Take her away at once and open up / the tomb I spoke of. Leave her there alone. / There let her choose: death, or a buried life. / No stain of guilt upon us in this case, / but she is exiled from our life on earth' (p. 189). Creon's oscillation between assuming and disclaiming responsibility runs through the whole play. Although eventually he does take responsibility for her death, at the conclusion he ultimately attributes his actions to fate. It is ironical, after Creon's efforts to disclaim responsibility for his acts, that when Antigone hangs herself with her veil in the cave, Haemon immediately blames Creon for her death, and Creon accepts his own agency in it. At the moment of his punishment, finally, Creon claims that a god sent him madness at the moment of making a decision (against Antigone, his son, the people and Tiresias' advice): 'It was a god who struck, / who has weighted my head with disaster; he drove me to wild strange ways, / his heave heel on my joy' (p. 201). At the end of the play, in any case, both Creon and the Chorus reaffirm fate's power. Chorus: 'Pray not again. No

mortal can escape / the doom prepared for him.' Creon: 'Take me away at once, the frantic man who killed / my son, against my meaning. I cannot rest. / My life is warped past cure. My fate has struck me down' (p. 203).

47. 'Untouched by wasting disease, / not paying the price of the sword, / of your own motion you go' (trans. Wyckoff, p. 187). In reply, Antigone attributes her death to a god ('My own putting to death a god has planned like hers [Tantalus' daughter's]' p. 188) and to her fate (p. 189). The Chorus largely supports Creon, reaffirming his right to rule as he pleases ('For you can make such rulings as you will / about the living and about the dead', p. 166), accusing Antigone of being too daring ('You went to the furthest verge / of daring, but there you found / the high foundation of justice, and fell', p. 188), suggesting that Antigone was driven by mad love for Creon's son, who has just opposed his father's decision ('Love unconquered in fight, love who falls on our havings. / Your rest in the blood of a girl's unwithered face. / . . . Who has you within him is mad', pp. 186–7), that she is as uncontrolled as her father Oedipus ('The girl is bitter. She's her father's child. / She cannot yield to trouble; nor could he', p. 174; 'The same tempest of mind / as ever, controls the girl', p. 190). Finally, the Chorus reproaches Antigone's self-sufficiency ('Your self-sufficiency has brought you down', p. 189), which has here the sense of stubbornness and disobedience.

48. 'Quick as you can. The gods move very fast / when they bring ruin on misguided man' (trans. Wyckoff, p. 196). Only in one more occasion, when the Guard announces that Polynices has been buried, does the Chorus cautiously suggest that perhaps Creon was not right: 'Lord, while he spoke, my mind kept on debating. / Isn't this action possibly a god's?' (p. 168), an insinuation that Creon angrily rejects.

49. 'The coherence of character is in fact shown by the way in which its individual qualities contradict one another', says Brecht, in John Drakakis and Naomi Conn Liebler, eds., *Tragedy* (London and New York: Longman, 1998), p. 103. By considering the inconsistency of character to be a need, Brecht's formulation about theater in general is more accurately descriptive of tragedy than Aristotle's idea of coherent incoherence: '[The character should be] consistent. If the model for the representation is somebody inconsistent, and such a character is intended, even so it should be consistently inconsistent' (Aristotle, *Poetics*, 54a26–28, 19).

50. The focus on character, not on action, in most modern and contemporary readings of tragedy, accounts for my decision to devote careful attention here to the oscillations of action.

51. Vernant, *Myth and Tragedy in Ancient Greece*, p. 45.

52. Aristotle discusses this rift in his *Nicomachean Ethics*, trans. Terence Irwin (Indianapolis: Hackett, 1984). See, for example, his discussion about voluntary and involuntary actions at the beginning of Book III, especially 1110a 28.

53. This is the kind of action that Aristotle describes as 'mixed' in *Nicomachean Ethics*, 1110a24–25.

54. *Antigone*, trans. Wickoff, pp. 201 and 203, respectively.

55. Walter Benjamin, *The Origin of German Tragic Drama*, p. 131.

56. Roland Barthes, *On Racine*, trans. Richard Howard (Berkeley and Los Angeles: University of California Press, 1992), p. 36. Barthes finds an excep-

tion to sterile formal deliberation in the *real* deliberation of King Danaos in Aeschylus' *Suppliants* (p. 36, footnote 2). Although the protagonist's deliberation is characteristic of tragedy, *Oedipus Rex* constitutes an exception, since Oedipus' lack of reflection and deliberation is due to lack of knowledge. See Chapter 2 below.

57. Barthes, *On Racine*, p. 36.
58. 'A heavy doom is disobedience, but heavy, too, if I shall rend my own child, the adornment of my house, polluting a father's hands with streams of slaughtered maiden's blood close by the altar. Which of these is without evils? How should I become a deserter, failing in my duty to the alliance?' Aeschylus, *Agamemnon*, trans. Martha Nussbaum, *The Fragility of Goodness* (Cambridge: Cambridge University Press, 1986), p. 35. As Nussbaum points out, here the need to fulfil one divine command is motivated by another one. If Agamemnon does not fulfil Artemis' demand of sacrificing Iphigenia, he also disobeys the god Zeus Xenio's command to lay siege to Troy, since his expedition will remain becalmed (p. 35). Vernant also uses Agamemnon's dilemma as an example of lack of choice (*Myth and Tragedy in Ancient Greece*, p. 72), arguing that this sort of decision 'does not belong to the category of will' (p. 75). See also pp. 51ff. and 75–84.
59. *Seven against Thebes*, in Aeschylus, *The Suppliant Maidens and The Persians. Seven against Thebes and Prometheus Bound*, eds David Greene and Richmond Lattimore, trans. David Greene (Chicago: The University of Chicago Press, 1956), pp. 113–14. Eteocles refers explicitly to his lack of choice, and locates its origin in a defilement attached to the kin of Laius, the race of Oedipus: 'It is the God that drives this matter on. / Since it is so – on, on with favouring wind / this wave of hell that has engulfed for its share / all kin of Laius . . .' (p. 114).
60. Nussbaum, *The Fragility of Goodness*, pp. 34–5.
61. Vernant, *Myth and Tragedy in Ancient Greece*, p. 52. Ricoeur locates the origin of the tragic lack of choice in the fact that divine power is not defined or personalized: '*Moira* denotes the most impersonal aspect of that power [of a reserve of non-personalized power]; it is the "portion", the "share", the "lot" imparted to a man beyond his choice; it is the non-choice of choice, the necessity that sur-charges and over-determines his acts. . . . Thus the theology of fault tends to sustain a reserve of divinity that resists the tendency, triumphant everywhere else, to individualize and visualize divine powers' (*The Symbolism of Evil*, pp. 215–16).
62. Ricoeur, *The Symbolism of Evil*, p. 215.
63. Nussbaum, *The Fragility of Goodness*, p. 50. See also Ricoeur, *The Symbolism of Evil*, p. 228.
64. Ricoeur, *The Symbolism of Evil*, p. 228.
65. Nussbaum, *The Fragility of Goodness*, p. 35 and Vernant, *Myth and Tragedy in Ancient Greece*, p. 72.
66. Aeschylus, *Agamemnon*, quoted in Nussbaum, *The Fragility of Goodness*, p. 35.
67. Vernant, *Myth and Tragedy in Ancient Greece*, p. 72.
68. *Agamemnon*, Nussbaum's translation, p. 35.
69. *Seven against Thebes*, Nussbaum's translation, p. 38. As Nussbaum observes, the Chorus is concerned not with the course of action the heroes are to take,

which they perceive as inevitable, but with the passion with which they have come to comply with the gods' desire, and to forget the opposing claim (p. 38). 'Why are you so eager, child?' the Chorus asks Eteocles, once he has decided to fight his brother Polynices. 'Do not let some spear-craving delusion, filling your spirit, bear you away. Cast out the authority of this bad passion' (p. 38). Eteocles replies: 'Since it is clear that the situation is controlled by a god, it is fitting to go quickly' (pp. 38–9). Similarly, in *Agamemnon*: 'And when he had slipped his neck through the yoke-strap of necessity, blowing his thought in an impious change of direction, from that moment he changed his mind and turned to thinking the all-daring. For men are made bold by base-counseling wretched madness' (p. 36).

70. See Vernant, *Myth and Tragedy in Ancient Greece*, p. 53.
71. On the retroactive character of tragic guilt, see Barthes, *On Racine*, pp. 38–40 and 46–7, and Ricoeur, *The Symbolism of Evil*, pp. 213–17.
72. Vernant, *Myth and Tragedy in Ancient Greece*, p. 62.
73. Barthes, *On Racine*, pp. 39–40.
74. See Barthes, *On Racine*, pp. 38–40, Ricoeur, *The Symbolism of Evil*, pp. 214–17.
75. Lattimore, 'Introduction' to *Oresteia*, p. 15.
76. Aristotle, *Poetics*, 52a23.
77. About the unexpected result of tragic action, see Vernant, *Myth and Tragedy in Ancient Greece*, p. 32 and Aryeh Kosman, 'Acting: Drama as the Mimesis of Praxis', in *Essays on Aristotle Poetics*, ed. Amélie O. Rorty (Princeton: Princeton University Press, 1992), p. 65.
78. For a fascinating study of reversal in *Oedipus Rex*, see Vernant, *Myth and Tragedy in Ancient Greece*, pp. 117–39, and also Charles Segal, *Oedipus Tyrannus* (New York: Twayne, 1993), pp. 114–33.
79. Barthes, *On Racine*, p. 43.
80. See George Steiner, *The Death of Tragedy* (New York, Oxford: Oxford University Press, 1980), p. 353. This section is inspired in Barthes, *On Racine*, pp. 44–7 and Ricoeur, *The Symbolism of Evil*, pp. 212–20.
81. Ricoeur, *The Symbolism of Evil*, p. 212.
82. 'Thus the non-distinction between the divine and the diabolical is the implicit theme of the tragic theology and anthropology. Perhaps, . . . it was this non-distinction that could not be thought through right to the end and that caused the downfall of tragedy and its vehement condemnation by philosophy in the second book of the Republic. But if the feeling that good and evil are identical in God resists thought, it is projected in dramatic works that give rise to indirect, but nevertheless troubling, reflection' (Ricoeur, *The Symbolism of Evil*, p. 214).
83. Barthes, *On Racine*, pp. 44–7. Ricoeur, *The Symbolism of Evil*, pp. 212–20. 'If there is a tragic vision of man', remarks Paul Ricoeur, 'that is because it is the other face of a tragic vision of the divine' (p. 212).
84. Ricoeur, *The Symbolism of Evil*, p. 219.
85. Benjamin, *The Origin of German Tragic Drama*, pp. 109–10.
86. Ibid., p. 109. What seemed to be a judgment of the hero becomes, according to Benjamin, a trial of the Olympians in which the hero acts as a witness (p. 109).
87. Ricoeur, *The Symbolism of Evil*, p. 219.

88. Ibid., p. 214.
89. On the retroactive character of guilt, see Barthes, *On Racine*, pp. 38–40 and 46–7, and Ricoeur, *The Symbolism of Evil*, pp. 213–17.
90. Ricoeur, *The Symbolism of Evil*, p. 217.
91. Ibid.
92. Barthes, *On Racine*, p. 45.
93. Ibid., p. 124.
94. See ibid., pp. 45–7.
95. Ricoeur, *The Symbolism of Evil*, p. 217.
96. Barthes, *On Racine*, p. 46. 'This is what Racine expresses so well apropos of Phaedra when he says that for her, crime itself is a punishment. Phaedra's entire effort consists in fulfilling her transgression, i.e., in absolving God' (p. 124).
97. Ibid., p. 46.
98. Ibid., pp. 38–40, and Ricoeur, *The Symbolism of Evil*, pp. 313–17.
99. Barthes, *On Racine*, p. 44.
100. Ricoeur, *The Symbolism of Evil*, p. 215. On the non-individualization of divine power and its abstraction as 'daimon', see also Vernant, *Myth and Tragedy in Ancient Greece*, p. 36.
101. Barthes, *On Racine*, p. 45.
102. Ibid.
103. The words are George Steiner's. In his definition, tragedy is 'the dramatic testing of a view of reality in which man is taken to be an unwelcome guest to the world' (*The Death of Tragedy*, p. xi). The word 'testing' implies that when reenacted in each drama, the tragic view of reality undergoes a process of redefinition. Since the tragic fable does not provide any solution, each tragic drama becomes an extensive exploration (thus the word 'testing') of tragic conflict.
104. Slavoj Žižek, *The Plague of Fantasies* (London: Verso, 1997), p. 219.
105. For this conception of agency see Slavoj Žižek, *The Sublime Object of Ideology*, (London: Verso, 1989), p. 220.
106. Žižek, *The Plague of Fantasies*, p. 221.
107. See Chapter 5 below.

Chapter 2

1. Euripides, *Hippolytus*, in *Alcestis. The Medea. The Heracleidae. Hippolytus*, eds David Grene and Richmond Lattimore, intro. Lattimore, trans. David Green (Chicago: University of Chicago Press, 1955), p. 171. The interpretation of these lines has posed critical difficulties, as evidenced in the diverging translations offered. W.S. Barret proposes the following literal translation: 'But whatever else there may be that is dearer than life, darkness enwraps it from our sight in cloud. Love-lorn we show ourselves for this glittering something here on earth, through ignorance of another life and the non-revealing of what lies below; they are mere tales whereon we are borne' (*Hippolytos*, ed., intro. and commentary by W.S. Barret [Oxford: Clarendon Press, 1964], p. 196). Unless the Nurse is taken to be '*affirming* our love of life', remarks Barret, these lines are inconsistent with the rest of the play, and on this ground they should be considered spurius.

For information about this critical disagreement, of great interest to us in so far as it manifests the resistance that these lines have provoked among Greek scholars, see Barret's edition of *Hippolytos*, pp. 196–9.

2. Jacques Lacan, *The Seminar, Book VII. The Ethics of Psychoanalysis, 1959–1960*, trans. Denis Porter (New York: Norton, 1992), p. 313, comma added.

3. Sophocles, *Oedipus at Colonus* in *Three Teban Plays*, trans. Robert Fagles (London: Penguin, 1984), p. 358.

4. Lacan, *Le séminaire, Livre VIII. Le transfert* (Paris: Éditions du Seuil, 1992), p. 358.

5. See Alenka Zupančič, *Ethics of the Real. Kant, Lacan* (London: Verso, 2000), p. 250.

6. *Agamemnon*, Nussbaum's translation in *Fragility of Goodness: Luck and Ethics in Greek Tragedy and Philosophy* (Cambridge: Cambridge University Press, 1986), p. 35.

7. See Alenka Zupančič's *Ethics of the Real*.

8. On the creation of 'necessary fictions' see Chapter 3.

9. Lacan, *Le transfert*, p. 384.

10. Zupančič, *Ethics of the Real*, p. 186.

11. On different occasions, Lacan himself proposes diverging readings of the character of Oedipus, sometimes as willingly assuming a position within the framework of guilt, others as unyielding to the end and refusing to be reconciled with his destiny. For an account of these different readings, see Zupancic, *Ethics of the Real*, p. 178–80.

12. When the leader of the Chorus tells him 'Better to die than be alive and blind', Oedipus, who has just gouged out his eyes, replies: 'What I did was best – Don't lecture me!' (Sophocles, *Oedipus the King* in *Three Theban Plays*, pp. 242–3).

13. Sophocles, *Oedipus at Colonus*, p. 358.

14. This passage, quoted by Franz Rosenzweig in *The Star of Redemption*, trans. William W. Hallo (Notre Dame, IN: Notre Dame Press, 1985), is in turn cited by Walter Benjamin in *The Origin of German Tragic Drama*, trans. John Osborne (London and New York: Verso, 1992).

15. Hegel, *Lectures on Fine Art*, in Lionel Abel, *Moderns on Tragedy* (Greenwich, Conn.: Fawcett Publications, 1967), p. 374. For complete text see Hegel, *Aesthetics: Lectures on Fine Art*, trans. T.M. Knox (Oxford: Clarendon Press, 1975), vol. 2, p. 1215.

16. All references to Jean Racine's *Phèdre* are to *Phèdre*, ed. Christian Delmas and Georges Forestier (Paris: Gallimard, 1995). With minor adaptations, I have used Margaret Rawling's translation in *Phèdre* (London: Penguin, 1989).

17. For an excellent study of the emergence of a new subjectivity in seventeenth-century absolutist states and theatrical stages, see Mitchell Greenberg, *Canonical States, Canonical Stages. Oedipus, Othering, and Seventeenth-Century Drama* (Minneapolis and London: University of Minnesota Press, 1994).

18. My writing on Racine's *Phédre* was initially inspired by Simon Critchley's suggestive essay 'I Want to Die, I Hate my Life – Phaedra's Malaise' (forthcoming). I am grateful to Critchley, from whose essay I borrow freely here, and to which I respond. My complete response, 'I Love to Hate My Life or

the Allure of Guilt: A Response to Simon Critchley', will appear together with his essay (forthcoming).

19. Roland Barthes, *On Racine*, trans. Richard Howard (Berkeley and Los Angeles: University of California Press, 1992), p. 36.

20. Just after confessing her secret to Onenone, she narrates the beginning of her dark passion at the first sight of Hippolytus:

> 'Je le vis, je rougis, je pâlis à sa vue;
> Un trouble s'éleva dans mon âme éperdue;
> Mes yeux ne voyaient plus, je ne pouvais parler;
> Je sentis tout mon corps et transir et brûler . . .
> Je l'évitais partout. O comble de misère!
> Mes yeux le retrouvaient dans les traits de son père' (Racine, *Phèdre*, Act I.iii, pp. 48–9).

I saw him. First I blushed and then grew pale; At sight of him my troubled soul was lost. My eyes no longer saw, I could not speak; I felt my blood run icy and then burn . . . I fled his presence everywhere, but found him – Crowing misery! – in his father's face! (trans. Margaret Rawlings, pp. 51 and 53).

21. See Jean Racine, *Phèdre*, Act II.v, pp. 66–7. See Critchley's comments on this remarkable passage.

22. Racine, *Phèdre*, Act IV.vi, pp. 94–5.

23. Racine, *Phèdre*. trans. Margaret Rawlings, pp. 138–9.

24. Critchley, 'I Want to Die, I Hate my Life'.

25. See Zupančič, *The Ethics of the Real*, p. 182 for a similar formulation.

26. Slavoj Žižek underscores this important distinction by rereading Kant's *'Du kannst, denn du sollst!* (You can, because you must) as 'There is no excuse for *accomplishing* one's duty!' (*The Plague of Fantasies* [London: Verso, 1997], p. 222). See also Chapter 2 of *The Indivisible Remainder* (London: Verso, 1996).

27. On Phaedra's inability to die, see Critchley, 'I Want to Die, I Hate my Life'.

28. Racine, *Phèdre*, Act IV,vi, pp. 94–5.

29. Racine, *Phèdre*, trans. Margaret Rawlings, pp. 138–9.

30. See Barthes, *On Racine*, p. 21, and Critchley, 'I Want to Die, I Hate my Life'.

31. Barthes, *On Racine*, p. 21.

32. See Critchley's reflections on languor.

33. Barthes, *On Racine*, and Critchley, 'I Want to Die, I Hate my Life'.

34. Critchley, 'I Want to Die, I Hate my Life'.

35. See Chapter 5.

36. See the final session of Lacan's *Seminar VII*, 'The Paradoxes of Ethics *or* Have You Acted in Conformity with Your Desire?' in *The Ethics of Psychoanalysis*, pp. 311–25. See also 'The Jouissance of Transgression' and 'The Death Drive', in *The Ethics of Psychoanalysis*, pp. 191–204 and pp. 205–217, and especially the six sessions under the rubric 'The Transference and the Drive' in Seminar XI, *The Four Fundamental Concepts of Psychoanalysis*, ed. Jacques-Alain Miller, trans. Alan Sheridan (New York: Norton, 1998), pp. 123–200.

37. Her own desire, now located in the desiring self, becomes the unknowable 'desire of the other', that is, the object-cause of our own desire: 'the image of Antigone . . . causes the Chorus to lose its head, makes the just appear

unjust, and makes the Chorus transgress all limits, including casting aside any respect it might have for the edicts of the city. Nothing is more moving than ... the desire that visibly emanates from the eyelids of this admirable girl' (Lacan, *The Ethics of Psychoanalysis*, p. 281). For a ground-breaking reading of Antigone from the viewpoint of kinship, see Judith Butler, *Antigone's Claim. Kinship Between Life and Death* (New York: Columbia University Press, 2000).

38. Lacan, *The Ethics of Psychoanalysis*, p. 280, my italics. See also p. 270.
39. Quoted in Lacan, ibid., p. 271.
40. In my view, the tragic character in *Antigone* is not Antigone herself, but Creon. Creon is the one who is torn between two impossible alternatives, between enforcing the rules of the city or fulfilling his familial duties. Unlike Creon, Antigone is never divided, she is clear about her course of action from the beginning, and no one's entreaties will make her change her mind. As Hegel writes, she 'knows beforehand the law and the power' she opposes, and nevertheless she 'knowingly commits the crime' (*Phenomenology of Spirit*, trans. A.V. Miller, foreword J.N. Finlay [Oxford: Oxford University Press, 1977], p. 284).
41. Lacan, *The Ethics of Psychoanalysis*, p. 313. See Zupančič, *Ethics of the Real*, p. 253.
42. For the distinction between classical and modern ethics, between the ethics of the slave and the ethics of the master, see Lacan, *The Four Fundamental Concepts of Psychoanalysis*, pp. 212–13 and 219–20.
43. See Jacques Lacan, 'Le non de Sygne' in Seminar VIII, *Le transfert*, pp. 315–32. See also Zupančič, *Ethics of the Real*, pp. 229 and 256–9.
44. Lacan, *Le transfert*, p. 328.
45. Zupancic, *Ethics of the Real*, p. 258.
46. See Lacan, *Le tranfert*, pp. 326–7.
47. See Chapter 5 below.
48. Lacan, *The Four Fundamental Concepts of Psychoanalysis*, p. 275.
49. Aristotle, *Poetics*, in *Poetics I with Tractatus, Coislinianus, A Hypothetical Reconstruction of Poetics II, The Fragments of On Poets*, trans. Richard Janko (Indianapolis: Hackett Publishing Co., 1987), 53b24–6, p. 18. I have modified the translation slightly.
50. Ibid., 52a20–1, p. 14.
51. Recognition and reversal 'should arise from the actual structure of the plot, so it happens that they arise either by necessity or by probability as a result of the preceding events' (52a19–21, p. 14).
52. See Ricoeur, *Time and Narrative*, Vol. 1, p. 41.
53. Aristotle, *Poetics*, 55b1, p. 23.
54. Ibid., 52a22–3, p. 14.
55. Ibid., 51b16, p. 12.
56. Ibid., 60a26–7 (p. 36) and 61b10–11 (p. 40).
57. Ibid., 52a4, p. 13.
58. Ricoeur, *Time and Narrative* Vol. 1, pp. 43–4.
59. Aristotle, *Poetics*, 60a26–7 (p. 36) and 61b10–11 (p. 40).
60. Žižek, *The Plague of Fantasies*, p. 215.
61. Ibid., p. 215, my emphasis.
62. Jacob Rogozinski, *Kanten. Esquisses Kantiennes* (Paris: Éditions Kimé, 1966).

63. Žižek, *The Plague of Fantasies*, p. 218.
64. Ibid., p. 219.
65. Ibid.
66. See Rogozinski, *Kanten*, pp. 124–32.
67. Žižek, *The Plague of Fantasies*, p. 220.
68. See Kant, *Critique of Pure Reason*, pp. 454–88, as well as Žižek's explanation in *The Plague of Fantasies*, p. 220.
69. Žižek, *The Plague of Fantasies*, p. 220.
70. Ibid.
71. This is the manner of the inexorable imperatives of the tragic causality that we examined in Chapter 1.
72. See Naomi Conn Liebler, *Shakespeare's Festive Tragedy: the Ritual Foundations of Genre* (New York and London: Routledge, 1995), pp. 42–3, and Drakakis and Liebler, eds, *Tragedy* (London and New York: Longman, 1998), p. 8. For other arguments against the interpretation of *hamartia* as 'flaw', see, for example, Amélie Rorty, ed., *Essays in Aristotle's Poetics* (Princeton: Princeton University Press), pp. 10–11, and Nussbaum, *The Fragility of Goodness*, p. 383.
73. Drakakis and Liebler, *Tragedy*, p. 9.
74. Ibid., pp. 8 and 9.
75. Žižek, *The Sublime Object of Ideology*, p. 176.
76. Žižek, *The Plague of Fantasies*, p. 218.
77. Ibid., p. 218.
78. See Chapter 4.
79. F.W.J. Schelling, *Philosophical Letters on Dogmatism and Criticism*, in *The Unconditional in Human Knowledge: Four Early Essays, 1794–1796*, trans. Fritz Marti (Lewisburg, PA: Bucknell University Press, 1980), pp. 192–3.

Chapter 3

1. When speaking of modern subjectivities I refer to state-based subjectivities, that is, to accounts based on the rationalization and universalization imposed by the state. They are literally modern in that they are historically determined (by the birth of the state), just as Greek tragedy is also historically determined though in a very different way.
2. Zygmunt Bauman, *Postmodern Ethics* (Oxford: Blackwell, 1993), p. 84.
3. Nietzsche's later work abounds with descriptions of irrational or nonconscious forces acting over the human self. See, for example, his account of conscience in *On the Genealogy of Morals*, trans. and intro. by Douglas Smith (Oxford: Oxford University Press, 1996), pp. 64–7.
4. Raymond Williams, *Modern Tragedy* (Stanford: Stanford University Press, 1987), p. 61.
5. Emmanuel Levinas, *Totality and Infinity. An Essay on Exteriority*, trans. A. Lingis (Pittsburgh: Duquesne University Press, 1969), p. 228.
6. See Judith Butler, *The Psychic Life of Power. Theories in Subjection* (Stanford: Stanford University Press, 1997), especially p. 11.
7. Jonathan Strauss, 'Death-Based Subjectivity', in *Subjects of Terror, Nerval, Hegel and the Modern Self* (Stanford: Stanford University Press, 1998), pp. 23–73.

8. See Strauss, *Post-Mortem: The State of Death as a Modern Construct, Diacritics,* 30.3 (Fall 2000, monographic issue) and Alphonso Lingis, *Death-Bound Subjectivity* (Bloomington: Indiana University Press, 1989).
9. See the works of these thinkers studied below, and also Butler, *The Psychic Life of Power.*
10. Louis Althusser, 'Ideology and Ideological State Apparatuses', *Lenin and Philosophy,* trans. Ben Brewster (New York: Monthly Review Press, 1971), p. 182; Michel Foucault, 'The Subject and Power', in Hubert L. Dreyfus and Paul Rabinow, *Michel Foucault: Beyond Structuralism and Hermeneutics (Second Edition with an Afterword by and an Interview with Michel Foucault)* (Chicago: The University of Chicago Press, 1983), p. 212; Butler, *The Psychic Life of Power.*
11. See Foucault, 'The Subject and Power', and Butler, *The Psychic Life of Power.*
12. See, for instance, Williams, *Modern Tragedy,* p. 189. See also George Steiner, *Antigones* (New Haven: Yale University Press, 1984), Simon Critchley, 'Comedy and Finitude: Displacing the Tragic-Heroic Paradigm in Philosophy and Psychoanalysis' in *Ethics–Politics–Subjectivity. Essay on Derrida, Levinas and Contemporary French Thought* (London: Verso, 1999), pp. 217–238, or, more recently, Terry Eagleton, *Sweet Violence: the Idea of the Tragic* (Oxford: Blackwell, 2003). Here I borrow freely from Simon Critchley's account of the tragic character of post-Kantian philosophy at the beginning of 'Comedy and Finitude' (*Ethics–Politics–Subjectivity,* pp. 217–19).
13. Heidegger, *An Introduction to Metaphysics,* trans. R. Manheim (New Haven: Yale University Press, 1959), pp. 146–65.
14. See Chapter 2.
15. See Chapter 1.
16. See Alenka Zupančič, *Ethics of the Real. Kant, Lacan* (London: Verso, 2000), pp. 175–186, and Chapter 2 above.
17. See Peter Szondi, *An Essay on the Tragic,* trans. Paul Fleming (Stanford: Stanford University Press, 2002).
18. Zupančič, *Ethics of the Real,* p. 186, quoting Lacan's formulation in his reading of Claudel's *L'otage* in *Le séminaire, Livre VIII. Le transfert* (Paris: Éditions du Seuil, 1992) p. 380. I have developed this idea in chapter 2.
19. At least not in *Oedipus Rex.* And is his disappearance at the end of *Oedipus at Colonus* indeed a form of death? If so, his death is of an exceptional kind.
20. *Phenomenology,* p. 62. See Strauss, *Subjects of Terror,* p. 17.
21. See Strauss, *Subjects of Terror,* pp. 7–8.
22. Here Hegel understands the 'I' primarily as a denominator of identity, and not only as an empty category or position that anybody who designs itself as a speaker can occupy. It is not by universalizing the self, but rather by providing a position from which the self can speak and establish communication with another, that the linguistic sign enables identity. As Emile Benveniste explains, it is precisely by designating oneself as an 'I' and getting involved in a dialogue with a 'you' that subjectivity in language is achieved. See *Problems in General Linguistics* (Coral Gables: University of Miami Press, 1971), p. 225.
23. Strauss, *Subjects of Terror,* p. 22.
24. The otherness of the outside world only exists for self-consciousness as a negative object, that is, as that which must lose its independence by being

superseded or consumed by the self. 'Self-consciousness which is simply for itself and directly characterizes its object as a negative element, or is primarily desire, will therefore, on the contrary, learn through experience that the object is independent' (*Phenomenology*, p. 106).

25. Ibid., p. 109, translation altered.
26. On desire's goal to perpetuate itself, see Jean Hyppolite, *Genesis and Structure of Hegel's Phenomenology of Spirit*, trans. Samuel Cherniak and John Heckman (Evanston: Northwestern University Press, 1974), p. 160.
27. See *Phenomenology*, p. 110.
28. On Hegel's idea of death as not inflicted from the outside, see Hyppolite, *Genesis and Structure of Hegel's Phenomenology of Spirit*, p. 154.
29. Hegel, *Phenomenology*, p. 114. Hegel continues: 'The individual who has not risked his life may well be recognized as a person, but he has not attained to the truth of this recognition as an independent self-consciousness. Similarly, just as each stakes his own life, so each must seek the other's death . . . The other . . . must regard its otherness as a pure being-for-self or as an absolute negation' (p. 114).
30. Ibid., pp. 113–14.
31. Ibid., p. 113.
32. Ibid., p. 111.
33. Hyppolite, *Genesis and Structure of Hegel's Phenomenology of Spirit*, pp. 149–50.
34. Ibid., 176.
35. *Phenomenology*, p. 117. Here I will refer to the master and slave as 'he' instead of 'it', for consistency with the quotations from Hegel's text, which use the second person masculine pronoun.
36. Ibid., p. 118.
37. It is significant that agency is enabled through authority. As Foucault observes, power acts only on agents, on those who act (see 'The Subject and Power', p. 221). It would seem that, according to Foucault, power first enables action and then exerts itself on acting beings and the other way around, in a process prefigured in Hegel's master and slave section.
38. *Phenomenology*, p. 119.
39. Ibid., p. 102. After quoting this paragraph from Hegel, Levinas observes that any alterity in the *Phenomenology* is nothing but 'the alterity of the I that takes itself for another', an alterity within the self. 'The difference is not a difference,' says Levinas; 'the I, as other, is not an "other". . . . The I that repels the self, lived as repugnance, the I riveted to itself, lived as ennui, are modes of self-consciousness and rest on the unrendable identity of the I and the self' (Levinas, *Totality and Infinity*, p. 36).
40. This divide within consciousness receives various characterizations in different narratives of subjectivity: what for Nietzsche was the tension between the Apollonian and the Dionysian, for Freud it is the split between superego and ego, and for Judith Butler the division between body and mind.
41. *Phenomenology*, p. 126.
42. Ibid., p. 127.
43. As authority re-emerges in the bondsman's conscience, observes Butler, aggression or accusation that the bondsman would have addressed to the master is readdressed to himself in the form of self-beratement (not unlike

what happens in Freud's description of melancholia). In this reflexive movement the bondsman now takes up the master's authority and exerts it over his own body, the alterity that must be suppressed. In Butler's bodily terms, the 'flight from that fear, a fear from death', which rids the subject of its thing-like character, 'entails vacating the body and clinging to what appears to be most disembodied: thought' (Butler, *The Psychic Life of Power*, p. 43). The unchangeable or universal (essential) and the changeable or particular (unessential) are, in other words, inseparable and must coexist, but the unhappy consciousness, unaware of the unity, attempts to repress one part.

44. Butler, *The Psychic Life of Power*, pp. 41 and 43. Although Hegel does not refer to fear of law specifically in this section, an ethical imperative seems to be presupposed and at work in the recurrent occasions in which he has self-consciousness turn against its changeable part, 'against its particular individuality' (*Phenomenology*, p. 136). Butler's acute reading interprets the invocation of the ethical norm as a move that allays fear: 'Consciousness clings or attaches to itself, and this clinging to consciousness is at the same time a disavowal of the body, which appears to signify the terror of death, "the absolute fear". The unhappy consciousness requires and engages this attachment by invoking an imperative. Its fear is allayed by legislating an ethical norm. Hence, the imperative to cling to oneself is motivated by this absolute fear and by the need to refuse that fear. Inasmuch as it is an ethical injunction, this imperative is the disarticulated refusal of absolute fear' (p. 43).

45. See Butler, *The Psychic Life of Power*, p. 43. The question that arises here is whether the ethical imperative to which the unhappy consciousness subjects itself, beyond emerging as a result of internalizing the master's authority, is not ultimately the result of identifying a universalizing principle, an ethical imperative, in exchange for subjective identity (i.e. for a position in an intelligible system).

46. *Phenomenology*, p. 137.

47. Ibid., p. 134.

48. See Butler, *The Psychic Life of Power*, p. 53.

49. 'Hegel, the philosopher of mind,' remarks Ricoeur, 'leaves us here in a state of indecision, halfway between an anthropological reading and a theological reading' (Paul Ricoeur, *Oneself as Another*, trans. Kathleen Blamey [Chicago: The University of Chicago Press, 1992], p. 353). Ricoeur refers here to a similar inconsistency in Hegel's next section on Morality.

50. See Strauss, *Subjects of Terror*, pp. 54–5.

51. See Butler, *The Psychic Life of Power*, pp. 51–3.

52. This possibility, implicitly opened by Hegel's text, although explicitly denied, may be thought of in terms of Sloterdijk's description of Nietzsche's reinvention of the enlightened subject: 'The subject of enlightenment could from this point forward no longer constitute itself as it had wanted to in accordance with the rules of Apollonian illusionism as an autonomous source of meaning, ethos, logic, and truth – but, instead, as something medial, cybernetic, eccentric, and Dionysian, as a site of sensibility within the ruling cycles of forces, as a point of alertness for the modulation of impersonal antagonisms, as a process of self-healing for primordial pain, and an instance of the self-composition of primordial pleasure – to speak

poetically, as an eye through which Dionysus observes himself' (Peter Sloterdijk, *Thinker on Stage. Nietzsche's Materialism*, trans. Jamie Owen Daniel [Minneapolis: University of Minnesota Press, 1989], p. 82).

53. Emmanuel Levinas, *Otherwise than Being or Beyond Essence*, trans. Alphonso Lingis (Pittsburgh: Duquesne University Press, 1998), pp. 15–16.

54. See ibid., pp. 14–15.

55. Ibid., p. 74.

56. Ibid., p. 15.

57. Ibid., p. 74.

58. Ibid.

59. See Butler, *The Psychic Life of Power*, p. 168.

60. See ibid., p. 168.

61. Sigmund Freud, 'Mourning and Melancholia', in *General Psychological Theory*, ed. Philip Rieff, trans. Joan Riviere (New York: Simon & Schuster, 1997), p. 166.

62. 'The occasions giving rise to melancholia for the most part extend beyond the clear case of a loss by death, and include all those situations of being wounded, hurt, neglected, out of favor, or disappointed, which can import opposite feelings of love and hate into the relationship or reinforce an already existing ambivalence' (Freud, 'Mourning and Melancholia', p. 172).

63. Freud, 'Mourning and Melancholia', p. 170. See also *The Ego and the Id*, ed. James Strachey, trans. Joan Riviere (New York and London: W.W. Norton and Company, 1989), p. 23.

64. Freud, 'Mourning and Melancholia', p. 170.

65. Butler writes: 'The power imposed upon one is the power that animates one's emergence, and there appears to be no escaping this ambivalence. Indeed, there appears to be no 'one' without ambivalence, which is to say that the fictive redoubling necessary to become a self rules out the possibility of strict identity' (*The Psychic Life of Power*, p. 198).

66. 'Mourning and Melancholia', pp. 168–9. See also Sigmund Freud, *The Ego and the Id*, p. 12. In *The Ego and the Id* Freud writes: 'Whereas the ego is essentially the representative of the external world, of reality, the super-ego stands in contrast to it as the representative of the internal world, of the id. Conflicts between the ego and the ideal will, as we are now prepared to find, ultimately reflect the contrast between what is real and what is psychical, between the external world and the internal world' (p. 32). Butler, in turn, remarks: 'Melancholia produces a set of spatializing tropes for psychic life, domiciles of preservation and shelter as well as arenas for struggle and persecution. Such tropes do not 'explain' melancholia: they constitute some of its fabular discursive effects' (p. 171).

67. See Butler, *The Psychic Life of Power*, p. 171.

68. Freud, *The Ego and the Id*, pp. 23–4 and 48.

69. Ibid., p. 30.

70. See Freud, *The Ego and the Id*, especially pp. 30 and 48–9.

71. 'In melancholia,' writes Butler, 'not only is the loss of an other or an ideal lost to consciousness, but the social world in which such a loss became possible is also lost. . . . The ego thus becomes a "polity" and conscience one of its "major institutions", precisely because psychic life withdraws a social world into itself in an effort to annul the losses that world demands' (*The Psychic Life of Power*, pp. 181–2).

72. Freud, 'Mourning and Melancholia', p. 165.
73. Butler, *The Psychic Life of Power*, pp. 182–3.
74. The possibility of a melancholic turn demands a strong fixation to the object and simultaneously a weak resistance of the object-cathexis: 'The narcissistic identification with the object then becomes a substitute for the erotic cathexis, the result of which is that in spite of the conflict with the loved person the love-relation need not be given up. This kind of substitution of identification for object-love is an important mechanism in the narcissistic affections' (Freud, 'Mourning and Melancholia', pp. 170–1. See also *The Ego and the Id*, pp. 24–5).
75. Such is the case, Butler argues, of homoerotic desire, a desire foreclosed and therefore unavowable as a loss. On the foreclosure of homoeroticism, see Butler, *The Psychic Life of Power*, pp. 139 and 190–1.
76. Ibid., pp. 183 and 190–1.
77. Ibid., p. 191.
78. Of course, this poses political problems. For if we are libidinally attached to subjection and punishment, may not that be used as an excuse for historical abuse? May not totalitarian systems advertise, rightly, that in subjecting us they are offering us the occasion to be 'authentic', to 'realize ourselves'?
79. See Butler, *The Psychic Life of Power*, pp. 190–1.
80. See Michel, Foucault, 'The Subject and Power' and *Discipline and Punish. The Birth of the Prison*, trans. Alan Sheridan (New York: Vintage Books, 1995).
81. Ibid., p. 212. I alter Foucault's original words in English following the French translation.
82. 'This form of power applies itself to immediate everyday life which categorizes the individual, marks him by his own individuality, attaches him to his own identity, imposes a law of truth on him which he must recognize and which others have to recognize in him. It is a form of power which makes individuals subjects.' ('The Subject and Power', p. 212).
83. Butler, *The Psychic Life of Power*, p. 12.
84. Louis Althusser, 'Ideology and Ideological State Apparatuses', in *Lenin and Philosophy*, trans. Ben Brewster (New York: Monthly Review Press, 1971), p. 182. Althusser explains the self's submission to ideology, the way ideology 'recruits subjects' or 'transforms the individuals into subjects' through the much debated scene of interpellation. When somebody is hailed by the police in the street, the one hailed almost invariably recognizes that the hail has been addressed to him, a recognition that feelings of guilt do not sufficiently elucidate. This scene explains how ideology calls subjects into being, but unlike the example, the existence of ideology and the interpellation of individuals as subjects do not happen in succession: both moments occur simultaneously; in fact, they are 'one and the same thing' (p. 175). Moreover, clarifies Althusser in a footnote, '[h]ailing as an everyday practice subject to a precise ritual takes a quite "special" form in the policeman's practice of "hailing" which concerns the hailing of "suspects"' (p. 174, footnote 18).
85. Ibid., p. 182.
86. Ibid. Foucault develops a similar line of thought in 'The Subject and Power'.
87. See Butler, *The Psychic Life of Power*, p. 13.
88. Althusser, 'Ideology and Ideological State Apparatuses', p. 170.

89. Blaise Pascal, *Pensées*, trans. A. J. Krailsheimer (London: Penguin Books, 1995), p. 125.

90. Franz Kafka, *The Trial*, trans. Breon Mitchell (New York: Schocken Books, 1998), p. 8.

91. Ibid., pp. 8–9.

92. See Butler, *The Psychic Life of Power*, p. 108.

93. Ibid., p. 109.

94. See Paul Ricoeur, *The Symbolism of Evil*, trans. Emerson Buchanan (Boston: Beacon Press, 1993), p. 216.

95. Ibid., p. 219.

96. See Roland Barthes, *On Racine*, trans. Richard Howard (Berkeley and Los Angeles: University of California Press, 1992), p. 45.

97. See Chapters 2 and 5.

98. Freud, 'Mourning and Melancholia', pp. 166–7.

99. Judith Butler, Ernesto Laclau and Slavoj Žižek, *Contingency, Hegemony, Universality* (London: Verso, 2000) p. 28.

100. See Chapter 4.

101. See Slavoj Žižek, *The Plague of Fantasies* (London: Verso, 1997), p. 216.

102. Foucault, 'The Subject and Power', p. 212.

103. Ibid., p. 219.

104. See Ricoeur, *The Symbolism of Evil*, p. 216.

105. See Chapter 2.

106. See Butler, *Contingency, Hegemony, Universality*, p. 28.

107. Foucault argues that while each subject reiterates the conditions of its heteronomous emergence by reaffirming its attachment to subjection (to the state), this reiteration disseminates the seed for resistance because repetition of the conditions of power is never exact (see Butler, *The Psychic Life of Power*, p. 93). But is this resistance simply absorbed by the system, strengthening the power it resists, as happens in tragedy, or is it ultimately capable of altering conditions of power? Can subjective agency really succeed in reformulating the terms of the social power by which it was spawned? This is what Foucault intimates in 'The Subject and Power', and what Butler suggests at the most optimistic moments of her argument: 'We might reread "being",' she writes, 'as precisely the potentiality that remains unexhausted by any particular interpellation. Such a failure of interpellation may well undermine the capacity of the subject to "be" in a self-identical sense, but it may also mark the path toward a more open, even more ethical, kind of being, one of or for the future' (p. 131). See also *The Psychic Life of Power* pp. 10–12, 15, 28–9, 64–5, 66, 101, 130–1, 190–1 and 193 on the possibility of altering conditions of power. Although Butler envisages here the possibility of being something else after escaping individuation by the state, in her study of concrete texts on subjectivity she is more pessimistic (pp. 12–13). Is it then possible to conceive a resistance to power that, emerging from existing conditions of power, is capable of reformulating those conditions? Narratives of subjectivity diverge on this point.

108. See Peter Sloterdijk, *Critique of Cynical Reason*, trans. Michael Eldred (Minneapolis: University of Minneapolis Press, 1987) and Slavoj Žižek, *The Sublime Object of Ideology* (London: Verso, 1989), pp. 30–5.

109. See Chapters 2 and 5.

110. Žižek, *The Plague of Fantasies*, p. 219, and *The Ticklish Subject*, pp. 25–8.
111. Immanuel Kant, *Critique of Practical Reason*, trans. Werner S. Pluhar (Indianapolis and Cambridge: Hackett Publishing Company Inc., 2002), 147–8, p. 185.
112. Ibid., 147–8, pp. 185–6.
113. Žižek, *The Sublime Object of Ideology*, pp. 79–80.
114. Immanuel Kant, 'What is Enlightenment?', in *Foundations of the Metaphysics of Morals and What is Enlightenment?*, trans. Lewis White Beck (Englewood Cliffs, NJ: Prentice Hall, 1990), pp. 85 and 89, my italics.
115. See Žižek, *The Sublime Object of Ideology*, pp. 79–80.
116. Or, as Žižek puts it, 'The main point is to perceive how this acceptance of given empirical, "pathological" (Kant) customs and rules is not some kind of pre-Enlightenment remnant – a remnant of the traditional authoritarian attitude – but, on the contrary, *the necessary obverse of the Enlightenment itself*: through this acceptance of the customs and rules of social life in their nonsensical, given character, through acceptance of the fact that "Law is law", we are internally freed from its constraints – the way is open for free theoretical reflection' (p. 80).
117. See Chapter 1.
118. Sophocles, *Oedipus at Colonus*, in *The Three Theban Plays*, trans. Robert Fagles (London: Penguin Books, 1982), 1614–18, pp. 167–8. See Zupančič's interpretation of these words in *Ethics of the Real*, p. 208.
119. Aeschylus, *Agamemnon*, trans. Martha Nussbaum, *The Fragility of Goodness. Luck and Ethics in Greek Tragedy and Philosophy* (Cambridge: Cambridge University Press, 1986), p. 35.
120. *Agamemnon*, Nussbaum's translation in *The Fragility of Goodness*, p. 35, my italics.
121. Lacan, *Le transfert*, p. 358.
122. See end of previous section, and also Chapter 2.
123. See analysis of Racine's *Phaedra* in Chapter 2.
124. G. W. F. Hegel, *The Jena System, 1804–5: Logic and Metaphysics*, ed. and trans. John W. Burbidge and George di Giovanni, intro. H. S. Harris (Kingston and Montreal: McGill-Queen's University Press, 1986).
125. See Slavoj Žižek, *Tarrying with the Negative. Kant, Hegel, and the Critique of Ideology* (Durham, NC: Duke University Press, 1993), p. 141.
126. Ibid., p. 143.
127. Mikhail Bakhtin, *Toward a Philosophy of the Act*, ed. Vadim Liapunov and Michael Holquist (Austin: University of Texas Press, 1993), p. 20.
128. Ibid., pp. 20–1.
129. Ibid., p. 42.
130. Ibid. In certain respects, Bakhtin's and Levinas's way of understanding the self's responsibility belong to a similar constellation. See Chapter 5.
131. Lacan, *Le transfert*, p. 358.
132. Žižek, *Plague of Fantasies*, p. 159. For Žižek, '"Word" stands here for the ideological doctrine which has lost its substantial bearings, it has the status of a pure semblance, but which – precisely as such, as a pure semblance, is essential'.
133. Althusser, 'Ideology and Ideological State Apparatuses', p. 182.

134. See again Sloterdijk, *Critique of Cynical Reason*, and Žižek, *The Sublime Object of Ideology*, pp. 30–5.
135. See Chapter 5.
136. See Lacan's reading of Antigone in the two last sessions of Seminar VII, *The Ethics of Psychoanalysis*, trans. Denis Porter (New York: Norton, 1992).
137. See Chapters 1 and 2.
138. On not taking one's duty as an excuse not to fulfil one's duty, see Žižek, *Plague of Fantasies*, p. 222.
139. See Chapter 5.
140. 'The Subject and Power', p. 216. Foucault continues: 'We have to promote new forms of subjectivity through the refusal of this kind of individuality which has been imposed on us for several centuries' (p. 216).
141. Gillian Rose, *Mourning Becomes the Law* (Oxford and Cambridge, Mass: Blackwell, 1992), p. 4.
142. 'Necessary fictions' belong to the group of artifacts whose fictionality is ultimately irrecoverable. Like every other artifact, these artifacts have been 'made up', and then, they have undergone a 'making-real' process (from which only works of art are exempt) whereby the trace of the human hand, the seams of its artificiality, have been erased. (Here I am borrowing Elaine Scarry's terms. See *The Body in Pain* [Oxford: Oxford University Press, 1985], p. 325 and 'The Made-Up and the Made-Real', *The Yale Journal of Criticism*, 5.2 [1992], pp. 243–4.) As compared with these 'necessary fictions', then, works of art display their artificiality overtly. And differently from non-artistic objects, whose fictionality has been erased but is recoverable upon reflection, the fabricated nature of 'necessary fictions' such as God, the Law, the Father or the Past, is impossible to retrieve. It is impossible to retrieve because these fictions are constitutive of their makers, because they play such a crucial role in the ways we represent ourselves as social beings that without them we would be undone as such.
143. These two forms of heteronomy are studied in Chapter 5.
144. We have already questioned the *objective* status of objective necessity by saying that tragic characters conceive of objective necessity as the inscrutable desire of the other, and by underscoring the self's participation in the *external* coercion that *usurps* its agency.

Chapter 4

1. Of Federico García Lorca's three tragic plays, this chapter will concentrate primarily on *Blood Wedding*. For a study of the process in which the characters in *Blood Wedding* construct fatality in language, see Gabriela Basterra, 'The Grammar of Fate in Lorca's *Bodas de sangre*', *Journal of Romance Studies*, 3.2 (2003) 48–67.
2. '¿Cómo no voy a hablar viéndote salir por esa puerta? Es que no me gusta que lleves navaja. Es que . . . que no quisiera que salieras al campo' (*How can I keep from talking when I see you go out that door? I don't want you to carry a knife. I just . . . I just wish you wouldn't go out to the fields*). *Blood Wedding*, Act I.1, p. 417. I use here Miguel García Posada's edition of the plays of Federico García Lorca, *Obras Completes II, Teatro*. For the English translation, I have contrasted and modified two published translations, one by

Langston Hughes and W.S. Merlin, the other by Michael Dwell and Carmen Zapata. I am indebted to both. Here I will give the reference of act, scene and page in Spanish.

3. At a climactic point of the play both Leonardo and the Bride declare they were irresistibly attracted to each other by an inexorable force, a claim that the Chorus-like group of Woodcutters substantiates: 'Han hecho bien en huir. . . . Hay que seguir el camino de la sangre' (*they were wise to run away. . . . One must follow the course of one's blood*). Act III.1, p. 455.

4. On the retroactive character of tragic guilt, see Roland Barthes, *On Racine*, trans. Richard Howard (Berkeley and Los Angeles: University of California Press, 1992), pp. 38–40 and 46–7, and Paul Ricoeur, *The Symbolism of Evil*, trans. Emerson Buchanan (Boston: Beacon Press, 1993), pp. 313–17. *Blood Wedding* instantiates literally the irreversible transmission of guilt through blood, so emblematic of tragedy. The Bridegroom inherits, by marrying, the fate of his 'casta de muertos en mitad de la calle' (*breed that dies in the middle of the street*) (Act III.1, p. 456). When the lovers elope after the wedding, the Woodcutters say: 'Hay que seguir el camino de la sangre' (*One must follow the course of one's blood*) (Act III.1, p. 455). The Mother's words at the moment of the elopement, 'Ha llegado otra vez la hora de la sangre' (*The hour of blood has come once again*), figuratively convey the repetitive sense of the tragic transmission of guilt, a guilt incarnated in the characters in spite of their temporary refusal to inherit it (Act II.2, p. 454). In turn, Leonardo, according to the Bride's Father, 'busca desgracia. No tiene buena sangre' (*is looking for trouble. He has bad blood*). 'Qué sangre va a tener' (*What blood could he have?*), replies the Mother. 'La de toda su familia. Mana de su bisabuelo, que empezó matando, y sigue en toda la mala ralea, manejadores de cuchillos y gente de falsa sonrisa' (*That of his whole family. It flows from his great-granfather, who started out killing, and runs through the whole evil clan, knife-slingers and people with false smiles*) (Act II.2, p. 446).

5. 'Hay que seguir el camino de la sangre', a Woodcutter says of Leonardo and the Bride (Act III.1, p. 455).

6. *Blood Wedding*, Act III.1, p. 456.

7. Ibid., pp. 459–60.

8. According to Barthes, the deliberation of tragic hero is only 'a spoken consciousness of division' (*On Racine*, p. 36).

9. *Blood Wedding*, Act II.1, p. 438.

10. G. H. Mead, *The Philosophy of the Present* (Chicago and London: Open Court, 1932), p. 12.

11. The reality-generating capacity of memory is based on memory's ability to disguise its fictionality. According to Susan Stewart, the narrativization or fictionalization of the past is an aesthetic operation, 'an attempt to erase the actual past in order to create an imagined past available for consumption.' Susan Stewart, *On Longing* (Durham, NC and London: Duke University Press, 1993), p. 143.

12. *Blood Wedding*, Act II.1, p. 437.

13. Lack of communication is, according to Rosenzweig and Benjamin, what makes erotic scenes alien to tragic drama: 'So it is that in Sophocles and Euripides the heroes learn "not to speak . . . only to debate"'; and this explains why 'the love-scene is quite alien to ancient drama' (Walter Benjamin, *The Origin of German Tragic Drama*, trans. John Osborne [London:

Verso, 1992], p. 116, quoting Franz Rosenzweig, *The Star of Redemption*, trans. William W. Hallo [Notre Dame, IN: Notre Dame Press, 1970–85] pp. 99–100). According to Barthes, for this very reason they are subjected to a protocol of repetition: 'The successful moments of Racinian Eros are always memories. . . . These erotic scenes are, in effect, veritable hallucinations, recalled in order to nourish pleasure or pain, and subject to a whole protocol of rehearsal and repetition' (*On Racine*, pp. 17–18).

14. *Blood Wedding*, Act I.1, p. 417.
15. Walter Benjamin, 'Theses on the Philosophy of History', in *Illuminations*, ed. Hannah Arendt, trans. Harry Zohn (New York: Hancourt, Brace & World, 1968), p. 255.
16. Jorge Luis Borges, 'Funes the Memorious', in *Labyrinths*, eds Donald A. Yates and James E. Irby, trans. James E. Irby (New York: Modern Library, 1983), pp. 59–66. In its lack of selection and abstraction, Funes's narrative of the past contradicts the synthetic activity of emplotment.
17. The traumatic power of the narrative of memory springs from the appearance of reality that it borrows from its supposedly historical origins, which in turn permits it to stand as a competent record of a historical context (see Susan Stewart, *On Longing* [Durham, NC and London: Duke University Press, 1993], pp. 22–3). The reality-generating capacity of memory, based on memory's ability to disguise its fictionality, can even make the past appear as more authentic than the present, because through its narrative organization of experience it confers on that experience the temporality and sense of causal sequence that lived experience often lacks.
18. Barthes describes a similar moment of image repetition in what he denominates 'the Racinian Tenebroso' (see *On Racine*, pp. 22–4).
19. *Blood Wedding*, Act III.2, p. 472.
20. Ibid., Act I.1, p. 421.
21. Emile Benveniste, *Problems in General Linguistics* (Coral Gables: University of Miami Press, 1971), p. 225. Benveniste refers here to reciprocity in interlocution, that is, to the first stage or 'linguistic basis' of the relation to the other, where the roles of speaker and listener are interchangeable. As Ricoeur observes in *Oneself as Another* (trans. Kathleen Blamey [Chicago: The University of Chicago Press, 1992]), the reversibility that takes place in interlocution, apparent in the exchange of personal pronouns, is not a reversibility of persons but of roles (p. 193). Persons are taken into account, in turn, in the idea of 'nonsusbtitutibility' (p. 193), where each of the persons that take part in an intersubjective relationship, still from the viewpoint of discourse, is irreplaceable due to the anchoring of the 'I' (the 'I' determines the spatio-temporal coordinates of the utterance, assigning concrete meanings to terms such as 'here' and 'now'). Finally, beyond the 'reversibility of roles' and 'nonsubstitutibility of persons' Ricoeur introduces the idea of 'similitude', which concerns all initial inequalities between oneself and another. 'Similitude' is based on an idea of asymmetry close to Levinas's, whereby the 'I' achieves subjectivity (*is oneself*) by *being for* another (p. 193).
22. *Blood Wedding*, Act II.1, p. 444.
23. Ibid., p. 462. The same ambiguity as to the subject of action is also reflected in Leonardo's words 'Con alfileres de plata / mi sangre se puso negra / y el

sueño me fue llenando / las carnes de mala hierba' (*With pins of silver / my blood turned black / and the sleep gradually filled / my flesh with bitter weeds*) (Act III.1, 463). Do 'pins of silver' pierce Leonardo's blood, or are the pins born precisely from his blood, piercing outwards? Does his blood, in other words, turn black by itself, 'producing' silver pins as a consequence, or do the pins 'author' the blackening (rotting?) action? Finally, does the sleep (or the dream? And whose sleep or dream?) 'plant' weeds on Leonardo's flesh, or do the weeds grow out of his flesh?

24. In *Blood Wedding* the main characters interrupt or suspend their verbal exchange, either by pushing other characters out of consciousness (as do the Mother and the Neighbour in Act 1.1), by replacing the potential interlocutors present on stage with absent or imaginary ones (that is, by narrating them instead of letting them speak, as do Leonardo and the Bride), by silencing them directly, or by remaining altogether silent. Since, according to Barthes, in tragedy one cannot die because one is always speaking, the characters who cannot speak, who leave the sphere of action either by remaining silent or by leaving the stage, must die.

25. According to Emile Benveniste, '[I]n the first two persons, there are both a person involved and a discourse concerning that person. . . . But in the third person a predicate is really stated, only it is outside "I-you"; this form is thus an exception to the relationship by which "I" and "you" are specified. Consequently, the legitimacy of this form as a "person" is to be questioned . . . : the "third person" is not a "person"; it is really the verbal form whose function is to express the non-person' (p. 197–8).

26. *Blood Wedding*, Act II.1, p. 438.

27. Ibid., 437 (my italics).

28. Ibid., 438 (my italics).

29. Ibid., 438 (my italics).

30. Furthermore, what drags the Bride towards ecstasy or death, what she says she cannot, or does not want to, hear, is not Leonardo's words, but rather the sound of his voice. The tension that underlies the conversation becomes manifest in the dissolution of verbal language itself: Leonardo's concrete words (and therefore what he attempts to communicate) have become indistinct, dissolved in an all-encompassing 'voice'. The impact that Leonardo's voice has on the Bride paradoxically erases Leonardo as a speaking 'I'. The power that drags the Bride, therefore, does not spring from Leonardo himself, whom she obliterates as a specific person, but rather from an image of Leonardo created in remembrance.

31. *Blood Wedding*, Act III.2, p. 472.

32. *Novia*: ¡Vámonos pronto a la iglesia!

Novio: ¿Tienes prisa?

Novia: Sí. Estoy deseando ser tu mujer y quedarme sola contigo, y no oír más voz que la tuya.

Novio: ¡Eso quiero yo!

Novia: Y no ver más que tus ojos. Y que me abrazaras tan fuerte, que aunque me llamara mi madre, que está muerta, no me pudiera despegar de ti.

Novio: Yo tengo fuerza en los brazos. Te voy a abrazar cuarenta años seguidos.

Novia: (*Dramática, cogiéndolo del brazo*) ¡Siempre! (Act II.2, p. 443).

Bride: *Let's leave for the church soon.*
Bridegroom: *Are you in a hurry?*
Bride: *Yes. I am longing to be your wife. And to be alone with you and hear no voice but yours.*
Bridegroom: *That is what I want!*
Bride: *And see no other eyes but yours. And have you hold me so tight that even if my dead mother called to me I couldn't pull myself away from you.*
Bridegroom: *My arms are strong. I am going to hold you for the next forty years.*
Bride: *(Dramatically, taking him by the arm) Always!*

33. Although in *Blood Wedding* this framework is acted out in dramatic time, emphasizing the contrast between it and the tragic events, other tragedies achieve a similar effect of distance from the events simply through the separation between stage and audience characteristic of the theatrical convention. The spectator's perspective is always wider than that of the character, who can see only death.

34. See Raymond Williams. *Modern Tragedy* (Stanford: Stanford University Press, 1987), p. 60, and Jean-Pierre Vernant and Pierre Vidal-Naquet, *Myth and Tragedy in Ancient Greece*, trans. Janet Lloyd (New York: Zone Books, 1988), p. 114.

35. Williams: 'This [evil recognized not as transcendent, but rather as actual and negotiable] is of course far from its simple abolition, which is the opposite and yet complementary effort to its recognition as transcendent' (*Modern Tragedy*, p. 60).

36. Ibid., p. 188.

37. *Blood Wedding*, Act III.2, p. 466.

38. Ibid., pp. 470–1.

39. The Little Girl's use of popular verse rescues the events from classical tradition, if only momentarily. She returns to eleven-syllable verse in her last sentence: '¡Qué ruiseñor de sombra vuela y gime / sobre la flor del oro!' This line echoes the fifth stanza of Luis de Góngora's *Polifemo*: '. . . caliginoso lecho, el seno oscuro / ser de la negra noche nos lo enseña / infame turba de nocturnas aves, / gimiendo tristes y volando graves' (*that the obscure recess is black night's caliginous bed is demonstrated to us by an infamous mob of nocturnal fowls, moaning sadly and flying heavily*) (in *Renaissance and Baroque Poetry of Spain*, ed. and trans. Elias Rivers [Prospect Heights, Illinois: Waveland, 1966]).

40. *Blood Wedding*, Act III.2, p. 473.

41. Ibid., p. 474.

42. Ibid., p. 475.

43. See Williams, *Modern Tragedy*, p. 59.

44. 'The affirmation of absolute Evil, which is now so current, is, under pressure, a self-blinding; the self-blinding of a culture which, lacking the nerve to inquire into its own nature, would have not only actors but also spectators put out their eyes. What is offered as tragic significance is here, as elsewhere, a significant denial of the possibility of any meaning' (ibid., p. 61).

45. *Blood Wedding*, Act III.2, 472.

46. This version is constructed by isolating some events and then recontextualizing them within a temporal structure devised to produce the illusion of causal sequence, and therefore of intelligibility. Reframing the events and giving them a closure renders the past safe and secures the resumption of life. In the process suffering is naturalized and presented as inevitable, since it now appears inflicted by an external predetermining will.
47. Williams, *Modern Tragedy*, p. 60.
48. Ibid., p. 199.
49. Levinas, *Totality and Infinity*, p. 228. See also Walter Benjamin, 'Theses on the Philosophy of History, VI', in *Illuminations*, p. 255.
50. See Williams, *Modern Tragedy*, p. 56.
51. Benjamin, *The Origin of German Tragic Drama*, p. 114. Benjamin's life-seeking 'ordinary creature' needs to be qualified, since we are arguing that modern subjects are death-bound.
52. Ibid.
53. See Williams, *Modern Tragedy*, p. 202.
54. Ricoeur, *Oneself as Another*, p. 189.
55. Peter Sloterdijk, *Thinker on Stage. Nietzsche's Materialism*, trans. Jamie Owen Daniel, Foreword by Jochen Schulte-Sasse (Minneapolis: Universitu of Minnesota Press, 1989), p. 90.
56. See Martha Nussbaum, *The Fragility of Goodness. Luck and Ethics in Greek Tragedy and Philosophy* (Cambridge: Cambridge University Press, 1986), p. 7.
57. Levinas, *Totality and Infinity*, p. 39.
58. Levinas, *Time and the Other*, pp. 78–9. According to Levinas, the relationship with the Other involves mystery: 'The relationship with the other is not an idyllic and harmonious relationship of communion, or a sympathy through which we put ourselves in the other's place; we recognize the other as resembling us, but exterior to us; the relationship with the other is a relationship with a Mystery. The other's entire being is constituted by its exteriority, or rather its alterity, for exteriority is a property of space and leads the subject back to itself through light. . . . The relationship with the other will never be the feat of grasping a possibility' (pp. 75–6).
59. Emmanuel Levinas, *Otherwise than Being or Beyond Essence*, trans. Alphonso Lingis (Pittsburgh: Duquesne University Press, 1998) pp. 43–8.
60. Levinas, *Totality and Infinity*, p. 39.
61. Levinas, *Ethics and Infinity*, p. 98. See also *Time and the Other*, pp. 83–4 and 93–4.
62. See Ricoeur, *Oneself as Another*, p. 189.
63. See Levinas, *Totality and Infinity*, pp. 218–19.
64. The other's call for responsibility is an injunction to act for him or her that demands 'a response to the being who in a face speaks to the subject and tolerates only a personal response, that is, an ethical act' (*Totality and Infinity*, p. 219).
65. Ibid., pp. 218–19.
66. *Totality and Infinity*, p. 30, and *Otherwise than Being*, pp. 6 and 151–6.
67. See Knud E. Løgstrup, *The Ethical Demand*, trans. Theodor IJensen (Philadelphia Fortress Press, 1971), p. 46. '[T]he demand is radical because . . . no one but he alone, through his own unselfishness, is able to discover what

will best serve the other person. . . . The demand has the effect of making the person to whom the demand is directed an individual in the precise sense of the word' (pp. 19, 20).

68. See Chapter 3.

69. Nussbaum, *The Fragility of Goodness*. As Nussbaum observes, even when committed to the other and determined to act well, we find ourselves in insoluble situations of practical conflict where taking a certain course of action seems imperative, yet damages our relation with the other. In these situations, which are elaborately described in classical tragedy, our affection for, and commitment to the other interferes with the action we should apparently take (thus, for example, Agamemnon's dilemma between letting his men die in a calm sea instead of setting sail for Troy, on one side, and sacrificing his daughter Iphigenia following a god's command, on the other). Nussbaum classifies these 'interferences' in three groups. The first refers to all activities susceptible of reversal, such as 'friendship, love, political activity, attachments to property or possessions'. The second concerns the agent's likely commitment to two or more of these activities at once, in which incompatible alternatives create conflicts of value. Finally, Nussbaum asks about the ethical role to be assigned to 'our bodily sensuous nature, our passions, our sexuality, all [of which] serve as powerful links to the world of risk and mutability' (p. 7).

70. The fact that abstract forms that deny creation attest to the success of creation is illustrated by the struggle between form and life, as described by Georg Simmel in his 1918 essay 'The Conflict in Modern Culture', in *On Individuality and Social Forms* (Chicago: The University of Chicago Press, 1971) pp. 375–593.

71. Elaine Scarry, *The Body in Pain* (Oxford: Oxford University Press, 1985), p. 311. 'Such objects [must] be devoid not only of any personal signatures but also of the general human signature that tells us they are man-made. The object must have no seams or cutting marks that record and announce its human origins' (p. 312).

72. Cf. Scarry, *The Body in Pain* p. 325 and 'The Made-Up and the Made-Real', *The Yale Journal of Criticism*, 5.2 (1992), pp. 243–4.

73. On the overtness of the fictionality of art, see Elaine Scarry, 'The Structure of the Artifact', chapter 5 in *The Body in Pain*, especially pp. 311–14, and 'The Made-Up and the Made-Real', especially pp. 242–5.

74. See Scarry, 'The Made-Up and the Made-Real', pp. 244–5.

75. Judith Butler, *The Psychic Life of Power. Theories in Subjection* (Stanford: Stanford University Press), p. 68.

76. Gabriela Basterra, 'Destino, responsabilidad y creación en el escenario trágico de Lorca', *Anales de la literatura española contemporánea*, 24 (1999), pp. 411–31, and 424–8, and 'Choreography of Fate: Lorca's Reconfigurations of the Tragic.' *Re-Staging Cultural Theory: Politics, Tragedy, History*, ed. John Burt Foster and Wayne J. Froman (London: Continuum International Publishing Group, forthcoming).

77. Scarry, *The Body in Pain*, pp. 311–14 and 325, and 'The Made-Up and the Made-Real', pp. 242–5.

78. Sloterdijk, *Critique of Cynical Reason* and Žižek, *The Sublime Object of Ideology*, pp. 28–30.

79. The position of the spectator we are occupying in this chapter is equivalent to, and as impossible as, the gaze at play in the Chapter 3, where I wrote on the subject in the third person.

Chapter 5

1. For a highly suggestive exploration of the structure of the ethical demand in Kant, Levinas, Lacan and Badiou, see Simon Critchley, 'Demanding Approval: On the Ethics of Alain Badiou', *Radical Philosophy*, 100 (March/April 2000), pp. 16–27. See also Simon Critchley, *Ethics . . . My Way* (forthcoming).
2. For a fascinating study of this structure of demand and approval, see Critchley's new book *Ethics . . . My Way*.
3. See Chapters 2 and 4 above.
4. Leaving many differences momentarily aside, God may be considered to have played a similar role as tragic necessity in the Western philosophical tradition.
5. See Jacques Lacan, *Le séminaire, Livre VIII. Le transfert 1960–1961* (Paris: Éditions du Seuil, 1992), p. 358.
6. See Simon Critchley, *Ethics–Politics–Subjectivity. Essay on Derrida, Levinas and Contemporary French Thought* (London: Verso, 1999), pp. 217–19.
7. Immanuel Kant, *Grounding for the Metaphysics of Morals*, in *Ethical Philosophy. Grounding for the Metaphysics of Morals. Metaphysical Principles of Virtue (Part II of the Metaphysics of Morals)*, trans. James W. Ellington (Indianapolis: Hackett Publishing Company, 1983), 440, p. 44; see Jacob Rogozinski, *Le don de la Loi. Kant et l'énigme de l'étique* (Paris: Presses Universitaires de France: 1999), pp. 181–2. All quotations from Rogozinski are my own translation.
8. Immanuel Kant, *Critique of Practical Reason*, trans. Werner S. Pluhar (Indianapolis: Hackett, 2002), 89, p. 113, my italics.
9. G. W. F. Hegel, *Aesthetics: Lectures on Fine Art*, trans. T. M. Knox (Oxford: Clarendon Press, 1975), vol. 2, p. 1215.
10. It also explains the fact that Kantian ethics constitutes a crucial source of inspiration for Lacan (see 'Kant avec Sade' in Lacan, *Écrits II* [Paris: Éditions du Seuil, 1999], pp. 243–69) and his followers.
11. Rogozinski, *Le don de la Loi*, p. 182.
12. Ibid.
13. Kant, *Grounding for the Metaphysics of Morals*, 434, p. 40.
14. Kant, *Critique of Practical Reason*, 82, p. 107.
15. Rogozinski, *Le don de la Loi*, pp. 187–8.
16. Ibid., p. 189.
17. Ibid.
18. Kant, *Philosophy of Religion*, quoted by Rogozinski in ibid., pp. 191–2.
19. Rogozinski, *Le don de la Loi*, p. 192.
20. Kant, *Opus Postumum*, quoted by Rogozinski in ibid., p. 192.
21. Kant, *The Metaphysical Principles of Virtue*, in Kant, *Ethical Philosophy*, 487, p. 157.
22. The Law, writes Rogozinski, could not 'impose itself as the Law *for* the subject without becoming the Law *of* the subject . . . unless the Law is *that*

which constitutes the subject: unless in the same movement as the Law gives itself to the subject, the subject *is constituted as subject* by the Law' (*Le don de la Loi*, p. 198).

23. Ibid., p. 199.
24. Ibid., p. 199: 'This subjection (*sujétion*) is equivalent to an unconditional submission to a Law whose author is not the subject (law "of the Other" in this sense) and which the subject does not even understand, although it is in truth its own Law, which makes him become (*advenir*) and brings him to existence (*le porte à l'existence*).'
25. See Chapter 3.
26. Ibid.
27. Ibid., p. 186.
28. Ibid., p. 184, my italics.
29. See Rogozinski's question quoted above (ibid., p. 184).
30. Kant, *Grounding for the Metaphysics of Morals*, 463, p. 62.
31. Ibid.
32. Ibid. My italics, translation slightly altered.
33. Alenka Zupančič, *Ethics of the Real. Kant, Lacan* (London: Verso, 2000), pp. 4–5 and 16–17.
34. See Kant, *Grounding for the Metaphysics of Morals*, 434, p. 40 and *Critique of Practical Reason* 82, p. 107.
35. Emmanuel Levinas, *Totality and Infinity. An Essay on Exteriority*, trans. A. Lingis (Pittsburgh: Duquesne University Press, 1969), p. 79.
36. On the *Faktum der Vernunft* and the *Faktum des Anderen*, see Critchley, *Ethics-Politics-Subjectivity*, p. 277 and 'Demanding Approval', pp. 17–18.
37. Emmanuel Levinas, 'Philosophy and the Idea of Infinity' in *Collected Philosophical Papers*, A. Lingis (Pittsburgh: Duquesne University Press, 1998), p. 59. 'Philosophy and the Idea of Infinity', first published in 1957, constitutes a condensed version or outline of many of the central themes of *Totality and Infinity*. Since the essay and the book reflect very similar moments in Levinas's thought, on some occasions I will offer quotations from the essay to illustrate ideas from the book.
38. In distinguishing between the Saying and the Said, Levinas also strives to escape the ontological language used in *Totality and Infinity*, and more generally, the conceptualization inherent in all philosophical discourse. *Otherwise than Being* (trans. Alphonso Lingis [Pittsburgh: Duquesne University Press, 1998]) thus elaborates the distinction between the instances of the Said that philosophy produces and the Saying that precedes and transcends them. This new focus on the saying materializes in the very language with which the work is written. As Critchley has shown, while *Totality and Infinity* expresses the interruption of ontology effected by ethics with the language of ontology, *Otherwise than Being* performatively enacts that interruption time and again, pushing language to its very limits (*The Cambridge Companion to Levinas*, eds Robert Bernasconi and Simon Critchley [Cambridge: Cambridge University Press, 2002], p. 19).
39. 'We call a face the epiphany of what can thus present itself directly, and therefore also exteriorly, to an I' ('Philosophy and the Idea of Infinity' in *Collected Philosophical Papers*, p. 55). See also, for example, *Totality and Infinity*, pp. 39 and 51: 'The way in which the other presents himself, exceed-

ing *the idea of the other in me*, we here name face. This *mode* does not consist in figuring as a theme under my gaze, in spreading itself forth as a set of qualities forming an image. The face of the Other at each moment destroys and overflows the plastic image it leaves me, the idea existing to my own measure and to the measure of its *ideatum* – the adequate idea. It does not manifest itself by these qualities . . . . It *expresses itself.* The face brings a notion of truth which, in contradistinction to contemporary ontology, is not the disclosure of an impersonal Neuter, but expression' (*Totality and Infinity*, p. 51).

40. 'Freedom is put into question by the other, and revealed to be unjustified, only when it knows itself to be unjust' ('Philosophy and the Idea of Infinity', in *Collected Philosophical Papers*, p. 50).

41. Ibid., p. 51.

42. 'Its [freedom's] knowing itself to be unjust is not something added on to spontaneous and free consciousness, which would be present to itself and know itself to be, in addition, guilty' (ibid., pp. 50–1).

43. 'And if the same does not peaceably rest on itself, philosophy does not seem to be indissolubly bound up with the adventure that includes every other in the same' ('Philosophy and the Idea of Infinity', in *Collected Philosophical Papers*, p. 51). 'Does not justice consist in putting the obligation with regard to the other before obligations to oneself, in putting the other before the same?' (p. 53).

44. For an illuminating and innovative exploration of the transfer of the traces of trauma from the other to the self, and on the 'matrixial' response-ability for those traces, see Bracha Lichtenberg Ettinger, *Regard et espace-de-bord matrixiels. Essais psychanalytiques sur le féminin et le travail de l'art* (Bruxelles: La Lettre Volée, 1999), especially 'Transcryptum: produire les traces mnésiques dans/pour/avec l'autre' (pp. 213–22).

45. See Jacques Derrida, 'Violence and Metaphysics', in *Writing and Difference*, trans. Alan Bass (Chicago, University of Chicago Press, 1978), pp. 79–153.

46. 'Philosophy and the Idea of Infinity' in *Collected Philosophical Papers*, pp. 53–4 and 58. See also *Totality and Infinity*, pp. 48–40 and 210–12, 'Transcendence and Height', in *Basic Philosophical Writings*, eds Robert Bernasconi, Simon Critchley and Adriaan Peperzak (Bloomington and Indianapolis: Indiana University Press, 1996), pp. 12, 21 and 25, and 'God and Philosophy' in *Basic Philosophical Writings*, p. 138.

47. 'Philosophy and the Idea of Infinity' in *Collected Philosophical Papers*, p. 57.

48. Levinas devotes the second section of *Totality and Infinity*, titled 'Interiority and Economy', to describing what he calls the 'egotistical self at home in the world'

49. Levinas, *Totality and Infinity*, p. 38. See also Adriaan Peperzak, *To the Other. An Introduction to the Philosophy of Emmanuel Levinas* (West Lafayette, Indiana: Purdue University Press, 1993), p. 121.

50. Levinas, *Totality and Infinity*, p. 36.

51. Ibid., p. 36, italics in the original. See also p. 38.

52. Levinas, *Otherwise than Being*, p. 25.

53. Levinas, *Totality and Infinity*, p. 26.

54. Ibid., p. 300.
55. See Lingis's 'Translator's Introduction' to *Otherwise than Being*, pp. xvii–xlviii, Critchley's 'Post-Deconstructive Subjectivity?' in *Ethics-Politics-Subjectivity*, pp. 51–82, and Bernasconi's 'What is the Question to which "Substitution" is the Answer?', in *The Cambridge Companion to Levinas*, pp. 234–51.
56. Levinas, *Totality and Infinity*, p. 40.
57. Levinas, *Ethics and Infinity*, p. 101.
58. Levinas, *Totality and Infinity*, p. 26.
59. See Peperzak, *To the Other*, pp. 25–6.
60. Levinas, *Totality and Infinity*, p. 300.
61. 'In welcoming the Other I welcome the On High to which my freedom is *subordinated*' (ibid.).
62. Levinas, *Otherwise than Being*, p. 158.
63. Ibid., p. 25, translation altered.
64. See Levinas, *Totality and Infinity*, p. 58.
65. About the need for 'a break from the break with participation' effected by philosophy, see Jill Robbins, *Altered Reading. Levinas and Literature* (Chicago: The University of Chicago Press, 1999), p. 88.
66. Levinas, *Totality and Infinity*, pp. 39 and 236, translation altered.
67. Levinas, 'Philosophy and the Idea of Infinity', in *Collected Philosophical Papers*, p. 58.
68. Levinas, *Totality and Infinity*, p. 88.
69. Levinas, 'Philosophy and the Idea of Infinity', in *Collected Philosophical Papers*, p. 58.
70. Levinas, *Totality and Infinity*, p. 200.
71. Ibid., p. 89.
72. See Peperzak, *To the Other*, p. 71: 'The subordination of freedom to the law of the Other, the heteronomy that links freedom with justice, avoids the impasses of an absolutized autonomy and avoids falling into one of the opposite traps. It does not violate free will but rather gives it direction in giving it a task and a meaning.'
73. Levinas, 'Freedom and Command', in *Collected Philosophical Papers*, p. 19, my emphasis.
74. Levinas, 'Philosophy and the Idea of Infinity', in *Collected Philosophical Papers*, p. 50, my emphasis.
75. Gillian Rose, *Mourning Becomes the Law. Philosophy and Representation* (Cambridge: Cambridge University Press, 1997), p. 38. Here Rose criticizes Levinas's 'passivity beyond passivity' for its inability to provide a basis for politics, overlooking the fact that for Levinas passivity is the condition of 'moral initiative' upon which political activity rests. See Rose's analysis of 'activity beyond activity' in *The Broken Middle* (Oxford and Cambridge, Mass: Blackwell, 1992).
76. Levinas, *Totality and Infinity*, p. 215. See also pp. 218–19 and 244–5.
77. Ibid., p. 219.
78. Levinas, 'Philosophy and the Idea of Infinity', in *Collected Philosophical Papers*, p. 58.
79. Levinas, 'Peace and Proximity', in *Basic Philosophical Writings*, p. 168.
80. Levinas, *Totality and Infinity*, pp. 218–19.

81. I refer here to Robbins' reflections on the talmudic maxim (*Altered Reading*, pp. 12–13), also explored by Lyotard, of 'doing before understanding' which Levinas formulates in 'The Temptation of Temptation' (*Nine Talmudic Readings*, trans. Annette Aronowicz (Bloomington: Indiana University Press, 1990).

82. As Robbins notes, this captures the reader of Levinas in a double bind, for shouldn't one act on Levinas's ethical discourse before one understands the work? See *Altered Reading*, p. 13.

83. Levinas, 'The Trace of the Other', ed. Mark C. Taylor, trans. Alphonso Lingis, in *Deconstruction in Context* (Chicago: University of Chicago Press, 1986), p. 349. See also Derrida's reading of the Levinasian idea of the gift in 'At This Very Moment in This Work Here I Am', in eds Robert Bernasconi and Simon Critchley, *Re-Reading Levinas* (Bloomington: Indiana University Press, 1991), pp. 11–48. For a reading of the economy of the gift, see Robert Bernasconi, 'What Goes Around Comes Around: Derrida and Levinas on the Economy of the Gift and the Gift of Genealogy', in Alan Schrift (ed.), *The Logic of he Gift* (New York: Routledge, 1997), pp. 256–73, and Robbins, *Altered Reading*, p. 7.

84. Levinas, *Totality and Infinity*, p. 244.

85. Robbins, *Altered Reading*, p. 16. See her reading of pages pp. 110–12 of Lyotard's *The Differend* on the same page.

86. Robbins, *Altered Reading*, p. 16.

87. See Rogozinski, *Le don de la Loi*, p. 184.

88. Levinas, *Otherwise than Being*, pp. 148–9. Translation slightly altered, italics in the original in French.

89. Levinas, *Otherwise than Being*, p. 146.

90. Rogozinski does the same in the reading of Kant discussed above.

91. Translation slightly altered.

92. See Critchley, 'Demanding Approval', p. 17.

93. Levinas, *Totality and Infinity*, p. 200.

94. Ibid., p. 79.

95. Levinas, *Otherwise than Being*, p. 157ff.

96. Levinas, 'Is Ontology Fundamental?', in *Basic Philosophical Writings*, p. 10.

97. I turn to the difference between guilt and responsibility below.

98. This angle, writes Levinas, does a violence to the face: 'Violence consists in ignoring this opposition, ignoring the face of a being, avoiding the gaze, and catching sight of an angle whereby the *no* inscribed on a face by the very fact that it is a face becomes a hostile or submissive force' ('Freedom and Command', in *Collected Philosophical Papers*, p. 19).

99. See, for example, Levinas, *Otherwise than Being*, p. 146.

100. See especially Chapters 2 and 3.

101. Levinas, *Totality and Infinity*, p. 203.

102. See Jacques Derrida, 'A Word of Welcome', in *Adieu to Emmanuel Levinas*, trans. Pascale-Anne Brault and Michael Naas (Stanford: Stanford University Press, 1999).

103. Ibid., pp. 23–4.

104. See Jacques Derrida, *Politics of Friendship*, trans. George Collins (London and New York: Verso, 1997), p. xi, and *Adieu to Emmanuel Levinas*, pp. 23–4. 'The

Other's Decision in Me' is the highly appropriate title of the last chapter of Critchley's *Ethics-Politics-Subjectivity*.

105. Critchley, *Ethics-Politics-Subjectivity*, p. 277. Critchley refers here to Derrida's notion of *the other's decision in me*.
106. Levinas, *Otherwise than Being*, p. 157.
107. Levinas, *Totality and Infinity*, p. 213.
108. Levinas, *Otherwise than Being*, pp. 158 and 160.
109. Ibid., p. 157.
110. Derrida, *Adieu*, p. 30
111. Levinas, *Otherwise than Being*, p. 157.
112. Ibid., p. 157.
113. Ibid., p. 158.
114. Ibid., p. 161.
115. Ibid., p. 158.
116. Ibid.
117. Ibid.
118. Ibid., p. 159.
119. Ibid., p. 158.
120. Ibid., p. 159.
121. Levinas, *Totality and Infinity*, pp. 308–9, 300.
122. It is the 'relationship with the other as neighbour' that 'gives meaning to my relations with all the others' (Levinas, *Otherwise than Being*, p. 159).
123. Ibid., p. 159.
124. Ibid., p. 148, my italics.
125. A third line of criticism targets (rightly, in my view) Levinas's problematical opinions on specific political situations. See Critchley, *Ethics-Politics-Subjectivity*, p. 278, and Howard Caygill, *Levinas and the Political* (London and New York: Routledge, 2002).
126. Critchley, *Ethics-Politics-Subjectivity*, p. 277.
127. Levinas, *Otherwise than Being*, p. 161.
128. See Critchley's introduction to Levinas's 'Peace and Proximity', in *Basic Philosophical Writings*, p. 162, and *The Cambridge Companion to Emmanuel Levinas*, pp. 24–5. See also Robert Bernasconi, 'The Third Party. Levinas on the Intersection of the Ethical and the Political', *Journal of the British Society for Phenomenology*, 30.1 (January 1999): 76–87; Annabel Herzog, 'Is Liberalism "All We Need"? Levinas's Politics of *Surplus*', *Political Theory*, 30.2 (April 2002), 204–27; and the essays in Charmaine Coyle and Simon Critchley, eds, *Levinas and Politics, Parallax*, p. 24 (monographic issue, July–September 2002).
129. For Levinas 'the one-for-the-other is not a commitment' (*Otherwise than Being*, p. 136).
130. Elaine Scarry, 'The Difficulty of Imagining Other People', in Martha Nussbaum and Joshua Cohen eds. *For Love of Country. Debating the Limits of Patriotism* (Boston: Beacon Press, 1996), pp. 98–110, p. 99, and Rose, *Mourning Becomes the Law*, p. 6.

Works Cited

Abel, Lionel. *Moderns on Tragedy* (Greenwich, Conn.: Fawcett Publications, 1967).

Aeschylus, *Oresteia. Agamemnon. The Libation Bearers. The Eumenides.* eds David Greene and Richmond Lattimore, trans. Richmond Lattimore (Chicago: The University of Chicago Press, 1953).

——*Seven against Thebes. Aeschylus II,* eds David Greene and Richmond Lattimore, trans. David Greene (Chicago: The University of Chicago Press, 1956).

Althusser, Louis. 'Ideology and Ideological State Apparatuses', in *Lenin and Philosophy,* trans. Ben Brewster (New York: Monthly Review Press, 1971).

Amin, Samir. 'Imperialism and Globalization', *Monthly Review* 53.2 (June 2001).

Arendt, Hannah. *The Human Condition* (Chicago: University of Chicago Press, 1958).

Aristotle. *Nicomachean Ethics,* trans. Terence Irwin (Indianapolis: Hackett, 1984).

——*Poetics I with The Tractatus Coislinianus, A Hypothetical Reconstruction of Poetics II, The Fragments of the On Poets,* trans. Richard Janko (Indianapolis: Hackett Publishing Company, 1987).

Badiou, Alain. *Ethics. An Essay on the Understanding of Evil,* trans. Peter Hallward (London: Verso, 2001).

Bakhtin, Mikhail M. *Toward a Philosophy of the Act,* eds Vadim Liapunov and Michael Holquist (Austin: University of Texas Press, 1993).

Barthes, Roland. *On Racine,* trans. Richard Howard (Berkeley and Los Angeles: University of California Press, 1992).

Basterra, Gabriela. 'The Grammar of Fate in Lorca's *Bodas de sangre', Journal of Romance Studies,* 3.2 (2003) 48–67.

——'Destino, responsabilidad y creación en el escenario trágico de Lorca', *Anales de la literatura española contemporánea,* 24 (1999) 411–31.

——'I Love to Hate My Life or the Allure of Guilt: A Response to Simon Critchley' (forthcoming).

——'Choreography of Fate: Lorca's Reconfigurations of the Tragic', *Re-Staging Cultural Theory: Politics, Tragedy, History,* ed. John Burt Foster and Wayne J. Froman (London: Continuum International Publishing Group, forthcoming).

Bauman, Zygmunt. *Postmodern Ethics* (Oxford: Blackwell, 1993).

——*In Search of Politics* (Stanford: Stanford University Press, 1999).

Benjamin, Walter. *Illuminations,* ed. Hannah Arendt, trans. Harry Zohn (New York: Hancourt, Brace & World, 1968).

——*The Origin of German Tragic Drama,* trans. John Osborne (London: Verso, 1992).

Benveniste, Emile. *Problems in General Linguistics* (Coral Gables: University of Miami Press, 1971).

Bernasconi, Robert. 'The Third Party. Levinas on the Intersection of the Ethical and the Political', *Journal of the British Society for Phenomenology,* 30.1 (January 1999) 76–87.

Bernasconi Robert and Critchley, Simon, eds. *The Cambridge Companion to Emmanuel Levinas* (Cambridge: Cambridge University Press, 2002).

—— *Re-Reading Levinas* (Bloomington: Indiana University Press, 1991).

Blanchot, Maurice. *The Writing of the Disaster*, trans. Ann Smock (Lincoln: University of Nebraska Press, 1986).

Bollas, Christopher. *Forces of Destiny. Psychoanalysis and Human Idiom* (London: Free Associations, 1989).

Borges, Jorge Luis. 'Funes the Memorious', in *Labyrinths*, eds Donald A. Yates and James E. Irby, trans. James E. Irby (New York: Modern Library, 1983), pp. 59–66.

Buber, Martin. *I and Thou*, trans. Walter Kaufmann (New York: Simon and Schuster, 1970).

Butler, Judith.*The Psychic Life of Power. Theories in Subjection* (Stanford: Stanford University Press, 1997).

—— *Antigone's Claim. Kinship Between Life and Death* (New York: Columbia University Press, 2000).

Butler, Judith, Ernesto Laclau and Slavoj Žižek. *Contingency, Hegemony, Universality. Contemporary Dialogues on the Left* (London: Verso, 2000).

Canault, Nina. *Comme paye-t-on les fautes de ses ancêtres? L'inconscient transgénératione* (Paris: Descleé de Brouwer, 1998).

Cascardi, Anthony J. *The Subject of Modernity* (Cambridge: Cambridge University Press, 1992).

Caygill, Howard. *Levinas and the Political* (London and New York: Routledge, 2002).

Chanter, Tina. 'Antigone's Dilemma', in *Re-Reading Levinas*, eds Robert Bernascone and Simon Critchley (Bloomington and Indianapolis: Indiana University Press, 1991).

—— *Ethics of Eros. Irigaray's Rewriting of the Philosophers* (New York and London: Routledge, 1995).

Cohen, Richard A., ed. *Face to Face with Levinas* (Albany: State University of New York Press, 1986).

Copjec, Joan, ed. *Supposing the Subject* (London: Verso, 1994).

—— *Radical Evil* (London: Verso, 1996).

Critchley, Simon. *Very Little . . . Almost Nothing. Death, Philosophy, Literature* (London: Routledge, 1997).

—— *The Ethics of Deconstruction. Derrida and Levinas* (Edinburgh: Edinburgh University Press, 1999).

—— *Ethics–Politics–Subjectivity. Essay on Derrida, Levinas and Contemporary French Thought* (London: Verso, 1999).

—— 'Demanding Approval: On the Ethics of Alain Badiou', *Radical Philosophy*, 100 (March/April 2000) 16–27.

—— 'Ethics, Politics and Radical Democracy: The History of a Disagreement'. *Cultural Machine*, 4 (2002), the Ethico-Political Issue.

—— *Ethics . . . My Way* (forthcoming).

—— 'I Want to Die, I Hate My Life: Phaedra's Malaise' (forthcoming).

Critchley, Simon and Charmaine Coyle, eds. *Levinas and Politics. Parallax* 8.24 (July–September 2002, monographic issue).

De Beistegui, Miguel and Simon Sparks, eds. *Philosophy and Tragedy* (London: Routledge, 2000).

Derrida, Jacques. 'Violence and Metaphysics', in *Writing and Difference*, trans. Alan Bass (Chicago: University of Chicago Press, 1978).

——'At this Very Moment in this Work Here I Am', trans. Ruben Berezdivin, in Bernasconi and Critchley, *Re-Reading Levinas*, 1991.

——*Politics of Friendship*, trans. George Collins (London and New York: Verso, 1997).

——*Adieu to Emmanuel Levinas*, trans. Pascale-Anne Brault and Michael Naas (Stanford: Stanford University Press, 1999).

——*Of Hospitality. Anne Dufourmantelle Invites Jacques Derrida to Respond*, trans. Rachel Bowlby (Stanford: Stanford University Press, 2000).

Dougherty, Dru. 'El lenguaje del silencio en el teatro de García Lorca.' *Valoración actual de la obra de García Lorca / Lectures actuelles de García Lorca. Actas del coloquio celebrado en la Casa de Velázquez*, eds Alfonso Esteban and Jean-Pierre Etienvre (Madrid: Universidad Complutense, 1988), pp. 23–40.

Drakakis, John and Naomi Conn Liebler, eds. *Tragedy* (London and New York: Longman, 1998).

Eagleton, Terry. *Sweet Violence: the Idea of the Tragic* (Oxford: Blackwell, 2003).

Eaglestone, Robert. *Ethical Criticism. Reading After Levinas* (Edinburgh: Edinburgh University Press, 1997).

Euripides. *Hippolytus*, in *Alcestis. The Medea. The Heracleidae. Hippolytus*, eds. David Greene and Richard Lattimore, trans. David Greene (Chicago and London: The University of Chicago Press, 1955).

Fernández Cifuentes, Luis. *García Lorca en el teatro: la norma y la diferencia* (Zaragoza: Prensas Universitarias de Zaragoza, 1986).

Fisher, Philip. *The Vehement Passions* (Princeton: Princeton University Press, 2002).

Foucault, Michel. 'The Subject and Power', in Hubert L. Dreyfus and Paul Rabinow, *Michel Foucault: Beyond Structuralism and Hermeneuticsm (Second Edition with an Afterword by and an Interview with Michel Foucault)* (Chicago: The University of Chicago Press, 1982), pp. 208–26.

——*Discipline and Punish. The Birth of the Prison*, trans. Alan Sheridan (New York: Vintage Books, 1995).

——*La verdad y las formas jurídicas*, trans. Enrique Lynch (Barcelona: Gedisa, 1998).

Freud, Sigmund. *The Ego and the Id*, ed. James Strachey, trans. Joan Riviere (New York and London: W. W. Norton and Company, 1989).

——'Mourning and Melancholia'. In *General Psychological Theory*, ed. Philip Rieff, trans. Joan Riviere (New York: Simon & Schuster, 1997), pp. 164–79.

García Lorca, Federico. *Federico García Lorca. Three Plays*, trans. Michael Dewell and Carmen Zapata (New York: Farrar, Straus and Giroux, 1993).

——*Blood Wedding and Yerma*, trans. Langston Hughes and W. S. Merwin (New York: Theatre Communications Group, Inc, 1994).

——*Obras Completas II, Teatro*, ed. Miguel García-Posada (Barcelona: Galaxia Gutenberg, Círculo de Lectores, 1997).

Glendinning, Simon. *On Being with Others. Heidegger, Derrida, Wittgenstein* (London: Routledge, 1998).

Goldmann, Lucien. *The Hidden God. A Study of Tragic Vision in the Pensées of Pascal and in the Tragedies of Racine* (New York: Humanities Press, 1964).

Greenberg, Mitchell. *Canonical States, Canonical Stages. Oedipus, Othering, and Seventeenth-century Drama* (Minneapolis: University of Minnesota Press, 1994).

Hegel, G. W. F. *Aesthetics: Lectures on Fine Art*, trans. T. M. Knox (Oxford: Clarendon Press, 1975).
——*Phenomenology of Spirit*, trans. A. V. Miller, intr. and analysis J. N. Findlay (Oxford: Oxford University Press, 1977).
——*The Jena System, 1804–5: Logic and Metaphysics*, ed. and trans. John W. Burbidge and George di Giovanni, intr. H. S. Harris (Kingston and Montreal: McGill-Queen's University Press, 1986).
——*Phénoménologie d'esprit*, trans. Jean Hyppolite (Paris : Aubier, Bibliothèque philosophique, 1995).
Heidegger, Martin. *An Introduction to Metaphysics*, trans. R. Manheim (New Haven: Yale University Press, 1959).
Herzog Annabel, 'Is Liberalism "All We Need"? Levinas's Politics of Surplus', *Political Theory*, 30.2 (April 2002) 204–27.
Honneth, Axel. *The Struggle for Recognition. The Moral Grammar of Social Conflicts*, trans. Joel Anderson (Cambridge, MA: MIT Press, 1996).
Hyppolite, Jean. *Genesis and Structure of Hegel's Phenomenology of Spirit*, trans. Samuel Cherniak and John Heckman (Evanston: Northwestern University Press, 1974).
Kafka, Franz. *The Trial*, trans. Breon Mitchell (New York: Schocken Books, 1998).
Kant, Immanuel. *Ethical Philosophy. Grounding for the Metaphysics of Morals. Metaphysical Principles of Virtue (Part II of Metaphysics of Morals)*, trans. James W. Ellington (Indianapolis: Hackett Publishing Company, 1983).
——*Grounding for the Metaphysics of Morals* in *Ethical Philosophy*.
——*Metaphysical Principles of Virtue* in *Ethical Philosophy*
——'What is Enlightenment?' In *Foundations of the Metaphysics of Morals and What is Enlightenment?* trans. Lewis White Beck (Englewood Cliffs, NJ: Prentice Hall, 1990), pp. 83–90.
——*Critique of Judgment*, trans. Werner S. Pluhar (Indianapolis: Hackett, 1987).
——*Critique of Pure Reason*, trans. Werner S. Pluhar, intr. Patricia W. Kitcher (Indianapolis: Hackett, 1996).
——*Critique of Practical Reason*, trans. Werner S. Pluhar (Indianapolis: Hackett, 2002).
Kojève, Alexandre. *Introduction to the Reading of Hegel. Lectures on the Phenomenology of Spirit*, ed. Allan Bloom, trans. James H. Nichols, Jr. (Ithaca: Cornell University Press, 1980).
Kosman, Aryeh. 'Acting: Drama as the Mimesis of Praxis'. *Essays on Aristotle's Poetics*, ed. Amélie O. Rorty (Princeton: Princeton University Press, 1992), pp. 51–72.
Lacan, Jacques. *Le séminaire, Livre VII. L'éthique de la psychanalyse 1959–1960* (Paris: Éditions du Seuil, 1986).
——*Le séminaire, Livre VIII. Le transfert 1960–1961* (Paris: Éditions du Seuil, 1992).
——*The Seminar of Jacques Lacan, Book VII. The Ethics of Psychoanalysis, 1959–1960*, trans. Denis Porter (New York: Norton, 1992).
——*The Seminar of Jacques Lacan, Book XI. The Four Fundamental Concepts of Psychoanalysis*, ed. Jacques-Alain Miller, trans. Alan Sheridan (New York: Norton, 1998).
Laclau, Ernesto. *Reflections on the New Revolutions of Our Time*. London: Verso, 1990.
——*Emancipation(s)* (London: Verso, 1996).

——'Ethics, Politics and Radical Democracy: A Response to Simon Critchley', *Cultural Machine*, 4 (2002), the Ethico-Political Issue.

Laclau, Ernesto, and Chantal Mouffe. *Hegemony and Socialist Strategy. Towards a Radical Democratic Politics* (London: Verso, 1985).

Laruelle, François. *Textes pour Emmanuel Levinas* (Paris: Jean-Michel Place, 1980).

Lefort, Claude. *Democracy and Political Theory*, trans. David Macey (Minneapolis: University of Minnesota Press, 1988).

Levinas, Emmanuel. *Totality and Infinity. An Essay on Exteriority*, trans. A. Lingis (Pittsburgh: Duquesne University Press, 1969).

——*Ethics and Infinity. Conversations with Philippe Nemo*, trans. Richard Cohen (Pittsburgh: Duquesne University Press, 1985).

——'The Trace of the Other', in *Deconstruction in Context*, ed. Mark C. Taylor, trans. A. Lingis (Chicago: University of Chicago Press, 1986).

——*Time and the Other*, trans. Richard Cohen (Pittsburgh: Duquesne University Press, 1987).

——*Nine Talmudic Readings*, trans. Annette Aronowicz (Bloomington: Indiana University Press, 1990).

——*Difficult Freedom: Essays on Judaism*, trans. Seán Hand (Baltimore: The Johns Hopkins University Press, 1991).

——*Basic Philosophical Writings*, eds Robert Bernasconi, Simon Critchley and Adriaan Peperzak (Bloomington and Indianapolis: Indiana University Press, 1996).

——'Is Ontology Fundamuntal?' in *Basic Philosophical Writings*.

——'Peace and Proximity', in *Basic Philosophical Writings*.

——*Collected Philosophical Papers*, trans. A. Lingis (Pittsburg: Duquesne University Press, 1998).

——'Freedom and Command'. *Collected Philosophical Papers*, pp. 15–24.

——'Philosophy and the Idea of Infinity' (PII). *Collected Philosophical Papers*, 47–50.

——*Otherwise than Being or Beyond Essence*, trans. Alphonso Lingis (Pittsburgh: Duquesne University Press, 1998).

Lichtenberg Ettinger, Bracha. *Regard et espace-de-bord matrixiels: Essais psychanalytiques sur le féminin et le travail de l'art* (Bruxelles: La Lettre Voleé, 1999).

Liebler Conn, Naomi, *Shakespeare's Festive Tragedy: the Ritual Foundations of Genre* (New York and London: Routledge, 1995)

Lingis, Alphonso. *Deathbound Subjectivity* (Bloomington: Indiana University Press, 1989).

Løgstrup, Knud E. *The Ethical Demand*, trans. Theodor I. Jensen (Philadelphia: Fortress Press, 1971).

Lyotard, Jean-François. 'Levinas's Logic'. *Face to Face with Levinas*, ed. Richard A. Cohen (Albany: State University of New York Press, 1986).

——*The Differend: Phrases in Dispute*, trans. Georges Van Den Abbele (Minneapolis: University of Minnesota Press, 1988).

Mead, G. H. *The Philosophy of the Present* (Chicago and London: Open Court, 1932).

Nietzsche, Friedrich. *The Birth of Tragedy* and *The Case of Wagner*, trans. Walter Kaufmann (New York: Vintage Books, 1967) (first published in 1872 and 1888, respectively).

——*On the Genealogy of Morals*, trans. and intro. by Douglas Smith (Oxford: Oxford University Press, 1996).

Nussbaum, Martha. *The Fragility of Goodness. Luck and Ethics in Greek Tragedy and Philosophy* (Cambridge: Cambridge University Press, 1986).

——'Tragedy and Self-Sufficiency: Plato and Aristotle on Fear and Pity'. *Essays on Aristotle Poetics*, ed. Amélie O. Rorty (Princeton: Princeton University Press, 1992), pp. 261–90.

Nussbaum, Martha and Joshua Cohen, eds. *For Love of Country. Debating the Limits of Patriotism* (Boston: Beacon Press, 1996).

Pascal, Blaise. *Pensées*, trans. A. J. Krailsheimer (London: Penguin Books, 1995).

Peperzak, Adriaan. *To the Other. An Introduction to the Philosophy of Emmanuel Levinas* (West Lafayette, Indiana: Purdue University Press, 1993).

Racine, Jean. *Phèdre*, trans. Margaret Rawlings (London: Penguin Books, 1991).

——*Phèdre* (Paris: Éditions Gallimard, 1995).

Reiss, Timothy J. *Tragedy and Truth. Studies in the Development of a Renaissance and Neoclassical Discourse* (New Haven and London: Yale University Press, 1980).

——*Against Autonomy. Global Dialectics and Cultural Exchange* (Stanford: Stanford University Press, 2002).

Ricoeur, Paul. *Time and Narrative* (3 vols), trans. Kathleen McLaughlin and David Pellauer (Chicago: The University of Chicago Press, 1984 [vol. I] 1985 [vol. II] and 1988 [vol. III]).

——*Oneself as Another*, trans. Kathleen Blamey (Chicago: The University of Chicago Press, 1992).

——*The Symbolism of Evil*, trans. Emerson Buchanan (Boston: Beacon Press, 1993).

Rivers, Elias. *Renaissance and Baroque Poetry of Spain* (Prospect Heights, Illinois: Waveland, 1966).

Rivier, André. 'Remarques sur le "nécesaire" et la "nécessité" chez Eschyle'. *R.E.G.* 81 (1968) 5–39.

Robbins, Jill. *Altered Reading. Levinas and Literature* (Chicago: The University of Chicago Press, 1999).

Rogozinski, Jacob. *Le don de la Loi. Kant et l'énigme de l'étique* (Paris: Presses Universitaires de France, 1999).

——*Kanten. Esquisses Kantiennes* (Paris: Editions Kimé, 1996).

Rorty, Amélie O., ed. *Essays in Aristotle's Poetics* (Princeton: Princeton University Press, 1992).

Rose, Gillian. *The Broken Middle* (Oxford and Cambridge, Mass: Blackwell, 1992).

——*Hegel Contra Sociology* (London and Atlantic Highlands, NJ: Athlone, 1995).

——*Mourning Becomes the Law. Philosophy and Representation* (Cambridge: Cambridge University Press, 1997).

Rosenzweig, Franz. *The Star of Redemption*, trans. William W. Hallo (Notre Dame, IN: Notre Dame Press, 1970–85).

Rousseau, Jean-Jacques. *On the Social Contract*, trans. Donald A. Cress, intr. Peter Gay (Indianapolis: Hackett, 1987).

Scarry, Elaine. *The Body in Pain* (Oxford: Oxford University Press, 1985).

——'The Difficulty of Imagining Other People'. In *For Love of Country*, pp. 98–110.

——'The Made-Up and the Made-Real'. *The Yale Journal of Criticism*, 5.2 (1992) 239–49.

Schelling, F. W. J. *Philosophical Letters on Dogmatism and Criticism*, in *The Unconditional in Human Knowledge: Four Early Essays, 1794–1796*, trans. Fritz Marti (Lewisburg, PA: Bucknell University Press, 1980).

— Schiller, Friedrich. *On the Sublime*, trans. Julius A. Elias (New York: Frederick Ungar, 1966).

Schrift, Alan, ed. *The Logic of the Gift* (New York: Routledge, 1997).

Schulte-Sasse, Jochen. 'Foreword', in Peter Sloterdijk. *Thinker on Stage. Nietzsche's Materialism* (Minneapolis: University of Minnesota Press, 1989).

Segal, Charles. *Tragedy and Civilization* (Cambridge, Mass: Harvard University Press, 1981).

——*Interpreting Greek Tragedy* (Ithaca and London: Cornell University Press, 1986).

——*Oedipus Tyrannus* (New York: Twayne, 1993).

Simmel, Georg. *On Individuality and Social Forms* (Chicago: The University of Chicago Press, 1971).

Sloterdijk, Peter. *Critique of Cynical Reason*, trans. Michael Eldred, foreword Andreas Huyssen (Minneapolis: University of Minneapolis Press, 1987).

——*Thinker on Stage. Nietzsche's Materialism*, trans. Jamie Owen Daniel, foreword Jochen Schulte-Sasse (Minneapolis: University of Minnesota Press, 1989).

Sophocles. *Oedipus the King. Oedipus at Colonus. Antigone*, eds David Grene and Richmond Lattimore, trans. David Grene, Robert Fitzgerald and Elizabeth Wyckoff (Chicago: University of Chicago Press, 1954).

——*The Three Theban Plays: Antigone, Oedipus the King, Oedipus at Colonus*, trans. Robert Fagles (London: Penguin Books, 1984).

Steiner, George. *The Death of Tragedy* (New York, Oxford: Oxford University Press, 1980).

——*Antigones* (New Haven: Yale University Press, 1984).

Stewart, Susan. *On Longing* (Durham, NC and London: Duke University Press, 1993).

Strauss, Jonathan. *Subjects of Terror. Nerval, Hegel and the Modern Self* (Stanford: Stanford University Press, 1998).

——ed. *Post-Mortem: The State of Death as a Modern Construct*, in *Diacritics*, 30.3 (Fall 2000, monographic issue).

Szondi, Peter. *An Essay on the Tragic*. trans. Paul Fleming (Stanford: Stanford University Press, 2002).

Vernant, Jean-Pierre and Pierre Vidal-Naquet. *Myth and Tragedy in Ancient Greece*, trans. Janet Lloyd (New York: Zone Books, 1988).

⌐ Williams, Raymond. *Modern Tragedy* (Stanford: Stanford University Press, 1987).

Wright, Tamra, Peter Hughes and Alison Ailey. 'The Paradox of Morality: an Interview with Emmanuel Levinas', trans. Andrew Benjamin and Tamra Wrigh, in *The Provocation of Levinas. Rethinking the Other*, eds Robert Bernasconi and David Wood (London and New York: Routledge, 1988), pp. 168–80.

Žižek, Slavoj. *The Sublime Object of Ideology* (London: Verso, 1989).

——*For They Know Not What They Do. Enjoyment as Political Factor* (London: Verso, 1991).

——*Tarrying with the Negative. Kant, Hegel, and the Critique of Ideology* (Durham, NC: Duke University Press, 1993).

——*The Indivisible Remainder. An Essay on Schelling and Related Matters* (London: Verso, 1996).

—— *The Plague of Fantasies* (London: Verso, 1997).

—— *The Ticklish Subject. The Absent Centre of Political Ontology* (London: Verso, 1999).

—— *The Fragile Absolute. Or Why is the Christian Legacy Worth Fighting For?* (London: Verso, 2000).

—— *Did Somebody Say Totalitarianism?* (London: Verso, 2001).

Zupančič, Alenka. *Ethics of the Real. Kant, Lacan* (London: Verso, 2000).

Index